PARLIAMENT
and the
EXECUTIVE

PARLIAMENT and the EXECUTIVE

An Analysis with Readings

by

H. V. WISEMAN

(Professor of Government, University of Exeter)

LONDON

ROUTLEDGE & KEGAN PAUL

C
547

First published 1966
by Routledge & Kegan Paul Limited
Broadway House, 68-74 Carter Lane
London, E.C.4

Printed in Great Britain
by C. Tinling & Co., Ltd.
Liverpool, London and Prescot

© H. V. Wiseman 1966

No part of this book may be reproduced
in any form without permission from
the publisher, except for the quotation
of brief passages in criticism

710 263304-9

LEEDS POLYTECHNIC
92519
C V
547
10 JUN 1970
328.3 (942)

Contents

PART IV: THE ROLE OF THE HOUSE OF COMMONS

PART X: QUESTIONS

PART XI: THE USE OF COMMITTEES

overlap between the two, since exponents of one modern interpretation or another often 'seek to rewrite history in order to find room therein for their own ideas.' Sir Sidney Low was already, in 1903, writing of the shift of the 'centre and force' of the State from Parliament to Cabinet. Professor F. A. Ogg's *English Government and Politics* (1936) emphasised this theme and supported it by reference to Redlich's *Procedure of the House of Commons*.

In Ramsay Muir's *How Britain is Governed* we find a stern indictment of alleged Cabinet dictatorship. This thesis was equally sternly rejected by Professor Bassett in *Essentials of Parliamentary Democracy*. So, also, by Harold Laski, not only in his *Reflections on the Constitution* (1946), which represented a post-war upsurge of confidence in parliamentary institutions, but also in his much more critical (and generally less balanced) *Parliamentary Government in England* (1938).

The great debate of the 1930s, however, did not settle the argument. We quote at length from a House of Lords debate in 1950 on a motion deploring the growing power of the Cabinet as a danger to the democratic consitution of the country.

Few serious commentators, however, appear to share the views of Viscount Cecil of Chelwood. We quote a less alarmist and more representative point of view from Lord Morrison of Lambeth's *Government and Parliament*.

IV

Next, we turn to a more specific examination of how the role of the House of Commons has been seen at different times by various commentators. Lord Campion, in *British Government since 1918* corrects the view which sees Parliament as virtually impotent, and this more moderate view is supported by Sir Ivor Jennings. We also quote a moving tribute to the House in war-time, delivered by Sir Winston Churchill. But it is necessary once more to look further back into history, for, as we have seen, not even the mid-nineteenth 'Liberal' view asserted that the House of Commons should be as all-powerful as modern *laudatores tempori acti*, such as Christopher Hollis and Professor Keeton, appear to claim.

First, we cite the views of Bagehot, and follow them by more modern comments, partly of historical interpretation, partly analytical, from Laski, Mr Nigel Nicolson, and Professor A. H. Birch. This is by way of general introduction to a more detailed analysis of *The Proper Functions of Representative Bodies* by J. S. Mill and a very similar analysis in Bagehot's *English Constitution*. Some of the points contained in these classical expositions are taken up—for refutation, confirmation, or extension—by Amery, Laski and Ogg.

Specifically on the House of Commons in relation to administration, we supplement these primarily 'academic' analyses by extracts from evidence given to the Committee on Ministers Powers, 1932, (Sir Maurice L. Gwyer); the Select Committee on Procedure (1931) (Lord Eustace Percy) and the Select Committee on Procedure (1946) (Sir Gilbert Campion, Clerk to the House).

For attempts to summarise the main arguments we turn to Jennings and to Dr Crick.

V

'It is not untrue to say that the most important part of Parliament is the Opposition in the House of Commons', says Sir Ivor Jennings in the first of our extracts in this section, devoted to the role of the Opposition. President Lowell of Harvard makes the same point much earlier in his *Government of England*. We have included some more material from Lord Campion's writings which develops this point and relates it to the procedure of the House of Commons and the division of parliamentary time between Government and Opposition. These aspects are further developed by Jennings. An interesting 'governmental' point of view is contained in evidence given to the Select Committee on Procedure (1931) by Ramsay Macdonald. Lord Morrison of Lambeth, while deploring unnecessary obstruction, gives the Opposition a somewhat wider role, though he emphasises that the Government must take action to protect itself where desirable. We conclude with two extracts from the memoirs of a valiant back-bencher, Lord Winterton, and with a brief note by Mr R. H. Crossman which suggests that the Opposition cannot, today, always be as perfervid as the noble lord demands.

VI

Neither the working of the House of Commons as a whole, nor the role of the Opposition, can be understood without reference to party. Indeed, it has been argued that party discipline is one of the principal causes of the excessive control of the Commons by the Cabinet.

We begin with Bagehot's analysis of the role of party as he saw it in his day. We then relate the party system to the 'Liberal' view of the Constitution through some extracts from Professor Birch's *Representative and Responsible Government* which also recall the views of such commentators as Ostrogorski, Goldwin Smith, President Lowell and Sir Sidney Low. The effect of the party system on the doctrine of ministerial responsibility is discussed by Marshall and Moodie.

The possible dangers of excessive party control are discussed by Amery in his *Thoughts on the Constitution* and there is the usual counterblast by Laski in his *Reflections*. Mr R. Rose puts a somewhat different view from either in his discussion of the actual working of the party system and 'the unstable policy parties *within* the formally united governing party'.

Such groups within a particular party make considerable use of party committees which, as declared in a Report from the Committee of Privileges in 1947, are a 'normal and everyday incident of parliamentary procedure'. We include a discussion of the work of such committees taken from Mr Nigel Nicolson's *People and Parliament*.

VII

Does the party system, combined with the excessive power of the Cabinet, undermine the position of the private member and perhaps reduce him to the role of 'lobby fodder'? Sir Courtenay Ilbert presents a balanced interpretation which certainly does not see the back-bencher as a mere cipher. This is confirmed by Lord Winterton, who replies forcefully to critics of the system of Whips. Lord Morrison, in somewhat more detail, also seeks to show that a reasonable balance is maintained between government (or opposition front-bench) and private member. Laski, from the outside, does not differ significantly from Lord

Morrison. Of great interest are the views of Mr Nigel Nicolson, who, as a private member, felt the discipline of his constituency party to be far more severe than that of the parliamentary party. With this view, may be compared some opinions of Aneurin Bevan. Professor Birch analyses the factors which tend to diminish the significance of the back-bencher, but we include also his detailed analysis of the opportunities for useful and effective work still open to the private member.

Finally, we raise the general question in the specific form of the proper place of 'free votes'. This is discussed by Mr Nigel Nicolson and Lord Morrison from the point of view of the parliamentarian—with back-bencher and ministerialist in considerable agreement, and by Marshall and Moodie as outside observers of the parliamentary scene.

VIII

The supremacy of Parliament has always rested firmly on its legislative powers, since no court can declare such legislation 'unconstitutional'. When, however, we examine in detail the part played by the House of Commons in legislation, we find that neither in practice, nor in the theories of the commentators, is its role supreme or even predominant.

Our extract from J. S. Mill's *Representative Government* begins with the assertion that 'a numerous assembly is as little fitted for the direct business of legislation as for that of administration'. Bagehot held that he would have dismissed his attorney if he had done his business as the legislature did the nation's business. Our extract gives reasons for this opinion. Sir Henry Maine, in his *Popular Government* (1885) describes how the House of Commons 'has turned over to the Executive Government, the most important part of the business of Legislation.' More briefly, Sir Sidney Low makes the same point and goes on to comment on Lord Salisbury's theme that 'discussion of a measure . . . for any effective or useful purpose . . . is rapidly becoming an impossibility in the House of Commons'. President Lowell suggests that 'the Cabinet legislates with the advice and consent of Parliament'. The general position is well summarised in an extract from Professor Ogg's once standard work, *English Government and Politics* (1936).

Yet there is, of course, no doubt about the volume and significance of legislation passed by the House of Commons; this is well illustrated by an extract from a Memorandum presented by the Clerk to the House to the Select Committee on Procedure in 1946. It is worth-while looking, therefore, at the stage where the most effective legislative work of the House is done, namely in Standing Committee. Mr Hore-Belisha, in evidence to the Select Committee on Procedure in 1931, argued the case for greater and more effective use of such committees. On the other hand, Lord Morrison told the Select Committee on Procedure in 1946 that he would not like to turn such committees into groups of specialists. Professor Wheare tries to show, in fact, that the British system has considerable advantage.

An even greater inroad into the legislative predominance of Parliament has, of course, been made by the growth of delegated legislation. This is well illustrated by yet another section of the evidence given by the Clerk to the House to the Select Committee on Procedure in 1946. It is interesting to set his argument for a Select Committee against the views expressed by Sir Maurice Gwyer to the Committee on Ministers' Powers in 1932. Mr Amery expressed strong views about the danger of delegated legislation in his *Thoughts on the Constitution*. Inevitably, strong refutation of these views is contained in Laski's *Reflections*. A balanced account of the procedures involved is to be found in Lord Morrison's *Government and Parliament*. We conclude with a judicious summary of the basic elements of the problem taken from an article by Mr Ernest H. Beet in *Public Administration* (1955) on *Parliament and Delegated Legislation, 1945–53*.

IX

Our historical survey showed the importance of financial control in the fight for parliamentary supremacy. Yet even the mid-nineteenth century exponents of the 'liberal' theory of the constitution had reservations about the role of the House of Commons in finance. We have included extracts from Mill and Bagehot. Sir Sydney Low and President Lowell both write of the increasing—and salutary—control exercised by the Cabinet over expenditure and taxation. The same point is made, for a later period by Professor Ogg. For once, too, we see Amery and Laski in broad agreement that the House could find no means of exercising effective control over finance except by greater use of Select Committees. Indeed, as Sir Frank Tribe shows from his experience as Comptroller and Auditor-General, it is doubtful whether the House as a whole wants to reduce the amount of government expenditure as opposed to exercising some control over its direction. This view was expressed to the Select Committee on Procedure in 1931 by Mr Chuter Ede, Captain Bourne, and Sir Malcolm Ramsay, the then Comptroller and Auditor-General.

X

If parliamentary control of legislation and finance is attenuated, what shall we say of the functions of the House of Commons as 'the grand inquest of the Nation'? This section deals with Question Time. Here, to quote President Lowell, we have 'a method of dragging before the House any acts or omissions by the departments of state, and of turning a searchlight upon every corner of the public service . . . It helps very much to keep the administration of the country up to the mark, and it is a great safeguard against neglect or arbitrary conduct, or the growth of bureaucratic arrogance which is quite unknown in England'. We begin with a standard account of Question Time taken from Professor Ogg's *English Government and Politics*. Changes since 1936 do not alter the broad picture significantly. This is followed by Laski's estimate of its importance at a time when, in his *Parliamentary Government in England*, he was somewhat critical of parliamentary institutions. The role of Questions as a check on the Administration, and also the limitations of Question Time, are well discussed in an article by Mr Nevil Johnson in *Public Administration* (1961). But we have drawn most freely on the authoritative study of *Questions in Parliament* by Chester and Bowring, and especially from their concluding observations.

XI

It is not the purpose of this book to examine in detail the various proposals for increasing the influence of the House of

Commons over the executive. One aspect of reform, however, deserves some attention since it has been considered for many years and may possibly be the basis for moderate changes in the future. This is the proposal to extend and strengthen the use of parliamentary committees.

To go no further back, the Haldane Report on the Machinery of Government recommended such committees in 1918. Before the Select Committee on Procedure (1931), Mr David Lloyd George spoke in favour of this mode of increasing parliamentary control over the Administration. However, Mr Speaker produced for the Select Committee on Procedure (1946) what he considered to be pertinent arguments against such committees and Lord Morrison was even more uncompromising in his opposition. The Select Committee on Procedure (1958) received a memorandum from the Clerk to the House which included a proposal for an experiment with a Colonial Affairs Committee. Lord Morrison repeated his objections, which he had already elaborated in *Government and Parliament.* The Report of the Select Committee rejected the suggestion. We include a review of Lord Morrison's book by Mr David Widdicombe which states in clear terms the arguments against Lord Morrison's attitude.

Not all politicians have been as strongly opposed to the idea as Lord Morrison—whose views are shared by Mr R. A. Butler. We quote an opinion in its favour from Mr Amery's *Thoughts on the Constitution.* From academic students of the problem we offer an extract from Professor Wheare's *Government by Committee* and a judicious summing-up by Professor Hanson. The subject is discussed further in the next section.

SECTION C

New battles are frequently fought out in old terms. The debate on the Machinery of Government Bill (19 November, 1964) produced some interesting confusions between the time of Queen Anne and that of Queen Elizabeth II. The proposal to increase the permitted number of ministers in the House of Commons from seventy to ninety-one raised once more the question of Executive-Legislative relations. No less a person than Mr R. A. Butler 'looked back at past history'.

> In this House it is quite easy to make fun of Queen Anne . . . But if they look back on the history of Stuart times, or at the Act of 1707, or at the developments since, hon. Members will find that our predecessors who lived and worked in this House were always jealous about increasing the Executive in relation to the Legislative.[25]

But as Mr Douglas Houghton, Chancellor of the Duchy of Lancaster, replied:

> The history of this matter is very fascinating indeed, because we see that originally the House of Commons was not criticising patronage exercised by Prime Ministers, but was afraid of patronage exercised by the Crown.[26]

Nevertheless, Mr Ian Perceval was right to comment that:

> . . . some Ministers should be in the House of Commons in order that the House of Commons can exercise control over the Executive . . . Why then have a limit on them? It is because . . . we may slip into the paradoxical situation where the Executive may get such strength in the House of Commons that it will itself exercise undue control over the very people who one supposed to be there to control it.[27]

As Mr Grimond expressed it:

> The objection to the appointment of an unlimited number of people in the Government . . . is not the eighteenth century objection that they are likely to be venal, but the twentieth century objection that it deprives the House of Commons and the Government side of its talents.[28]

Realistically, he referred also to the growth of the party system and the failure to adapt procedure to the new situation. This, at least, was a more useful contribution than Sir Derek Walker-Smith's reference to 'a deliberate exercise in increasing the power of the Executive over Parliament, thereby diminishing parliamentary control and derogating, in fact if not in form, from the great concept of the sovereignty of Parliament'[29]; as if the House of Commons is 'Parliament' in this context (see

[25] H. C. Debates, vol. 702, c. 738.
[26] ibid., col. 749.
[27] ibid., cols. 700–701.
[28] ibid., col. 682.
[29] ibid., col. 671.

Extracts, Section I) and 'the Executive' i.e. the ministers are not—as an essential feature of parliamentary government on the Westminster model—members of the House, sharing in its share of 'Parliamentary Sovereignty'. Nevertheless, if the distinction between parliamentary attempts to limit the power of the Crown and the problem of parliamentary 'control' over the Executive is clearly made, the same speaker was justified in saying that:

> the very genesis of Parliament lies in seeking to exercise control over the Executive, and that has been the primary occupation of the House of Commons through the generations.[30]

The weakening of such controls is the primary reason for such gloomy publications as *The Passing of Parliament*, *Can Parliament Survive? Parliament in Danger! Has Parliament a Future?* and *Change or Decay?* Parliament has, possibly, sunk in prestige somewhat. Excellent men have given up a parliamentary career, parties have come to dominate deliberation and decision, there has, according to Sir Edward Fellowes, been an unfortunate tendency to question the authority of Mr Speaker. The power of the Government is clear. Estimates are never reduced and control over finance is largely non-existent except in so far as committees are effective. Longer sessions and extended hours are used primarily to get government business through and the government's power is greatly enhanced and that of Parliament reduced, by the extended use of delegated legislation, by the insulation of public corporations from parliamentary control (except, again, through committees), and by the development of direct contacts between M.P.s and departments. Even at question time, the House concentrates more and more on matters of general policy.

Yet it is on such matters that the government is most secure. It may be more vulnerable on smaller matters, but these are often paid inadequate attention. Moreover M.P.s are inadequately informed on matters of fact and on the nature of technical problems or the advice on which the government attempts to solve them.

We noted Mr Grimond's reference to parties. M. Duverger, an eminent French student of parliamentary government considers that 'Executive and Legislative, Government and

[30] ibid., col. 665.

Parliament, are consitutional façades; in reality the party alone exercises power'. Debate, so the argument runs, is futile; government is no longer 'open', being more amenable to party influence than Opposition criticisms voiced in public debate. In so far as all this is true, the House as such tends to lose respect and seldom is able to present a 'House view'.

It is natural that the emergence of a government with a majority of only five should have exacerbated the argument about the proper role of the Executive and the Legislature. But whatever party, and with whatever majority, had been returned to power in October, 1964, there would almost certainly have been a new Select Committee on Procedure to consider the above and other problems. The imminence of such reconsideration of the procedures for performing essential roles such as legislation (mostly governmental), 'control' of finance, and scrutiny of policy-making and administration, justifies some attempt in this book to look ahead. It may be assumed that the Select Committee's recommendations will be firmly rooted in the historical and traditional influences described earlier in this introduction and further illustrated in the extracts which follow. A brief examination of the suggestions for reform likely to be made or accepted may, therefore, be useful. Brief, because it is not our purpose to prescribe remedies for alleged defects, useful, because when once again the procedure of the House is to be under official scrutiny, there is some point in trying to put together the lessons of the past, the orthodox interpretation of the role of the House, and possible future developments to meet the needs of the second half of the twentieth century.

Both the history and orthodox interpretation suggest that any changes must take into account the power and stability of the Executive. Though parliamentary scrutiny of the Executive is fundamental to the working of parliamentary democracy, it must be understood that the role of the Government is to govern; the role of Parliament is to criticise the policies and acts of the Government. Control means influence, not direct power; advice, not command; criticism, not destruction; scrutiny, not initiative; publicity, not secrecy. But strong government needs strong opposition; it can benefit from such opposition and stand up to it. Political control, thus conceived, does not directly hinder governments; sometimes it can even help them to anticipate trouble. But to be effective, such control necessitates informed contribution to deliberation by M.P.s and a fairer balance between Government and Private Member. There is good reason to believe that all this necessitates a greater degree of specialisation by M.P.s and an extended use of more specialised committees. (see Extracts: Part XI).

To judge by the reception of proposals along these lines by previous Select Committees and the House itself, it will be necessary to establish that they do not in any way infringe the principle of ministerial responsibility (in as far as this is now a reality—see Extracts, Part II(a)); that they would not, to quote Mr R. A. Butler, introduce a 'muddle' into our constitutional arrangements, nor constitute a 'radical constitutional innovation'; that they would certainly not involve the oft-cited 'weaknesses' and 'defects' of the French and American committees which operate with entirely different powers and in entirely different constitutional and political conditions. It will also be necessary to show that the taking of more work 'upstairs' in committees would in no way derogate from the dignity of the House as a whole; that it would not replace debate on the Floor of the House, but rather give such debate 'authoritative depth'; it would not infringe but rather make more real M.P.s' 'rights'. To these points we return.

First, however, it is clear from suggestions already made that some consideration may be given to the possibility of altering the hours of sitting so as to provide for morning sittings and the avoidance of those late sittings and all-night debates which cause frayed tempers in the House and frustrated M.P.s outside the Chamber who are waiting to participate in a division. One possible objection to this, however, is that it may lead to the 'full-time professionalisation' of M.P.s and deprive them of the alleged advantage of outside contacts and experience. More important from the point of view of Executive-Legislative relations is that Ministers are already overburdened and need their mornings for essential departmental work. From the point of view of the House, any suggestions for a greater use of committees might make it impossible to *add* to the length of sittings, though it is possible for committees to meet while the House is sitting, or for the House to adjourn at certain times so that Committees may sit. Other suggestions for relieving the pressure of work such as better arrangements for divisions, the provision of proxy votes at least for Ministers and possibly for the sick, time-limits on speakers, and many others, are too technical for further discussion here.

We return, therefore, to the question of scrutiny and control, and first to finance. The suggestion has been made that there are four stages of control of expenditure: the total; the balance between services; the total of individual services; economy within individual services. Each should be matched by four processes of parliamentary scrutiny or debate. It is further suggested that present opportunities for such scrutiny or debate are inadequate (see Extracts, Part IX). It may be suggested, therefore that on the basis of appropriate Government White Papers, a Select Committee on Expenditure should attempt to produce factual information and interpretation to aid subsequent debate in the House. Such committee might also review continuing services. With some extension of Supply Days it would then be possible to debate the reports of this committee as well as those of the Public Accounts and Estimates Committees. The latter would continue to perform its functions of a general and 'inter-departmental' nature, and, initially, might set up more sub-committees to deal with particular departments. Later, this latter job might be handed over to the specialist committees suggested below.

Before we turn to them, however, we look briefly at the other side of finance, revenue as opposed to expenditure. There has been much discussion about sending the Finance Bill in whole, or in part, 'upstairs'. The traditional role of the House is so conceived as to make it unlikely that the whole Bill would be entrusted to a Committee, even though the Report stage would still be taken on the Floor of the House. It may be possible, however, to send those clauses raising technical taxation problems to a Select Committee which, as far as possible, would report in time to suggest any desirable amendments at the Report stage.

To return to specialist committees, it is suggested that these are needed to hold a watching brief on administration, to scrutinise the actions of government in their own fields, to collect, discuss and report evidence relevant to proceedings in Parliament whether legislative or other. Such committees might eventually cover the whole field of administration, though initially experiments might be of a limited nature, related either to a particular department e.g. the Home Office, or to particular subjects e.g. Scientific Development, the Machinery of Government, the Social Services. Some suggestions even involve the 'sensitive' policy-making Foreign Office and Defence Department.

We have indicated above that the examination of the appropriate Estimates might eventually be handed over to these committees. They might also, by themselves, or as the nucleus of a larger committee, take the Committee Stage of Public Bills. Indeed, it has been suggested that the 'Gladstonian' principle of examination of legislative proposals before Bills are drafted might be re-established through these committees. Whatever may be the ultimate decision with regard to a fully-fledged committee system, it seems very likely that the House will make greater use of *ad hoc* Select Committees for specific purposes.

There are a number of other changes which seem likely, at least, to be discussed. Could better use be made of Question Time? (see Extracts: Part X). Questions addressed to the Secretaries of State for Scotland and Wales might be taken in the Scottish and Welsh Grand Committees. Question Time might be extended and/or the numbers of questions permitted to M.P.s reduced. There is the vexed problem of control of supplementary Questions. Still on the subject of 'Private Members' Opportunities', more use might be made of Adjournment Debates; for example two topics might be taken at the end of each sitting. Similarly, additional scope might be given to Private Members' Motions on Fridays. For some time now, also, it has been felt that it ought to be somewhat easier to obtain an Urgency Debate under S.O. No. 9, though this might cut across another important requirement of orderly parliamentary work, namely, that the business of the day should be as certain as possible.

Another aspect of effective supervision of administration is that related to the possible appointment of an Ombudsman or Parliamentary Commissioner. The question is so much in the public eye at present that it seems unnecessary to say more than that Parliament is unlikely to accept any new institution which might reduce the significance of the individual M.P. as the channel for raising 'constituents' grievances' and that any

Parliamentary Commissioner ought, like the Comptroller and Auditor-General, to be responsible to the House, preferably through a Select Committee. Neither proviso would seem to prevent the establishment of such an officer.

We have left the question of legislation until the last. The role of the House at present is made sufficiently clear in our Extracts, Part VIII. It needs only to be said that there is a growing feeling (expressed, for example, by Sir Edward Fellowes to the Select Committee on Procedure, 1958) that the detailed discussion of legislation should largely be removed from the floor of the House and that the House should concentrate upon approving the principle of any legislative proposal (on Second Reading); approving or perhaps recommitting in certain respects, the Report of the Committee on the Bill, and, finally (on Third Reading), deciding whether or not to pass the Bill. It has further been suggested that much more of the detail of legislation might be embodied in statutory instruments—delegated legislation has not only come to stay but is likely increasingly to be used. This, however, would mean further opportunity for the scrutiny of such statutory instruments. The existing 'Scrutiny Committee' would clearly be needed to continue its 'lawyer's' job. A further committee would be needed to discuss the 'merits' of statutory instruments, with opportunity for debating its reports in the House. Eventually, the examination of delegated legislation might be conducted by the appropriate specialist committees.

What prospect is there of these proposals being adopted? The record of the Select Committee of 1945 and 1958 is not encouraging. Readers will judge for themselves how far the suggestions would cut across the traditional functions and procedures of the House and individual M.P.s, as these have been described in our Extracts. Would they create a new danger of tension between the Executive and the Legislative? Or would they provide new machinery for the more effective performance of those traditional functions? The report of the new Select Committee on Procedure will be examined with considerable interest by those who, after studying the material of this book, have come to their own conclusion about the nature, past, present, and future, of Executive-Legislative relations.

PART I
The Sovereignty of Parliament

1. UNLIMITED LEGISLATIVE AUTHORITY OF PARLIAMENT

[from Blackstone, *Commentaries*, in Dicey, *Law of the Constitution*, Macmillan, pp. 160–161, 9th Edition]

The power and jurisdiction of Parliament, says Sir Edward Coke, is so transcendent and absolute, that it cannot be confined, either for causes or persons, within any bounds. And of this high court, he adds, it may be truly said, '*Si antiquitatem spectes, est vetustissima; si dignitatem, est honoratissima; si jurisdictionem, est capacissima!* It hath sovereign and uncontrollable authority in the making, confirming, enlarging, restraining, abrogating, repealing, reviving, and expounding of laws, concerning matters of all possible denominations, ecclesiastical or temporal, civil, military, maritime, or criminal: this being the place where that absolute despotic power, which must in all governments reside somewhere, is entrusted by the constitution of these kingdoms. All mischiefs and grievances, operations and remedies, that transcend the ordinary course of the laws, are within the reach of this extraordinary tribunal. It can regulate or new-model the succession to the Crown; as was done in the reign of Henry VIII and William III. It can alter the established religion of the land; as was done in a variety of instances in the reigns of king Henry VIII and his three children. It can change and create afresh even the constitution of the kingdom and of parliaments themselves; as was done by the act of union, and the several statutes for triennial and septennial elections. It can, in short, do everything that is not naturally impossible; and therefore some have not scrupled to call its power, by a figure rather too bold, that omnipotence of Parliament. True it is, that what the Parliament doth, no authority upon earth can undo. So that it is a matter most essential to the liberties of this kingdom, that such members be delegated to this important trust, as are most eminent for their probity, their fortitude, and their knowledge; for it was a known apophthegm of the great lord treasurer Burleigh, 'that England could never be ruined but by a Parliament': and, as Sir Matthew Hale observes, this being the highest and greatest court over which none other can have jurisdiction in the kingdom, if by any means a misgovernment should any way fall upon it, the subjects of this kingdom are left without all manner of remedy. To the same purpose the president Montesquieu, though I trust too hastily, presages; that as Rome, Sparta, and Carthage have lost their liberty and perished, so the constitution of England will in time lose its liberty, will perish: it will perish whenever the legislative power shall become more corrupt than the executive.

2. RIGHT OF SUPREME POWER TO MAKE LAWS

[from Bentham, *A Fragment on Government*, (ed.) Harrison, Blackwell, 1948, pp. 89; 95–96; 98–99.]

14. The vehemence of this passage is remarkable. He ransacks the language: he piles up, one upon another, four of the most tremendous epithets he can find; he heaps Ossa upon Pelion: and, as if the English tongue did not furnish expressions strong or imposing enough, he tops the whole with a piece of formidable Latinity.

26. Let us avow then, in short, steadily but calmly, what our Author hazards with anxiety and agitation, that the authority of the supreme body cannot, *unless where limited by express convention*, be said to have any assignable, any certain bounds—That to say there is any act they *cannot* do,—to speak of anything of their's as being *illegal*,—as being *void*;—to speak of their exceeding their *authority* (whatever be the phrase)—their *power*, their *right*,—is, however common, an abuse of language.

27. The legislature *cannot* do it? The legislature *cannot* make a law to this effect? Why cannot? What is there that should hinder them? Why not this, as well as so many other laws murmured at, perhaps, as inexpedient, yet submitted to without any question of the *right?* With men of the same party, with

men whose affections are already lifted against party, with men whose affections are already lifted against the law in question, any thing will go down: any rubbish is good that will add fuel to the flame. But with regard to an impartial bystander, it is plain that it is not denying the right of the legislature, their *authority*, their *power*, or whatever be the word—it is not denying that they *can* do what is in question—it is not that, I say, or any discourse verging that way that can tend to give *him* the smallest satisfaction.

28. Grant even the proposition in general:— What are we the nearer? Grant that there are certain bounds to the *authority* of the legislature:— Of what use is it to say so, when these bounds are what no body has ever attempted to mark out to any useful purpose; that is, in any such manner whereby it might be known beforehand what description a law must be of to fall *within*, and what to fall *beyond* them? Grant that there *are* things which the legislature *cannot* do;—grant that there *are* laws which exceed the *power* of the legislature to establish. What rule does this sort of discourse furnish us for determining whether any one that is in question is, or is not of the number? As far as I can discover, none. Either the discourse goes on in the confusion it began; either all rests in vague assertions, and no intelligible argument at all is offered; or if any, such arguments as are drawn from the principle of *utility:* arguments which, in whatever variety of words expressed, come at last to neither more nor less than this: that the tendency of the law is to a greater or less degree, pernicious. If this then be the result of the argument, why not come home to it at once? Why turn aside into a wilderness of sophistry, when the path of plain reason is straight before us? . . .

34. In denying the existence of any assignable bounds to the supreme power, I added,[1] unless where limited by express convention: for this exception I could not but subjoin. Our Author indeed, in that passage in which, short as it is, he is the most explicit, leaves, we may observe, no room for it. 'However they began,' says he (speaking of the several forms of government) 'however they began, and by what right soever they subsist, there is and must be in ALL of them an authority that is absolute,'—To say this, however, of *all* governments without

[1] V. supra, para. 26.

exception;—to say that no assemblage of men can subsist in a state of government, without being subject to some *one* body whose authority stands unlimited so much as by convention; to say, in short, that not even by convention can any limitation be made to the power of that body in a state which in other respects is supreme, would be saying, I take it, rather too much: it would be saying that there is no such thing as government in the German Empire; nor in the Dutch Provinces; nor in the Swiss Cantons; nor was of old in the Achaean League.

3. PARLIAMENT AND ELECTORATE

[from Austin, *Province of Jurisprudence determined*, ed. Library of Ideas, 1954, Weidenfeld and Nicolson, pp. 230–233]

Adopting the language of most of the writers who have treated of the British Constitution, I commonly suppose that the present parliament, or the parliament for the time being, is possessed of the sovereignty: or I commonly suppose that the king and the lords, with the members of the commons' house, form a tripartite body which is sovereign or supreme. But, speaking accurately, the members of the commons' house are merely trustees for the body by which they are elected and appointed: and, consequently, the sovereignty always resides in the king and the peers, with the electoral body of the commons. That a trust is imposed by the party delegating, and that the party representing engages to discharge the trust, seems to be imported by the correlative expressions 'delegation' and 'representation'. It were absurd to suppose that the delegating empowers the representative party to defeat or abandon any of the purposes for which the latter is appointed: to suppose, for example, that the commons empower their representatives in parliament to relinquish their share in the sovereignty to the king and the lords.—The supposition that the powers of the commons are delegated absolutely to the members of the commons' house probably arose from the following causes. 1. The trust imposed by the electoral body upon the body representing them in parliament, is tacit rather than express: it arises from the relation between the bodies as delegating and representative parties, rather than from oral or written instructions given by the former to the latter. But since it arises from that relation, the trust is general and vague. The representatives are merely bound, generally and vaguely, to abstain from any such exercise of the delegated sovereign powers as would tend to defeat the purposes for which they are elected and appointed. 2. The trust is simply enforced by moral sanctions. In other words, that portion of constitutional law which regards the duties of the representative towards the electoral body, is positive morality merely. Nor is this extraordinary. For (as I shall show hereafter) all constitutional law, in every country whatever, is, as against the sovereign, in that predicament: and much of it, in every country, is also in that predicament, even as against parties who are subject or subordinate to the sovereign, and who therefore might be held from infringing it by legal or political sanctions.

If a trust of the kind in question were enforced by legal sanctions, the positive law binding the representative body might be made by the representative body and not by the electoral. For example: If the duties of the commons' house towards the commons who appoint it were enforced by legal sanctions, the positive law binding the commons' house might be made by the parliament: that is to say, by the commons' house itself in conjunction with the king and peers. Or, supposing the sovereignty resided in the commons without the king and the peers, the positive law binding the commons' house might be made by the house itself as representing the sovereign or state.—But, in either of these cases the law might be abrogated by its immediate author without the direct consent of the electoral body. Nor could the electoral body escape from that inconvenience, so long as its direct exercise of its sovereign or supreme powers was limited to the election of representatives. In order that the electoral body might escape from that inconvenience, the positive law binding its representatives must be made directly by itself or with its direct concurrence. For example; In order that the members of the commons' house might be bound legally and completely to discharge their duties to the commons, the law must be made directly by the commons themselves in concurrence with the king and the lords: or, supposing the sovereignty resided in the commons without the king and the peers, the law must be made directly by the commons themselves as being exclusively the sovereign. In either of these cases, the law could not be abrogated without the direct consent of the electoral body itself. For the king and the lords with the electoral body of the commons, or the electoral body of the commons as being exclusively the sovereign, would form an extraordinary and ulterior legislature: a legislature superior to that ordinary legislature which would be formed by the parliament or by the commons' house. A law of the parliament, or a law of the commons' house, which affected to abrogate a law of the extraordinary and ulterior legislature, would not be obeyed by the courts of justice. The tribunals would enforce the latter in the teeth of the former. They would examine the competence of the ordinary legislature to make the abrogating law, as they now examine the competence of any subordinate corporation to establish a by-law or other statute or ordinance. In the state of New York, the ordinary legislature of the state is controlled by an extraordinary legislature, in the manner which I have now described. The body of citizens appointing the ordinary legislature, forms an extraordinary and ulterior legislature by which the constitution of the state was directly established: and any law of the ordinary legislature, which conflicted with a constitutional law directly proceeding from the extraordinary, would be treated by the courts of justice as a legally invalid act.—That such an extraordinary and ulterior legislature is a good or useful institution, I pretend not to affirm. I merely affirm that the institution is possible, and that in one political society the institution actually obtains.

4. PARLIAMENTARY SOVEREIGNTY AND AUSTIN

[from Dicey, *Law of the Constitution*, Macmillan, 9th ed. 1919, pp. 72–74; 75–76]

As to Austin's theory of sovereignty in relation to the British constitution.—Sovereignty, like many of Austin's conceptions, is a generalisation drawn in the main from English law, just as the ideas of the economists of Austin's generation are (to a great extent) generalisations suggested by the circumstances of English commerce. In England we are accustomed to the existence of a supreme legislative body, i.e. a body which can make or unmake every law; and which, therefore, cannot be bound by any law. This is, from a legal point of view, the true conception of a sovereign, and the ease with which the theory of absolute sovereignty has been accepted by English jurists is due to the peculiar history of English constitutional law. So far, therefore, from its being true that the sovereignty of Parliament is a deduction from abstract theories of jurisprudence, a critic would come nearer the truth who asserted that Austin's theory of sovereignty is suggested by the position of the English Parliament, just as Austin's analysis of the term 'law' is at bottom an analysis of a typical law, namely, an English criminal statute.

It should, however, be carefully noted that the term 'sovereignty,' as long as it is accurately employed in the sense in which Austin sometimes uses it, is a merely legal conception, and means simply the power of law-making unrestricted by any legal limit. If the term 'sovereignty' be thus used, the sovereign power under the English constitution is clearly 'Parliament.' But the word 'sovereignty' is sometimes employed in a political rather than in a strictly legal sense. That body is 'politically' sovereign or supreme in a state the will of which is ultimately obeyed by the citizens of the state. In this sense of the word the electors of Great Britain may be said to be, together with the Crown and the Lords, or perhaps, in strict accuracy, independently of the King and the Peers, the body in which sovereign power is vested. For as things now stand, the will of the electorate, and certainly of the electorate in combination with the Lords and the Crown, is sure ultimately to prevail on all subjects to be determined by the British Government. The matter indeed may be carried a little further, and we may assert that the arrangements of the constitution are now such as to ensure that the will of the electors shall by regular and constitutional means always in the end assert itself as the predominant influence in the country. But this is a political, not a legal fact. The electors can in the long run always enforce their will. But the courts will take no notice of the will of the electors. The judges know nothing about any will of the people except in so far as that will is expressed by an Act of Parliament, and would never suffer the validity of a state to be questioned on the ground of its having been passed or being kept alive in opposition to the wishes of the electors. The political sense of the word 'sovereignty' is, it is true, fully as important as the legal sense or more so. But the two significations, though intimately connected together, are essentially different, and in some part of his work Austin has apparently confused the one sense with the other.

Austin owns that the doctrine here laid down by him is inconsistent with the language used by writers who have treated of the British constitution. It is further absolutely inconsistent with the validity of the Septennial Act. Nothing is more certain than that no English judge ever conceded, or, under the present constitution, can concede that Parliament is in any legal sense a 'trustee' for the electors. Of such a feigned 'trust' the courts know nothing. The plain truth is that as a matter of law Parliament is the sovereign power in the state, and that the 'supposition' treated by Austin as inaccurate is the correct statement of a legal fact which forms the basis of our whole legislative and judicial system. It is, however, equally true that in a political sense the electors are the most important part of, we may even say are actually, the sovereign power, since their will is under the present constitution sure to obtain ultimate obedience. The language therefore of Austin is as correct in regard to 'political' sovereignty as it is erroneous in regard to what we may term 'legal' sovereignty. The electors are a part of and the predominant part of the poltically sovereign power. But the legally sovereign power is assuredly, as maintained by all the best writers on the constitution, nothing but Parliament.

It may be conjectured that the error of which (from a lawyer's point of view) Austin has been guilty arises from his feeling, as every person must feel who is not the slave to mere words, that Parliament is nothing like an omnipotent body, but that its powers are practically limited in more ways than one. And this limitation Austin expresses, not very happily, by saying that the members of the House of Commons are subject to a trust imposed upon them by the electors.

5. A MODERN ANALYSIS

[from Marshall and Moodie, *Some Problems of the Constitution*, Hutchinson, 1959, pp. 16–18]

Later writers have treated Austin's definition of the sovereign authority as an elementary confusion and adopted the distinction popularised by Dicey between 'legal sovereignty' exercised by the Queen-in-Parliament, and 'political sovereignty' exercised by the electorate. ('Electorate', 'People', and 'Nation', it should be noticed, cannot be used for this purpose entirely interchangeably, since the last two contain many persons who are not in fact electors.) But Dicey's definitions are clumsy in implying that the distinction between the two sets of persons can be matched by the entirely different kind of distinction between the function of legislation and the function or right of exerting political influence to secure legislation. Clearly if the exercise of political sovereignty is the bringing to bear of non-legal power or influence it is not something which is confined to the electorate. Members of Parliament, as well as the Government and Civil Service collectively, are themselves part of the political sovereign as well as the electorate. Exercising political sovereignty is not what the electorate does as distinct from Parliament, but what everybody (including Parliament) does in his or their political capacity. Similarly legal sovereignty is not what Parliament has as distinct from the electorate, but what everybody (including the electorate) has in his or their legal capacity or status. But can it be argued that the electorate has a legal capacity? Austin at least, in including the electorate in his definition of the sovereign legal authority, was saying that it had, but that it had conferred the function of legislating upon its representatives; and there is no obvious reason why his description of the Constitution should be regarded as less apposite than Dicey's. He was not, after all, under any misapprehension as to the way in which legislation came about. It is conceded on this view that the people may not impress their will on a court of law directly, but must legislate through their representatives. As Sir Frederick Pollock remarked, an identical resolution passed by the electors of every constituency in England would have no legal force and no court of justice would be entitled to pay any attention to it. But exactly the same is true in the United States or in India, whose constitutions explicitly declare that legislative institutions are founded upon the authority of the people. The claim does not of course imply either that the people legislate directly or that their assent is necessary to the validity of individual rules in a legal system. In its elective function at least it might be said that the British electorate is a creature known to the law.

Dicey's distinctions tend to obscure this constitutional, as distinct from political, influential, or agitatory, role of the people. That legislators are the product of a specific legal process of election and not of any other process (e.g. self-appointment, nomination, or insurrection) is a fact which could hardly be omitted from any accurate account of the rules of our constitutional system. It is said that the office of Prime Minister is no longer entirely unknown to the law since several statutes now refer to it. A similar claim might be made on behalf of the People or the Nation. There must, after all, be some collectivity of the kind referred to by the Representation of the *People* Acts, or even (though more obliquely) to be inferred from the existence of such appellations as *British* Railways and the *National* Trust.

6. THE NATURE OF PARLIAMENTARY SOVEREIGNTY

[from Dicey, *Law of the Constitution*, Macmillan, 9th ed. 1919, pp. 39–40]

Parliament means, in the mouth of a lawyer (though the word has often a different sense in ordinary conversation), the King, the House of Lords, and the House of Commons; these three bodies acting together may be aptly described as the 'King in Parliament,' and constitute Parliament.

The principle of Parliamentary sovereignty means neither more nor less than this, namely, that Parliament thus defined has, under the English constitution, the right to make or unmake any law whatever; and, further, that no person or body is recognised by the law of England as having a right to override or set aside the legislation of Parliament.

A law may, for our present purpose, be defined as 'any rule which will be enforced by the courts.' The principle then of Parliamentary sovereignty may, looked at from its positive side, be thus described: Any Act of Parliament, or any part of an Act of Parliament, which makes a new law, or repeals or modifies an existing law, will be obeyed by the courts. The same principle, looked at from its negative side, may be thus stated: there is no person or body of persons who can, under the English constitution, make rules which override or derogate from an Act of Parliament, or which (to express the same thing in other words) will be enforced by the courts in contravention of an Act of Parliament.

7. SOVEREIGNTY OF PARLIAMENT

[from Wade, 'Introduction to Dicey', *Law of the Constitution*, Macmillan, 9th ed. 1919, pp. xli–xlv]

Recent events have shown that the limitation of the legal rule in fact goes further than Dicey would have admitted. He described the external limit to the real power of a sovereign as consisting in the possibility or certainty that his subjects, or a large number of them, will disobey or resist his laws. His examples are chiefly concerned with the actions of despotic monarchs. As a prophet he has been unhappy in his predictions of resistance to Parliament. For it has without resistance both changed the succession to the throne by His Majesty's Declaration of Abdication Act, 1936, and on more than one occasion prolonged the life of the existing House of Commons. Granted that political expediency may be a *de facto* limitation upon the working of a legal rule, it must be admitted that the question of where lies sovereignty as a political concept remains unanswered, except that the power of government rests in the last resort in the result of a general election. Nor need it be answered by a lawyer . . .

There is in the sphere of internal government a limitation upon the supremacy of Parliament which was hardly recognisable in 1885. The presence in the State of organisations reflecting the views of every trade, profession or business has led to the practice of consultation prior to the introduction of a measure into Parliament between the Government Department whose task it may be to present a Bill to Parliament and the organisations whose members are most concerned with the contents of the proposed legislation. The result is that Parliament may be asked by the Government to enact what is more or less an agreed measure . . . Governments can no longer afford to disregard public opinion. The exercise of the law-making power by Parliament is controlled almost exclusively by the Government of the day, placed in power by the possession of a majority in the Commons. But it is only used to coerce the subject after the subjects—through Chambers of Commerce, Federations of Industry, Trade Unions (of manufacturers as well as of employees) professional, technical and manual—have been consulted.

Rule by advisory committees is a device much favoured since 1918. This gives the force of law to the obligation to consult beforehand, where as is often the case, such advisory committees are expressly provided by statute.

The result is that before the sovereignty of Parliament is invoked to make or unmake laws the normal process, at all events as regards internal administrative organisation, is for the Minister either by obligation of law or on grounds of expediency to seek advice from the appropriate advisory committee. He may also take into consultation as many other bodies of a representative character as he chooses. When the resulting Bill comes before Parliament which alone can give it the force of law, it may well be, except in details, an agreed measure which those most affected are prepared, however reluctantly, to put into operation. Delegated legislation too has weakened the control of Parliament, though without it Parliament could not have enlarged the sphere of administration. This type of legislation is not confined to Government Departments, but extends also to the numerous independent statutory authorities which cannot be regarded as Departments of State directly responsible to the legislature; the Unemployment Assistance Board and the Agricultural Marketing Boards will suffice as illustrations.

Thus the political supremacy of Parliament as a law-making organ becomes more and more a fiction. Legislation is a compromise of conflicting interests. Parliament can no longer compel, save in outward form. It must be left to the political scientist to say, if he can, where lies the political sovereign. This much is clear, that truly representative government can but imperfectly be achieved by a legislature acting alone. Other methods are essential to produce coincidence between the organ exercising legal power and the subject.

It may be well to add that a convention which secures consultation before framing legislation does not involve a Government accepting dictation upon major matters of policy. It would be a dangerous doctrine to admit, for example, control of the foreign policy of the State by the refusal of members of an important trade union to make munitions of war. Consultation of private interests by Government Departments is in practice directed to matters of detail in framing legislation rather than to the determination of fundamental issues of policy.

8. THE MEANING OF SUPREMACY

[from Jennings, *The Law and the Constitution*, U.L.P., 5th ed. 1959, pp. 144–149;–170–171]

The dominant characteristic of the British Constitution is, as has previously been emphasised, and as Dicey pointed out, the supremacy or sovereignty of Parliament. This means, in Dicey's words, that Parliament has the right to make or unmake any law whatever, and that no person or body is recognised by the law of England as having a right to override or set aside the legislation of Parliament.

The consequence is that not only the courts but everybody in the United Kingdom regard that as binding law which Parliament has enacted. It is not possible for any person to refuse to obey the orders of Parliament because they are not law, though it is possible for him to disobey on the ground that they ought not to be law. Nor is it possible, as it is in some countries such as the United States and most Commonwealth Countries, for the courts to declare that an Act of Parliament need not be obeyed because it is *ultra vires* or beyond the powers of Parliament. These two assertions, it should be noted, are not the same. For though in most countries the powers of the legislature are limited, it is not necessarily the prerogative of the courts to refuse to obey legislation. The notion that a court of law could determine the legality of legislation comes from the United States, where the Supreme Court assumed the power of declaring the statutes of Congress to be not applicable because they did not conform with the Constitution. The same power has either been assumed by the courts or provided by the constitutions in Canada, Australia, India, Pakistan, Ceylon, Ghana, and the Federation of Malaya. But many continental countries continue to follow the old principle that excess of legislative authority is a matter between the legislature and the electors. Consequently, the fact that the *courts* do not regard themselves as competent to restrict the exercise of the legislative power is not in itself conclusive of the extent of that power.

Dicey has emphasised the authority which this supremacy of its legislation gives to Parliament . . . The powers which it exercised with the King's consent and authority it claimed to exercise as of right under the Stuarts. Though for a long time it was not clear what its power was, the result of the revolutions was firmly to establish the doctrine that the King in Parliament can do anything.

Thus Parliament may remodel the British Constitution, prolong its own life, legislate *ex post facto*, legalise illegalities, provide for individual cases, interfere with contracts and authorise the seizure of property, give dictatorial powers to the Government, dissolve the United Kingdom or the British Commonwealth, introduce communism or socialism or individualism or fascism, entirely without legal restriction.

Dicey has called this enormous legal power the 'sovereignty' of Parliament. But this is a word of quasi-theological origin which may easily lead us into difficulties. Sovereignty was a doctrine developed at the close of the Middle Ages to advance the cause of the secular State against the claims of the Church. 'Sovereignty', said Bodin in 1576, 'is supreme power over citizens and subjects unrestrained by the Laws.' Though the sovereign was bound by divine law and the law of nature, he could within these limits make what laws he liked: and in every community there must be such a sovereign. Developed by Hobbes, Bentham, and Austin, this theory has passed into the current legal theory of England. It appears particularly appropriate to us because it seems to fit the facts of English political institutions.

Yet if sovereignty is supreme power, Parliament is not sovereign. For there are many things, as Dicey and Laski both point out, which Parliament cannot do. 'No Parliament,' says Professor Laski, 'would dare to disfranchise the Roman Catholics or to prohibit the existence of trade unions.' Parliament is not the permanent and personal sovereign contemplated by Bodin. It consists of two groups of men, of which the members of one will within five years at most cease to have anything to do with Parliament, and who, if they wish to join 'the best club in Europe' once again, must offer themselves through a complicated political organisation for re-election by a heterogeneous group of their fellow citizens. Since, if they wish for re-election, they may be called upon to give an account of their actions, they must consider in their actions what the general opinion about them may be. Parliament passes any laws which many people do not want. But it never passes any laws which any substantial section of the population violently dislikes . . .

These considerations made Austin a little doubtful about the seat of sovereignty in England. Dicey felt compelled to draw a distinction between legal sovereignty and political sovereignty. 'Legal sovereignty,' he said, 'is a merely legal conception, and means simply the power of law-making unrestricted by any legal limit.' Whereas 'that body is politically sovereign or supreme in a State the will of which is ultimately obeyed by the citizens of the State.' Thus Parliament is the legal sovereign and the electors the political sovereign.

If this is so, legal sovereignty is not sovereignty at all. It is not supreme power. It is a legal concept, a form of expression which lawyers use to express the relations between Parliament and the courts. It means that the courts will always recognise as law the rules which Parliament makes by legislation; that is, rules made in the customary manner and expressed in the customary form . . .

Parliamentary supremacy means essentially two things. It means, first, that Parliament can legally enact legislation dealing with any subject-matter whatever. There are no limitations except political expediency and constitutional conventions. De Lolme's remark that Parliament can do anything except make a man into a woman and woman into a man is often quoted. But, like many of the remarks which de Lolme made, it is wrong. For if Parliament enacted that all men should be women, they would be women so far as the law is concerned. In speaking of the power of Parliament, we are dealing with legal principles, not with facts. Though it is true Parliament cannot in fact change the course of nature, it is equally true that it cannot in fact do all sorts of things. The supremacy of Parliament is a legal fiction, and legal fiction can assume anything.

Parliamentary supremacy means, secondly, that Parliament

can legislate for all persons and all places. If it enacts that smoking in the streets of Paris is an offence, then it *is* an offence. Naturally, it is an offence by English law and not by French law, and therefore it would be regarded as an offence only by those who paid attention to English law. The Paris police would not at once begin arresting all smokers, nor would French criminal courts begin inflicting punishments upon them. But if any Frenchman came into any place where attention was paid to English law, proceedings might be taken against him. If, for instance, a Frenchman who had smoked in the streets of Paris spent a few hours in Folkestone, he might be brought before a court of summary jurisdiction for having committed an offence against English law.

9. DOES THE CABINET REALLY EXERCISE PARLIAMENT'S 'SOVEREIGNTY'?

[from Jennings, *The Law and the Constitution*, U.L.P., 5th ed. 1959, pp. 180–184]

With the nineteenth century the Cabinet became at once more homogeneous and more powerful. George IV and William IV might still exercise great influence. The first official act of George IV was to send for the Foxite Whigs. Only because of his death was the Reform Government possible in 1830. The death of William IV prolonged for four years a ministry which would have expired long before if he had lived. But certainly after the accession of Victoria the policy of the country was that of the Cabinet, and the Cabinet existed because it could command a majority in the House of Commons. The strange experiment of William IV in 1834 failed because Peel could not control the House of Commons. The dissolution did not give Peel the majority which he expected, and Lord John Russell turned him out when he thought fit. It is true that 'the Bedchamber Plot' in 1839 kept in the Whigs and kept out the Tories because the Queen objected to changing her ladies. But this was only because neither party had a majority upon which it could rely. When Peel obtained his vast majority in 1841 there was no longer any doubt that the Tories had to 'COME IN'. After that, the Cabinet resigned as soon as it had lost its majority. Disraeli with his customary realism correctly estimated the nature of the new Constitution when, after the defeat of his party at the general election of 1868, he resigned without meeting Parliament. It is useless for a Cabinet to remain in office if it has lost its majority.

It is commonly asserted that the Cabinet system enables Parliament to control the Government. That may be true of France, where any Government is necessarily a Coalition, and where real deference is shown to the opinions of the committees of the legislature. It is not true in the United Kingdom. The Cabinet, or a Department under the control of the Cabinet, formulates the policy, and Parliament must either accept the policy or risk a dissolution.

Under the two-party system this is obvious, at least so far as the House of Commons is concerned. The Cabinet contains the leaders of the party having the majority in the House of Commons. It places the policy before the House and expects the party to vote in its favour. If the party does as it is told, the Cabinet's majority is assured. No matter what the Opposition may say or do, the policy is definitely determined and cannot be overridden. Not only can the Government be certain of a majority for its legislative proposals, but also it can control the procedure of the House in order to pass the legislation in its own way and at its own time. The Standing Orders give great preference to Government business. From the beginning of the session until Whitsuntide, Government business has precedence on all days except Fridays; and from Whitsuntide or thereabouts until the end of the session the Government occupies the whole time of the House.

It is true that matters can be discussed in various ways at the instance of private members. A question can be asked on any subject though it need not be answered. Any member can move the adjournment of the House to discuss any definite matter of urgent public importance. If the Speaker thinks fit and forty members support him, a debate takes place the same evening. But the Government can use its majority to secure a favourable verdict. When the House is about to go into committee on the Civil Estimates, the Army Estimates, and the Navy Estimates, any matter relevant to those Estimates may be debated in the House. When any individual vote is discussed in committee, the service for which the vote is proposed may be discussed. By convention, too, it is the Opposition which determines what votes are discussed. But at the end of the debate the whips are put on, and the Government majority votes in its favour. Also, only twenty-six days are available for discussing all the Estimates, Supplementary Estimates and other Supply business, so that the number of subjects debated is limited, and the longer the debate the fewer of them there are to debate. By convention, again, the Government gives precedence for a vote of censure by the Opposition, but the Government majority determines the result.

Yet even these rights of the Opposition may be swept away by the Government, for the Standing Orders may be suspended or altered by a majority vote. It is not uncommon for the Government to move to suspend some Standing Orders, in order that it may take all the time of the House; and the Government majority passes the motion. The extent of debate upon legislation and the result of the debate are similarly determined by the Government. Though under Standing Orders a Bill may be debated on its introduction (in some cases), on second reading, on the financial resolution and the report of the financial resolution (if there is one), in committee, on the report stage, and on third reading, and these normally take place on different days, the Government majority can suspend Standing Orders so as to take all the steps on the same day. A 'guillotine resolution' may be moved by the Government and passed by the Government majority to determine the times at which the votes must be taken; and the majority supports the Government on these votes. Also, if a minister moves the closure of any debate, and the Speaker or Chairman accepts the motion, the majority vote brings the debate to an end. Bills introduced by private members can be rejected or passed, as the Government thinks fit, by the use of its majority.

Thus a Government backed by its majority can determine what legislation shall be debated, for how long it shall be debated, and what the result of the debate shall be. Naturally, it does not exercise its powers too stringently, for the House dislikes to feel 'the whip' too much. Ministers try to persuade, rather than to coerce, the House to adopt their timetable. Moreover, the fact that the Government has the power enables it to make agreements with the Opposition leaders, so that a reasonable amount of business is done with a reasonable amount of criticism.

PART II

(a) Collective and Individual Ministerial Responsibility
(b) The "Weapon" of Dissolution

(a)

10. COLLECTIVE RESPONSIBILITY: THE BASIC CONVENTION

[from E. C. S. Wade and G. Godfrey Phillips, *Constitutional Law*, Longmans, 4th ed. 1950, pp. 63–65]

It is not the fear of legal liability, but the desire to operate the machinery of government on consitutional lines which influences Ministers in their conduct of affairs and their relationship with Parliament. Accordingly there has been evolved since 1688 the rule of collective responsibility which rests upon convention alone. During the great part of the eighteenth century the Cabinet was still a body of holders of high office whose relationship with one another was ill defined, and thus the body remained not responsible to Parliament. The Government was the King's Government in fact as well as in name, and the King acted on the advice of individual Ministers. The advice tendered by a Minister might, or might not, agree with that acceptable to his nominal colleagues, some of whom were seldom, if ever, consulted by their Sovereign. Apart from the relatively homogeneous Ministries under Walpole's pre-eminent leadership Cabinets were formed of different groups with many different aims; this made collective responsibility impracticable. Moreover, the King sometimes consulted those who were out of office without the prior approval of his Ministers. Eventually the Representation of the People Act, 1832 (the great Reform Bill), brought realisation that for the future the Executive must hold the same political views as the majority in Parliament. The support of Parliament could no longer be secured by the expedients of sinecure offices, pensions, the gift of seats in rotten boroughs, and such-like devices which had not shocked eighteenth-century political morality. The Cabinet, all its members united by party ties, became the definite link between the King and Parliament and so acquired the whole control over the direction of public affairs. Thus collective responsibility developed later than the political responsibility of individual Ministers. Just as it became recognised that a single Minister could not retain office against the will of Parliament, so later it became clear that all Ministers must stand or fall together in Parliament, if the Government was to be carried on as a unity rather than by a number of advisers of the Sovereign acting separately.

By the middle of the nineteenth century collective responsibility, as it is understood to-day, was firmly established. *Lord Salisbury* said in 1878:

> For all that passes in Cabinet every member of it who does not resign is absolutely and irretrievably responsible and has no right afterwards to say that he agreed in one case to a compromise, while in another he was persuaded by his colleagues . . . It is only on the principle that absolute responsibility is undertaken by every member of the Cabinet, who, after a decision is arrived at, remains a member of it, that the joint responsibility of Ministers to Parliament can be upheld and one of the most essential principles of parliamentary responsibility established.

This statement explains why it is essential to draw the veil of secrecy over all that passes in Cabinet even in times when the requirements of security do not necessarily impose the ban of silence. It is impossible to preserve a united front, if disclosures are permitted of differences which have emerged in arriving at a decision. The fate of the minority of Ministers on the occasion of the single departure from the rule of unanimity reinforces its validity. In 1932 a coalition Cabinet issued an announcement to the effect that they had agreed to differ over the tariff issue, while remaining united on all other vital matters of national policy. The dissenting Ministers were given leave to oppose the majority view by speech and by vote. The convention of Cabinet unanimity was, however, reinforced when those Ministers decided a few months later to resign on the cognate issue of imperial preference.

Collective responsibility does not require that every Cabinet Minister must take an active part in the formulation of policy, nor that his presence in the Cabinet room is essential whenever a decision is taken. His obligations may be passive rather than active when the decision does not relate to matters falling within his own sphere of administrative responsibility. He must, however, be informed beforehand of what the proposal is and have an opportunity of voicing his doubts and objections. The size of modern Cabinets (in peacetime) would alone seem to preclude active participation by each Minister in forming conclusions. A body of some twenty or more is too large for effective committee work, but in the nature of things Ministers in Cabinet are, or should be, concerned more with decisions of principle rather than detail. Collective responsibility does, however, mean that a Cabinet Minister, and his Parliamentary Secretary, must vote with the Government in Parliament and, if necessary, be prepared to defend its policy. Neither in Parliament nor outside can a Minister be heard to say that he is in disagreement with a Cabinet decision, or for that matter with a decision of a colleague taken without reference to the Cabinet.

11. THE CHANGING PRACTICE OF COLLECTIVE RESPONSIBILITY

[from A. H. Birch, *Representative and Responsible Government*, Allen and Unwin, 1964, pp. 136–138]

It is clear that the doctrine of collective responsibility does not occupy the place in the present political system that is commonly claimed for it. It purports to provide an effective sanction for governmental blunders, but it does not normally do so . . . In times of peace a modern government is not more likely to resign or dissolve Parliament when its policies meet with a major reversal than when things are going well, but less likely to do so. In the months following the Suez expedition the opposition leaders frequently quoted the Government's alleged unpopularity in the country as a reason why it should resign, but they knew as well as every one else that they were simply playing a traditional and somewhat outdated Parliamentary game. A crisis that would have brought down a government a hundred years ago now acts as an opportunity for its Parliamentary supporters to give an impressive display of party loyalty, and stimulates its leaders to hold on to the reins of power until public attention is diverted to a sphere of policy which puts the government in a more favourable light.

To say this is not to say that the doctrine has no useful function. The convention that the government must always present a united front has important and possibly beneficial effects. It compels ministers to be discreet and prevents the sort of confusion that sometimes arises in other countries, for instance the United States, when government spokesmen make pronouncements which reveal differences of view within the administration. It tends to force inter-departmental disputes to the surface at cabinet meetings, when they are generally resolved one way or another. It identifies government policy in a way that provides a clear focus for public discussion, at least when the facts are generally known.

This maintenance of a united front is held in such high esteem by the general public that, significantly, and quite recently, a new linguistic usage has developed. A government is now commonly said to be 'taking responsibility' when it takes a collective decision and uses the whips to ensure Parliamentary support for it, and to be 'shedding' or 'evading responsibility' if it permits a free vote on the matter. The decision to allow a free vote on capital punishment in 1956 was criticised in these terms, and when the Government proposed to allow a free vote on the most controversial clauses of the Street Offences Bill in 1959 the objections from its own back-benchers were so numerous that it changed its mind and put on a two-line whip.

This usage of the term 'responsibility' involves something like a reversal of the traditional meaning, for in the new usage a government is acting 'responsibly' not when it submits to Parliamentary control but when it takes effective measures to dominate Parliament. Perhaps this reversal of meaning indicates as well as any description the gap between the doctrine of collective responsibility and the practice of contemporary politics.

12. COLLECTIVE RESPONSIBILITY TODAY

[from G. Marshall and Graeme C. Moodie, *Some Problems of the Constitution*, Hutchinson, 1959, pp. 72–74]

The substance of the Government's collective responsibility could be defined as its duty to submit its policy to and defend its policy before the House of Commons, and to resign if defeated on an issue of confidence. The defeat of any substantial bill is nowadays regarded as a loss of confidence. This was not always so. It was argued (for example by Lord Macaulay) that the ability to provide a stable administration—being the primary function of government—did not entail a duty to avoid defeat on mere legislative proposals. There may be something to be said for this view, though it is a principle which politicians in a predominantly two-party House of Commons might now find difficult to sustain in the face of the notion of Parliament as a legislative machine directed by Ministers and powered by a legislative mandate. The modern practice, however, is a stricter one than that of carrying major legislative measures. For governments now regard it as politically incumbent upon them to avoid defeat in the Commons on any issue whatsoever, whether on the floor of the House or in Committee. (Resignation does not, of course, follow upon a chance defeat in Committee, but the matter is regarded as one whose consequences must be put right at the earliest opportunity.) It is not perhaps self-evident that such a rigidity of principle is necessary to the successful working of the parliamentary system, or that it is required by any constitutional convention. In the Commons' debate of January 1958 on the procedure of the House some back-bench arguments in favour of a conscious relaxation of the practice were heard. It was suggested, for example, that the Government might 'let it be known that on all minor matters of the Committee stage of Bills, wherever they are taken, it will not be regarded as a world-shaking event justifying the resignation of the Government . . . if the Government are defeated'. The benefits, it was said, might include more freedom of action for individual Members of Parliament, and some lightening of the physical responsibility of attendance to vote in divisions. The Home Secretary, replying to the debate, thought that it was necesssary for Members to face a certain amount of discomfort in playing to the rules of the parliamentary contest. 'We are here,' he said, 'in a struggle for power. If we started to reach some sort of agreement between the parties that there could be a defeat of the Government of the day, it is doubtful if the parliamentary system would work'.[1] There is perhaps a suspicion of circularity in the argument here. That a defeat for the Government is a defeat in the parliamentary struggle for power is so because all such defeats are regarded as counting adversely according to the existing conventional practice. It is not inherent in the nature of an already artificial struggle that its rules could not be otherwise than they are. The contest for power is not, as matters stand, conducted without restriction. When for example in the Parliament of 1950–1, discomforting consequences were seen to follow from attempts to bring about snap defeats of the Government by late-night prayers against statutory instruments, it was not thought improper to suggest procedural remedies for the inconveniences to Members and thus in a minor way deliberately to relax the rules of parliamentary struggle for power. It is hard to see why a voluntary loosening of conventional practices on a minor scale by a government with a safe majority, or an extension of the number of occasions on which a free vote is permitted, must be incompatible with the principles of the parliamentary system. Any extension of free voting[2] is admittedly often opposed either on the ground that it exposes Members to outside pressures—a view which suggests its own remedy—or on the ground that 'governments should govern' and not evade their responsibility. It is slightly curious that 'responsibility' which originally stood for the amenability of the Crown and its servants to legislative control should have come to stand in this sense for an assertion of the executive's independence of parliamentary control.

[1] 581 H. C. Deb., c. 760.

[2] For further comments on the 'free vote' cf. section VII, pp. 36.

13. INDIVIDUAL MINISTERIAL RESPONSIBILITY: THE CONVENTION

[from E. C. S. Wade and G. Godfrey Phillips, *Constitutional Law*, Longmans, 4th ed. 1950, p. 65]

The individual responsibility of a Minister to Parliament is more positive in character. Each in his own sphere bears the burden of speaking and acting for the Government. When a Minister announces that His Majesty's Government have decided that they are prepared to take a certain course of action, it does not follow that the decision has been referred to the Cabinet. No doubt it would have been on an important issue of policy; but if the decision relates exclusively to the sphere for which the Minister is responsible, it must be at his discretion whom he chooses to consult beforehand; it is in the exercise of that discretion that he may decide to act without previous reference to his Cabinet colleagues. Nowadays so complex are results of governmental action that it is safe to assume that the practice of prior inter-departmental consultation is firmly established at all levels, and the experience of war should serve to ensure that there is no relapse into departmental isolationism. Be this as it may, a Minister knows that he will ultimately have to rely upon the support of his Cabinet colleagues if political criticism becomes vocal, and he must temper his decisions by reference to that consideration.

While collective responsibility ensures that the King's Government presents a united front to Parliament, individual responsibility in its political meaning ensures that for every act or neglect of his department a Minister must answer. Hence the rule of anonymity in the Civil Service is important. For what an unnamed official does, or does not do, his Minister alone must answer in Parliament and the official, who can not be heard in his own defence, is therefore protected from attack. This positive liability of a Minister is essential to the performance by Parliament, and more particularly by the House of Commons, of its role of critic of the Executive. No Minister can shield himself by blaming his official. 'It would be new and dangerous constitutional doctrine if Ministers of the Crown could excuse the failure of their policies by turning upon the experts whose advice they have taken or upon the agents whom they have employed.'[3] Nor can he throw responsibility on a ministerial colleague, once it is established that the matter under consideration is the responsibility of his own department.

14. INDIVIDUAL MINISTERIAL RESPONSIBILITY IN PRACTICE

[from S. E. Finer, *Public Administration*, xxxiv, 1956, pp. 393–394]

The convention implies a form of punishment for a delinquent Minister. That punishment is no longer an act of attainder, or an impeachment, but simply loss of office.

If each, or even very many charges of incompetence were habitually followed by the punishment, the remedy would be a very real one: its deterrent effect would be extremely great. In fact, that sequence is not only exceedingly rare, but arbitrary and unpredictable Most charges never reach the stage of individualisation at all: they are stifled under the blanket of party solidarity. Only when there is a minority Government, or in the infrequent cases where the Minister seriously alienates his own back benchers, does the issue of the individual culpability of the Minister even arise. Even there it is subject to hazards: the punishment may be avoided if the Prime Minister, whether on his own or on the Minister's initiative, makes a timely reshuffle. Even when some charges get through the now finely woven net, and are laid at the door of a Minister, much depends on his nicety, and much on the character of the Prime Minister. Brazen tenacity of office can still win a reprieve. And, in the last resort—though this happens infrequently—the resignation of the Minister may be made purely formal by reappointment to another post soon afterwards.

We may put the matter in this way: whether a Minister is forced to resign depends on three factors, on himself, his Prime Minister and his party. On himself—as Austen Chamberlain resigned though possessing the confidence of his Prime Minister and his party whereas Ayrton remained in office despite having neither. On the Prime Minister—as Salisbury stood between Matthews, his Home Secretary, and the party that clamoured for his dismissal. On the party, as witness the impotence of Palmerston to save Westbury, Balfour to save Wyndham,

[3] *The Times*, Leading Article, November 21, 1949.

Asquith to save Birrell. For a resignation to occur all three factors have to be just so: the Minister compliant, the Prime Minister firm, the party clamorous. This conjuncture is rare, and is in fact fortuitous. Above all, it is indiscriminate—which Ministers escape and which do not is decided neither by the circumstances of the offence nor its gravity. A Wyndham and a Chamberlain go for a peccadillo, a Kitchener will remain despite major blunders.

A remedy ought to be certain. A punishment, to be deterrent, ought to be certain. But whether the Minister should resign is simply the (necessarily) haphazard consequence of a fortuitous concomitance of personal party and political temper.

Is there then a 'convention' of resignation at all?

A convention, in Dicey's sense, is a rule which is not enforced by the Courts. The important word is 'rule'. 'Rule' does not mean merely an observed uniformity in the past; the notion includes the expectation that the uniformity will continue in the future. It is not simply a description; it is a prescription. It has a compulsive force.

Now in its first sense, that the Minister alone *speaks* for his Civil Servants to the House and to his Civil Servants for the House, the convention of ministerial responsibility has both the proleptic and the compulsive features of a 'rule'. But in the sense in which we have been considering it, that the Minister *may be punished, through loss of office* for all the misdeeds and neglects of his Civil Servants which he cannot prove to have been outside all possibility of his cognisance and control, the proposition does not seem to be a rule at all.

What is the compulsive element in such a 'rule'? All it says (on examination) is that if the Minister is yielding, his Prime Minister unbending and his party out for blood—no matter how serious or trivial the reason—the Minister will find himself without Parliamentary support. This is a statement of fact, not a code. What is more, as a statement of fact it comes very close to being a truism: that a Minister entrusted by his Prime Minister with certain duties must needs resign if he loses the support of his majority. The only compulsive element in the proposition in that if and when a Minister loses his majority he ought to get out rather than be kicked out.

Moreover, even as a simple generalisation, an observed uniformity, the 'convention' is, surely, highly misleading? It takes the wrong cases: it generalises from the exceptions and neglects the common run. There are four categories of delinquent Ministers: the fortunate, the less fortunate, the unfortunate, and the plain unlucky. After sinning, the first go to other Ministries; the second to Another Place; the third just go. Of the fourth there are but twenty examples in a century: indeed, if one omits Neville Chamberlain (an anomaly) and the 'personal' cases, viz., Mundella, Thomas and Dalton, there are but sixteen. Not for these sixteen the honourable exchange of offices, or the silent and not dishonourable exit. Their lot is public penance in the white sheet of a resignation speech or letter. (Sir Ben Smith is the only exception: neither shuffle nor white sheet for him, but highly uncommunicative disappearance: Sir Winston put it as *spurlos versunken*, 'sunk without trace.') It is on some sixteen or at most nineteen penitents and one anomaly that the generalisation has been based.

'*When Diagoras, the so-called atheist, was at Samothrace one of his friends showed him several votive tablets put up by people who had survived very dangerous storms. "See", he says, "you who deny a Providence, how many people have been saved by their prayers to the Gods." "Yes" rejoins Diagoras, "I see those who were saved. Now show me the tablets of those who were drowned."*'

15. HOW IMMUNE ARE MINISTERS TO PARLIAMENTARY SANCTIONS?

[from G. Marshall and Graeme C. Moodie, *Some Problems of Constitution*, Hutchinson, 1959, pp. 78–70]

What then are we to say of the rule which is often stated in the form that there exists a liability on a Minister to resign for errors in administration not connected with the general policy of his Cabinet colleagues? The efficacy of this principle as a sanction upon Ministers was strongly denied by Sidney Low half a century ago. The House cannot in fact, he pointed out, get rid of one Minister of whose conduct it disapproves, without getting rid of the Government, if its intended victim is sheltered behind the shield of joint responsibility. Acts unconnected with government policy can be treated by the administration as raising a question of confidence, and moreover a Minister, besides being aware of this, is also aware that when he does lose his office, his fall is likely to be the result of other ministerial shortcomings bearing no necessary relation to his own departmental conduct. 'He may,' Low wrote:—

> have cost the country thousands of lives and millions of pounds, launching an ill-arranged expedition into the heart of a distant continent, too late for it to be of any use; and his defeat eventually be brought about because his colleagues have decided—perhaps in opposition to his own wishes—to put an unpopular tax on bread and beer?[4]

With some small substitution of examples, Ministers experience similar immunities and contingencies today.

16. THE MEANING OF MINISTERIAL RESPONSIBILITY

[from D. N. Chester, 'Crichel Down and Ministerial Responsibility' in *Public Administration*, xxxii, Winter, 1954, pp. 399–401]

In replying to the general debate on the 20th July, (1954), the Home Secretary enlarged upon the doctrine of Ministerial responsibility to meet those critics who thought that the doctrine rendered civil servants effectively responsible to no one. After pointing out that all civil servants hold their office 'at pleasure' and can be dismissed at any time by the Minister concerned, Sir David Maxwell Fyfe went on to enumerate four different categories of cases in which there may be Parliamentary criticism of a Department and for which he said different considerations applied. They were:

1. Where a civil servant carries out an explicit order by a Minister, the Minister must protect the civil servant concerned.

2. Where a civil servant acts properly in accordance with the policy laid down by the Minister, the Minister must equally protect and defend him.

3. Where a civil servant 'makes a mistake or causes some delay, but not on an important issue of policy and not where a claim to individual rights is seriously involved, the Minister acknowledges the mistake and he accepts the responsibility, although he is not personally involved. He states he will take

[4] *The Governance of England*, 1904, pp. 148–9.

corrective action in the Department.' (530 H.C. Deb. 5s. cols. 1290).

4. '. . . where action has been taken by a civil servant of which the Minister disapproves and has no prior knowledge, and the conduct of the official is reprehensible, then there is no obligation on the part of the Minister to endorse what he believes to be wrong, or to defend what are clearly shown to be errors of his officers. The Minister is not bound to approve of action of which he did not know, or of which he disapproves. But, of course, he remains constitutionally responsible to Parliament for the fact that something has gone wrong, and he alone can tell Parliament what has occurred and render an account of his stewardship.' (Cols. 1290–91).

It is interesting to see Mr Herbert Morrison's view on the subject. Mr Morrison spoke just before the Home Secretary and on this particular issue he said:

> There can be no question whatever that Ministers are responsible for everything that their officers do, but if civil servants make errors or commit failures the House has a right to be assured that the Minister has dealt with the errors or failures adequately and properly, or that he will do so. That is a duty that falls on Ministers as well, and it would be wrong for a Minister automatically to defend every act of his officers or servants merely because they belong to his Department. Therefore, the House has to be satisfied that he is dealing with the matter adequately. (Col. 1278).

In his book *Government and Parliament*, published in April, 1954, Mr Morrison has more to say on this point:

> If a mistake is made in a Government Department the Minister is responsible even if he knew nothing about it until, for example, a letter of complaint is received from an M.P., or there is criticism in the Press, or a Question is put down for answer in the House; even if he has no real personal responsibility whatever, the Minister is still held responsible. He will no doubt criticize whoever is responsible in the Department in mild terms if it is a small mistake and in strong terms if it is a bad one, but publicly he must accept responsibility as if the act were his own. It is, however, legitimate for him to explain that something went wrong in the Department, that he accepts responsibility and apologizes for it, and that he has taken steps to see that such a thing will not happen again. (pp. 320–1.)

Later he says:

> Somebody must be held responsible to Parliament and the public. It has to be the Minister, for it is he, and neither Parliament nor the public, who has official control over his civil servants. One of the fundamentals of our system of government is that some Minister of the Crown is responsible to Parliament, and through Parliament to the public, for every act of the executive. This is a cornerstone of our system of parliamentary government. There may, however, be an occasion on which so serious a mistake has been made that the Minister must explain the circumstances and processes which resulted in the mistake, particularly if it involves an issue of civil liberty or individual rights. Now and again the House demands to know the name of the officer responsible for the occurrence. The proper answer of the Minister is that if the House wants anybody's head it must be his head as the responsible Minister, and that it must leave him to deal with the officer concerned in the Department.
>
> There is a circumstance in which I think a considerable degree of frankness is warranted. If a Minister has given a specific order within the Department on a matter of public interest and his instructions have not been carried out, then, if he is challenged in Parliament and if he is so minded, he has a perfect right to reveal the facts and to assure the House that he has taken suitable action. Even so he must still take the responsibility. It is, I think legitimate in such a case that disregard of an instruction should be made known, even if it involves some humiliation for the officer concerned and his colleagues knowing that he was the one who disobeyed; for the Civil Service should at all times know that the lawful orders of Ministers must be carried out. However, such a situation is rare, though I did experience one and told the House about it.
>
> In all these matters it is well for the Minister to be forthcoming in Parliament. Unless the matter is exceptionally serious nothing is lost by an admission of error. The House of Commons is generous to a Minister who has told the truth, admitted a mistake, and apologized; but it will come down hard on a Minister who takes the line that he will defend himself and his Department whether they are right or wrong or who shuffles about evasively rather than admit that a blunder or an innocent mistake has been made. (pp. 323–4).

What does all this add up to? In the first place it confirms the doctrine of Ministerial responsibility. Civil servants whatever their official actions, are not responsible to Parliament, but to a Minister. It is the Minister who is responsible to Parliament, and it is he who must satisfy the majority in the House of Commons that he has handled a particular policy or case properly. It is for the Minister, therefore, so to direct, control and discipline his staff that his policy and views prevail. But the fact that the Minister is responsible for everything done, or not done, by his Department does not render the civil servant immune from disciplinary action or dismissal by the Minister nor even from public admonition by him in extremely serious cases, nor does it prevent the Minister from admitting to Parliament that his Department is in error and reversing or modifying the decision criticised.

17. THE REAL MEANING OF ANSWERABILITY TO PARLIAMENT

[from G. Marshall and Graeme C. Moodie, *Some Problems of the Constitution*, Hutchinson, 1959, pp. 81–82]

It may of course be maintained both of governments and of Ministers individually that their 'responsibility', 'accountability', or 'answerability' imply merely the obligation of Ministers collectively and individually, to meet Parliament and provide information about their policies. If this is what 'answerable' means in the constitutional sphere, it must be allowed that the usage is slightly eccentric. 'Explaining' and 'answering to' are, in ordinary speech, terms with an entirely different flavour. The distinction between 'answerable *to*' and 'answerable *for*' is difficult to maintain. Where there is no relation of authority one may 'answer', but it is hardly appropriate to speak of being answerable at all—either 'to' or 'for'. We may, for example, answer questions about our heatlh or explain that we are in good health, but we do not normally 'answer to' anybody for our health. A Minister at the dispatch box, answering to the House, is at least acting as if his explanations were to a body with authority. He is not just reciting a part, or treating Members as curious or interested bystanders, or performing as a kind of parliamentary press and information officer. It is certainly true that censure by the House is not an effective remedy for administrative mismanagement. Nevertheless, that Ministers are constitutionally liable (as distinct from politically likely) to receive parliamentary censure may be part of the theory of the constitution whose denial we ought not—in Mr Morrison's phrase—to be 'shouting to the world'. There is indeed much parliamentary behaviour and language which is comprehensible only on the assumption of punitive authority on the part of the House, as distinct from a mere right to information. Governments which shield unpopular Ministers do not at any rate ever do so on the explicit ground that no such convention as answerability for departmental action is known to them, and on many occasions the convention in its punitive form seems to be taken for granted by Members of Parliament on both sides of the House.

(b)

18. IS DISSOLUTION A 'WEAPON'?

[from William G. Andrews, 'Some Thoughts on the Power of Dissolution', *Parliamentary Affairs*, xiii, No. 3, 1960]

This is an impertinent little article. In an interview with Lord Attlee about a year ago, I asked him if he considered the power of dissolution useful in maintaining party discipline. He replied with one of his longer answers of the evening: 'It's essential.' One purpose of this article will be to show not only that it is not essential, but that it is not even useful toward that end...

Prying further into Lord Attlee's views on dissolution, I asked if he had used it as a disciplinary weapon either in 1950 or 1951. He replied that he had not and, in answer to another query, denied ever having threatened to dissolve in order to bring recalcitrant Labour M.P.s into line. With what we Americans regard as typical British aplomb he resolved the apparent contradiction between his views on its power and his failure to avail himself of its aid by commenting that 'some of the most effective weapons are among the least used'. Attlee's chief lieutenant agrees, calling dissolution 'a deterrent to parliamentary revolt', often saving governments from defeat by the fear it instils in the back-benchers[5] and, to a leading British constitutional scholar, it is the 'big stick . . . intended never to be used' whose 'mere existence' is a 'psychological influence' inducing 'a private member to remain loyal to the Government'.[6] British writers are also fond of citing British experience with dissolution as a worthy example for the French. Peter Campbell explains French ministerial instability under the Fourth Republic as resulting partly from the fact that this 'weapon which British ministers could use against their avowed opponents and their disloyal supporters was denied to the French' and Sir Douglas Savory in a foreword to the same book agrees.

There was a time when the power of dissolution was regarded as a weapon in the hands of the cabinet against the House of Commons. With the rise of a disciplined two-party system, this is no longer a tenable argument, for everyone recognises that, as long as the parties remain disciplined, there can be no serious conflict between the cabinet and the House of Commons. Today, the discord exists only between the majority party in parliament and the cabinet on one hand, and the minority party in parliament, on the other. When the electorate resolves a question of policy today, it is argued, it does so by indicating its preference between the two great parties, not between parliament and cabinet. Even so, it is said that the power of dissolution still strengthens the executive arm of the majority party *vis-à-vis* its parliamentary supporters, not as a weapon against parliament *per se*, but only against the backbenchers of the ruling party. In short, it is considered a key weapon for the maintenance of party discipline.

The first reason dissolution is not an intra-party disciplinary weapon is that it is never used for this purpose. It may be, as Lord Attlee contends, that the most powerful weapons are sometimes little used. It is also true that unused powers tend to atrophy, to lose their edge. If no prime minister has used dissolution to prevent party indiscipline—and none has, at least not since the restoration of the two-party system in 1931—it seems unlikely that it will be so used in the future, unless

[5] Herbert Morrison, *Government and Parliament from the Inside*, 2nd ed. U.P., 1959, p. 94.

[6] Sir Ivor Jennings, *Parliament*, C.U.P., 2nd ed., 1957, p. 7. See also pp. 136, 414–415, and his *Cabinet Government*, C.U.P., 2nd ed., 1951, pp. 441–442.

conditions change significantly, and equally doubtful that party back-benchers believe it will be so used.

The second reason for doubting the efficacy of dissolution as a disciplinary tool is that it cuts both ways and cuts the prime minister most deeply. It may compel the M.P. to stand for re-election, but the prime minister is also driven to the hustings. Furthermore, his task in an election is much more gruelling, onerous, and difficult than that of the average back-bencher. The burden it places on him as his party's chief campaigner is many times heavier than the one it places on the back-bencher. Not only that, but the prime minister stands to lose much more in an election than does the back-bencher. The back-bencher might lose his seat and his small salary, but he stands to lose very little political power for he holds very little. The political insignificance of the back-bencher is well known. On the other hand, the prime ministership is by far the most powerful political office in the land. In many ways it is a dictatorial post between elections. With a united party behind him, he is impregnable in parliament and he appoints and removes cabinet ministers with a hand free even of party control. His office is much the most important centre of policy formulation. All this is placed in jeopardy by a dissolution. Furthermore, the risk he will lose the prime ministership is much greater than is the back-bencher's danger of losing his seat. Prime ministers have dissolved the House of Commons thirty-one times since 1833. Seventeen times they lost office as a result. Six of the sixteen dissolutions since 1900, and six of the eleven since 1918 have produced new prime ministers. Even when the prime minister retained office, he almost invariably was weaker. Only four times since 1933, has a prime minister increased his party's parliamentary strength by means of a dissolution. On the other hand, an average of about four out of every five M.P.s in the prime minister's party who have sought re-election have been successful since 1833. Thus, the prime minister has a greater burden placed on him by dissolution, he has more to lose, and he is more likely to lose it than the back-bencher against whom it is alleged to be used. Dissolution would not seem to be a very attractive weapon for a prime minister faced by the danger of party indiscipline, especially as a much less treacherous weapon is available to him.

This other weapon is the power of the party leadership to withdraw from rebellious M.P.s the party label at the next election. In recent times it has been virtually impossible for an independent candidate to win a seat in the House of Commons. Since 1945 only one independent candidate has been elected to parliament. Not a single M.P. expelled from his party for indiscipline has been able to retain his seat in a post-war election. Therefore, in the last analysis, the party leadership has the ultimate weapon to use against party rebels. It needs no other. Party expulsion means political death. Not only is dissolution ineffective and dangerous, it is unnecessary. This, I think, is the decisive reason why dissolution cannot validly be regarded as a device for maintaining party discipline.

PART III

The Power of the Cabinet: General

19. THE SHIFT OF POWER TO THE CABINET AFTER 1832

[from Sir Sidney Low, *The Governance of England*, Longmans, 1904, pp. 53–54]

It would be safe to say that Cabinet government MIGHT BE, rather than that it IS, all that is implied in the flattering estimates of its admiring critics. The model was nearer the reality, in the period between the two great Reform Bills, than at any other period; for in that era of middle-class supremacy, before the electoral flood-gates had been opened to the inrush of the masses, and at a time when legislation and internal affairs were of relatively greater importance than foreign policy, the relations between the executive, the legislature, and the constituencies, were much more like those imaged in the constitutional theory, than they can be said to be at the present day. Even in the 'sixties, the ideal of the textbook writers was often a long way from the facts; and the modifying influences have gained force in recent years. Account should be taken of the extent and real character of the relationship of members of the Cabinet to one another and to the Prime Minister; the development of the party system; and the diminished power and importance of the House of Commons as compared with the Ministry, on the one hand, and the electorate, on the other. The last is the most significant feature in our recent political evolution. 'The principal change,' says Todd, 'effected by the development of the English Constitution since the Revolution of 1688 has been the virtual transference of the centre and force of the State from the Crown to the House of Commons.' One might add that the principal change effected since 1832 has been the further tendency to shift this 'centre and force' from Parliament to the Cabinet, and to render the latter amenable to the control of the constituent bodies themselves rather than to that of their elected representatives.

20. IS THE CABINET THE 'SERVANT OF PARLIAMENT'?

[from F. A. Ogg, *English Government and Politics*, Macmillan, 2nd ed. 1936, p. 450]

[Most important] is the growth of the power of the Cabinet at Parliament's expense; indeed, the growing dominance of the cabinet represents probably the most important single development of the British constitution in the past fifty years. We know well enough what the theory of cabinet government is. The ministers are members of Parliament; they (in Britain, a limited group of the more important ones) formulate policy and introduce bills; they see to the carrying out of the measures enacted, and indeed of all other law; singly and collectively, they are responsible for all executive and administrative acts; this responsibility is to the House of Commons, of which, to all intents and purposes, the cabinet is a working committee; the group is in no sense an independent authority, but only the servant of the House, charged with its high duties for only so long as it can hold the confidence and support of that body. It was on these lines that Bagehot, seventy years ago, skilfully analyzed the relations existing between the cabinet and its parliamentary master. The theory, as a theory, still holds. But for a good while the facts have been growing more difficult to reconcile with it.

21. CABINET POWER AND PARLIAMENTARY PROCEDURE

[from J. Redlich, *The Procedure of the House of Commons*, Constable, 1907, I pp. 207–210]

In the British cabinet of today is concentrated all political power, all initiative in legislation and administration, and finally all public authority for carrying out the laws in kingdom and empire. In the sixteenth century and down to the middle of the seventeenth, this wealth of authority was united in the hands of the crown and its privy council; in the eighteenth century and first half of the nineteenth, Parliament was the dominant central organ from which proceeded the most powerful stimulus to action and all decisive acts of policy, legislation, and administration; the second half of the last century saw the gradual transfer from crown and Parliament into the hands of the cabinet of one after another of the elements of authority and political power . . . The union of all political power in the hands of the House of Commons and the simultaneous transfer of this concentrated living force to a cabinet drawn exclusively from Parliament are the dominant features of the modern development of public law and politics in England . . . The very completeness of its power, which, if we disregard technicalities, may be said to comprise the whole administration of domestic and foreign affairs, has compelled the House of Commons to abdicate the exercise of almost all its authority in favour of its executive committee, the ministry (*i.e.* cabinet). This was inevitable for the reason, if there were no other, that 670 members cannot initiate legislation, cannot even govern or administer. The evolution of the modern state has set before every nation the problem how the sovereignty of the people, realized in the form of representative institutions, can be rendered operative for the current work and constructive activity of the state . . . In . . . the United States of America, it has been solved by the careful division of political authority and legal power among several organs, each dependent on the popular will. In Great Britain on the contrary, a solution has been found in the completest possible concentration of actual and legal power in one and the same organ, the cabinet, which is part and parcel of Parliament.

22. CABINET, PARTY DISCIPLINE, AND THE ELECTORATE

[from Sir Gilbert Campion (ed.) *British Government since 1918*, Allen and Unwin, 1950, pp. 15–21]

It is generally put forward as a criticism of our system that the Government is unduly predominant over Parliament, and that this predominance has been increasing steadily with each successive extension of the franchise at least since the second Reform Act of 1867. The argument runs something like this. The huge constituencies which a wide franchise creates need elaborate and extensive machinery to spread the party gospel and bring supporters, and waverers, to the poll. The personality of the ordinary candidate counts for little at a general election, because the party managers find it profitable to focus attention on a few well-known leaders, and the electors have readily learnt to simplify the issues of the contest into a competition between rival Prime Ministers. This depresses the standing of the individual Member. And, in the House itself, parallel machinery, playing upon the Member's party loyalty turns him into a unit in a highly disciplined force whose main duty is to give unswerving support to the policy of its leaders. Since Ministers are the leaders of the majority party, the success of this doctrine has given them control of the powers properly belonging to Parliament as well as the executive powers which they possess as Ministers of the Crown. The conclusion is that unless there is some relaxation in the stringency of party discipline, on which ministerial power is based, the Government will continue to dominate, and may arrive at dictating to, Parliament. This is not quite how the parliamentary system was intended to work. The House of Commons acquired political power as an organ of control *over* the executive. The question we should ask ourselves is, is this diagnosis correct hitherto, and, if so, is the position likely to get better or worse?

Now it is true that, judging by certain obvious tests, it does look as though the Government tended more and more to act as though they were the sole source of parliamentary action and masters of the House of Commons, responsible only to the electors. Until well after the Reform Act of 1832, Ministers confined themselves almost entirely to the field of administration, and left the initiation of legislation to unofficial Members. Now they have acquired almost a monopoly in both Houses of this traditional function of Parliament. Up to 1868, it was the accepted constitutional doctrine that a Ministry, defeated at the polls, should come back to face the House and take their dismissal at its hands. Now, unless there is some real doubt about the result of an election (as in 1924), the defeated Prime Minister resigns at once and lets his opponents form a government and open Parliament. It seems as if the Government looked over the heads of Members to the electors, and regarded the electorate, and not the House, as their direct masters. Again, until well past the middle of last century, Ministers often left questions of policy to the free vote of the House, whereas now the Whips are 'put on' whenever Government policy is concerned, so as to show their supporters that they are expected to follow obediently. And this form of coercion is very effective. The result of this, it is concluded, is to reduce the House in matters of Government policy to a registration chamber; debate is unreal because it never changes a vote; whatever the arguments, the result of the division is known beforehand. At most, debate may affect public opinion outside and possibly weaken the Government against the next general election.[1]

23. PARLIAMENTARY CONTROL *is* UNREAL

[from Ramsay Muir, *How Britain is Governed*, 1930, Constable, Introduction]

According to accepted theory, then, the sovereign body in the British State is Parliament; and, since the Parliament Act of 1911 turned the House of Lords into a mere delaying and revising body, the ultimate sovereign power resides in the House of Commons, which derives its authority from the fact that it represents, and is freely elected by, the whole body of enfranchised citizens. As sovereign body, Parliament has absolute control over all legislation and taxation. It controls executive government also, through the Cabinet, which is a Committee of Parliament, drawn from that party which commands a majority in the House of Commons, or is, at all events, able to count upon the support of the House for its policy. Subject to the control of Parliament, the Cabinet directs and manages all the work of national government. Every other body in the country either derives its authority from an enactment of Parliament, like the Church of England, the municipalities and the Railway Companies, or exists at the discretion of Parliament and must submit to any regulations that Parliament may impose, like the Trade Unions, the Non-conformist Churches and all trading concerns.

Such is the theory, which remarkably magnifies the power of Parliament, making it the pivot and controlling factor in the

[1] We quote Campion later as modifying this view.

whole system. This theory seems to me to be very nearly as remote from the facts as the statement of formal constitutional law already set forth. Indeed, in one respect it is more remote from the facts, because it disregards the immense and largely independent power wielded by the Government. The power of the Government is in practice so much the most important element in our system that some commentators (Mr Ramsay MacDonald for one) have spoken as if the chief purpose of a General Election was to select a Government and to send to Parliament a body of supporters strong enough to maintain it in office; a view which does, in fact, largely accord with modern usage, and which explains why it is that Parliament—reduced to a mere intermediary, like the Electoral College in America—has lost so much of its prestige. The truth lies somewhere between the theory of the text books, which makes Parliament effectively supreme in every sphere, and the theory of Mr Ramsay MacDonald, which reduces it to a sort of Electoral College. It is, or ought to be, not merely a means of selecting a Government, or of formally embodying the decision of the electorate as to how the Government should be constituted: it is, or it ought to be, what Burke called it—a control over the Government on behalf of the people.

Almost every phrase in the popular theory as I have summarised it seems to me to be open to challenge. I do not stop to discuss the question whether Parliament is 'sovereign,' i.e. whether its power is absolute and unlimited. That is a highly technical question, much argued by professors of political science, some of whom are now inclined to contend that the claim of absolute and exclusive sovereignty for any single body in the State is invalid, seeing that all organised bodies, such as Churches or Trade Unions, draw their authority from the will of their members equally with the State and its supreme organ. We need not discuss this question, which is, when all is said, purely an academic one. There are certainly, in practice, limits to the sovereignty of Parliament: it can do nothing important to which public opinion is definitely opposed; and if it were to try (for example) to put an end to all Trade Unions, it would find the undertaking too great for its real powers, even if a majority of voters were in favour of it. The doctrine of sovereignty is purely theoretical; and in such an inquiry as we are undertaking it is best to keep aloof from the arid realm of abstractions in which political scientists love to wander.

But when we turn to the assertion that the sovereignty of Parliament is expressed in its absolute control over legislation and taxation, we are dealing with a more practical issue, an issue capable of being tested by the facts. And here it is plain that, whatever theory may say, Parliament has next to no independent control over either legislation or taxation. It is the Government, not Parliament, that the man in the street blames for bad laws and heavy taxes. And he is right, for, by modern usage, the Government frames all important legislation, and proposes all taxes, carrying them by the voting-power of its supporters in Parliament, who will risk the loss of their seats if they do not vote steadily for the Government they have been elected to support.

Still more out of relation with the facts is the assertion that Parliament controls executive government through the Cabinet which is a Committee of Parliament. This statement is exquisitely misleading. In the first place, it is a distortion of the meaning ordinarily attached to the word 'Committee' to describe the Cabinet as a Committee of Parliament. For Parliament does not in any sense appoint this 'Committee,' nor does it receive any regular reports as to what its 'Committee' does. The Chief of the Cabinet is, in fact, chosen partly by private agreement within a single section or party in Parliament, and partly by the result of a general election. Once chosen, he selects all the other members of the Cabinet, and assigns to them their offices: he must, indeed, choose from among the members of the two Houses of Parliament, but he can, if he likes, put a man into the House of Lords in order to make him eligible. And far from 'reporting' to Parliament, this so-called Committee only reports what it thinks fit, or what is formally demanded from it in a way that it seems dangerous to resist. Finally, this so-called 'Committee' has the power, if Parliament dares to differ from it, of advising the King to bring Parliament to an end and to order the election of a new one; and the King usually takes this advice. It is not easy to imagine a body more unlike what a 'Committee' is usually supposed to be.

Again, it is merely absurd to say that Parliament 'controls' the Cabinet in its executive functions. It sometimes criticises, so far as it is allowed to know what is going on, and the criticism is sometimes effective and may lead the Cabinet to change its policy; more often the criticism has no effect at all. There is never any attempt to review systematically the way in which this Department or that is carrying on its work. The nearest Parliament ever gets to the 'control' of executive government is a motion to reduce the salary of one Minister or another in order to call attention to some administrative failure. But these attacks are treated as votes of confidence; it is made clear that the Government will resign, and that every member of Parliament (or his supporters) will in effect be fined £1,000 in the form of the expenses of a general election, if the motion is carried; the disciplined voters pour into the division lobbies, and the perfunctory attempt at 'control' reaches its appointed destiny. To say that Parliament controls the Cabinet is an absurdity. The truth is that—except when it is not in command of a clear majority—the Cabinet absolutely controls Parliament. Even a Cabinet which has no independent majority has so wide a range of unfettered authority, and has access to so formidable a weapon in the prerogative of dissolution, that Parliamentary control is bound to be largely unreal. Nor, one may add, is it desirable that Parliament *should* control every aspect of the complex work of administration, a task which is wholly beyond its capacity. All the more reason why we should cease to talk about Parliament 'controlling' the Government. The only thing it can do is to turn the Government, out; and it cannot do this when the Government is in command of a disciplined majority of pledged supporters.

24. TOO MUCH POWER IN THE HANDS OF THE CABINET

[from Ramsay Muir, *How Britain is Governed*, Constable, pp. 23–26]

In short, the essence of the British system is that all power and all responsibility tend more and more to be concentrated upon what we call 'the Government'; and that, so long as 'the Government' commands a docile majority in Parliament, its power is practically unlimited and uncontrolled, except by the fear of alienating public opinion and therefore losing its power at the next general election. This statement is fully borne out by the ordinary forms of popular speech, and even by the political judgments of instructed commentators. If a recently made law works badly, we do not blame Parliament, the law-making body; we blame 'the Government,' which (we say) passed the law. If taxation is heavy and we are spending too much money, again we do not blame Parliament, which is supposed to 'hold the strings of the purse,' we blame 'the Government'; and it is always 'the Government', not Parliament, which we describe as being extravagant or unduly parsimonious.

Whether this is, or is not, a healthy state of things—whether 'the Government' ought, or ought not, to be brought under closer criticism, supervision and control, and, if so, by what means this could be done—are questions to which we shall later have to give some attention. But in the meanwhile, it is clear that the vast powers of 'the Government' are the dominating fact in our system. Our first task must therefore be to get some clear notion of the extent of these powers; and then to consider what exactly we mean when we speak of 'the Government,' of what elements it consists, how it is appointed, and how it works.

'The Government,' not merely in theory, but in reality, wields in the King's name all that vast complex of powers, largely undefined which are covered by the phrase 'the Royal Prerogative.' The King is the source of all authority, in legal theory; and he (or 'the Government' acting in his name) wields every power which has not been specifically withdrawn from him, or definitely limited, by law. All public officials of the State are his servants; the Navy and Army are his Navy and his Army; the rulers of all dependencies are his representatives; all treaties with foreign States are made in his name, and the ambassadors who 'lie abroad for the good of their country' are his spokesmen; he is the fountain not only of authority, but also of honours, and all titles and dignities (which are a potent means of rewarding service and securing loyalty) emanate from him. There is no limit to his power save that he cannot make or alter laws, or raise taxes, without the assent of Parliament, and that he must use his power in accordance with the law. But (in legal form) the King performs all these vast and indefinite functions on the advice of his Ministers, who are legally responsible for any misuse of them; for in the eye of the law the King himself 'can do no wrong'. And this means (in actual practice) that 'the Government' has annexed the whole of the Royal Prerogative, subject only to the safeguard (which is, so far as it goes, a real one) that the King can protest privately against anything being done in his name which he strongly disapproves.

It is not only the Royal Prerogative which 'the Government' has annexed. Whenever it commands a clear majority in the House of Commons, it also wields practically the whole power of Parliament. It does this, in the main, by means of an elaborate party organisation, which is normally controlled by the head of 'the Government,' since he commonly nominates the party officials by whom the secret party fund is raised and spent. Party organisation and party discipline have been so much elaborated during the last two generations that the members of Parliament who have been elected as representatives of a party hesitate long before showing any independence of their leaders—or, at any rate, before carrying their independence to the point of open revolt—because they know that they will thus endanger their seats: in a system of election based upon single-member constituencies, as ours is, the ablest man has little or no chance of election if a rival candidate is put up against him by his own party, and this will happen if he shows too much independence. And 'the Government' has a further means of ensuring the docility of its majority, in its power to use (or threaten the use of) the Royal Prerogative of dissolution. This weapon may even be used (if the precedent of 1924 holds good) by a Government which has no clear majority in the House of Commons. Hence it is little exaggeration to say that 'the Government' normally wields all the powers of the House of Commons as well as all the powers of the Crown. As for the House of Lords, its power has become almost negligible since the Parliament Act of 1911; and, when 'the Government' wants to impose its will upon the House of Lords, it has in reserve—for use in an extreme emergency—the Royal Prerogative of creating peers: a threat to use this power was enough to bring about a rapid collapse of the Lords' resistance to the Parliament Act in 1911. Finally, as we have seen, the boasted independence of the judicial bench—real as it is within its limits—provides no effective limitation of the autocracy of 'the Government'. If the judges give a decision which 'the Government' and its supporters dislike, it can always be reversed by an Act of Parliament.

We are thus justified in saying that the most distinctive feature of the British system is the concentration of all power and all responsibility, administrative, legislative and even (in the last resort) judicial, in the hands of 'the Government,' so long as it commands a majority in the House of Commons. This dictatorship (for such it essentially is) may be wielded by the heads of any organised political party which is able to win a majority of seats in the House of Commons by the skilful use of electioneering devices, even if this majority of seats represents (as it often does) a minority of votes. It may safely be said that no party ever has, or ever will have, a clear majority of satisfied and convinced supporters in the country. The dictatorship is qualified only—and is sometimes qualified very dangerously—by the necessity of not alienating that fluctuating margin of voters who have it in their power, by turning the scale in a few constituencies, to throw the handkerchief to one or another of the groups of party manipulators.

It will be observed that in this system very little independent power is left to Parliament, which the text-books are so fond of describing as the supreme controlling power in our system. In reality, so long as 'the Government' has a clear majority, Parliament is reduced to two functions. It is an *electoral machine*, by means of which the decision of the electorate is given as to who shall wield the immense powers of government; but normally this power is exhausted at the moment of election, which decides the main issue. It is also an *advisory body*, through which the all-powerful Government is enabled in some degree to feel the pulse of the country, and to modify its proposals so as to avoid alienating public opinion.

25. THE 'MYTHS' OF PROFESSOR MUIR

[from R. Bassett, *Essentials of Parliamentary Democracy*, Macmillan 1935, pp. 24–28]

What are the facts about the alleged dictatorship of the Cabinet? Professor Ramsay Muir's references to the subject in his *How Britain is Governed*, and elsewhere, merit attention. 'The truth,' he contends 'is that—except when it is not in command of a clear majority—the Cabinet absolutely controls Parliament.' The 'most distinctive feature of the British system is the concentration of all power and all responsibility, administrative, legislative, and even (in the last resort) judicial, in the hands of "the Government," so long as it commands a majority in the House of Commons. This dictatorship (for such it essentially is) may be wielded by the heads of any organised political party which is able to win a majority of seats in the House of Commons by the skilful use of electioneering devices, even if this majority of seats represents (as it often does) a minority of votes.'

The impression conveyed by these remarks, it is suggested, is highly misleading. It is quite true, as Professor Muir contends that the Cabinet in practice virtually monopolises the time of the House of Commons; that Government Bills, or Bills approved by the Government, alone stand any chance of becoming law; and that, in normal circumstances, and in so far as time permits, Government Bills do become law. It is true also that, by long established practice, no proposal for taxation or expenditure can be made except by a Minister of the Crown. These and other facts might seem to justify the view that there is a Cabinet 'dictatorship,' but these things are done by the Cabinet as a consequence of parliamentary decisions. The limitations placed upon the financial powers of members of the House of Commons, for instance, are the result of decisions by the House of Commons. They are self-imposed limitations, embodied in Standing Orders. The Cabinet's control over the time of the House of Commons is exercisable only with the consent of the House. Consent has to be obtained if the Cabinet wishes to take up more of the time of the House than the Standing Orders already allow, and, as a matter of fact, the general business of the House, including the allotment of time, is arranged, so far as possible, after consultation and by agreement with the party or parties in opposition.

So far from the Cabinet exercising a 'dictatorship,' it is dependent all the time upon the support of its party majority in the House of Commons. Its power is continuously limited by the necessity of maintaining that majority, and its general policy may have to be modified accordingly. Its Bills may have

to be modified. Professor Muir grants this, but says that 'if the Cabinet has a stable majority, the modification will only happen by its own consent.' It is true that Cabinet consent to the modification is requisite, but the Cabinet often has to consent, or sacrifice the measure, unless it is prepared to risk defeat and its possible consequences.

Professor Muir makes the 'dictatorship' of the Cabinet conditional upon the support of a majority. It is a rather far-reaching qualification, for without a majority the Cabinet, of course, is powerless; but its effect is minimised, and the allegation of 'dictatorship' rendered plausible, by the 'automatic' or 'docile' nature attributed to the majority. It is said that 'so long as the Government commands a docile majority in Parliament, its power is practically unlimited and uncontrolled.' But when does a Cabinet 'command' a majority? Is a majority ever 'docile,' or 'automatic?' Surely only under conditions such as obtain under the regimes of Mussolini or Hitler. Professor Muir has had, it is believed, some experience of the difficulties of getting a parliamentary minority to act in unison, and it would be unwise to assume that the task is easier in the case of a majority. That members of Parliament are deficient in a spirit of independence is very frequently asserted, especially by the Opposition of ministerialists. Paradoxically, the Opposition members denounce the Cabinet just as frequently for giving way to the clamour of their unruly and extremist followers. There is no basis for the assumption of 'docility.' Ministers and 'Whips' would doubtless tell a very different story. It is true that, as a rule, members hesitate 'to carry their independence to the point of open revolt,' but it is only political common-sense to exhaust every means of persuasion and influence before openly producing a breach in the party ranks. If it is the private member who is more often the person persuaded, that is only to be expected from the nature of the case.

Moreover, it would be stupid to run the risk of weakening or even overthrowing a 'government' to whom one gives general support, unless the matter in dispute is considered of such vital importance that everything else must be subordinated to it. A superficial appearance of tranquillity and docility is, no doubt, produced, but surely no student or practitioner of politics is deceived by it. Furthermore, Professor Muir allows that even with a docile majority behind it, the Cabinet is restrained 'by the fear of alienating public opinion and therefore losing its power at the next General Election.' That constitutes a highly powerful limitation upon its so-called 'dictatorship.' Nor is it merely, as is suggested, a case of 'not alienating that fluctuating margin of voters who have it in their power to turn the scale in a few constituencies.' It is a question of dealing with a complex of groups of various kinds, any or all of which may have to be considered at any particular time on any particular issue. The Cabinet's power, with or without a *Party* majority, is continuously limited by the necessity of securing the support of a majority in the House of Commons, and, normally, also in the House of Lords, and by the necessity of securing the assent, or not alienating the support, of a majority of the electorate. In the House of Commons itself, power resides essentially with the majority, not with the Cabinet. Indeed, the Cabinet and its supporters cannot be artificially separated in the manner implicit in the phrase 'Cabinet dictatorship.' The members of the Cabinet, after all, are leaders or influential members of their party or parties.

It seems clear from the general argument of Professor Muir's book that his real objection is not so much to what he calls the 'dictatorship' of the Cabinet, as to a position in which the Cabinet has the support of a majority composed of members of one party only. The central point of his attack, therefore, is the two-party system. He is clearly anxious to maintain efficient Cabinet Government, but while he recognises fully the need for harmony between the executive and Parliament, and also the necessity and value of party, he nevertheless objects to that harmony being attained by means of a one-party Cabinet backed by a one-party majority in the House of Commons. In such circumstances, his interesting argument has to follow a rather narrow path, and it is difficult to resist the impression that it has been influenced by the situation in recent years of the party with which Professor Muir is so closely associated. Whatever its merits may be, the case is weakened rather than strengthened by the unjustifiable attribution of dictatorial powers to the Cabinet.

26. CAN THE CABINET RELY UPON AUTOMATIC SUPPORT IN THE DIVISION LOBBY?

[from H. J. Laski, *Parliamentary Government in England*, Allen and Unwin, 1938, pp. 157–158]

It must not be forgotten that the theory of mechanized voting is, as a matter of proportion, a travesty of the facts. There are limits beyond which a Government dare not push its majority for fear of losing its majority. Mr Baldwin had to sacrifice Sir Samuel Hoare; Mr Chamberlain had to abandon the original form of his National Defence Contribution. In 1923, after Mr Bridgeman's blunder over *Ex parte O'Brien*, it was proposed to pass a Bill of Indemnity in which the arrested men were deprived of their legal right to compensation. The whole House protested against a principle which, it was urged on all sides, was a violation of 'fair play'; and the Government had to yield to the opinion of the House. The argument of a mechanical debate devoid of reality is, shortly, nonsense. It fails to take account of the long negotiations which usually precede the formulation of policy by parties, the weighing of the facts, the eliciting of opinions, the consultation of interests known to be affected. It misses the point that parties are unresting in their efforts to keep in touch with the opinions and sentiments of their supporters, that a vital test of good leadership in the House of Commons is the ability to gauge just how far the leader can take his followers. Debates do not normally overturn Governments just because the main art of a Government is to produce for its supporters what they expect. When a leader fails to do this, at the point where he produces a sense of outrage, he finds, like Peel in 1846, or Mr MacDonald in 1931, that his party throws him over. The secret of the division-lobby is not, as Mr Ramsay Muir seems to think, the fact the Government has the threat of dissolution in its hand. A government which could not live save by the constant invocation of that threat would very rapidly cease to be a Government.

27. LARGE MAJORITIES SOMETIMES BEND TO PUBLIC OPINION

[from H. J. Laski, *Parliamentary Government in England*, Allen and Unwin, 1938, pp. 172–173]

The Cabinet has to elicit consent; it cannot exact it. The difference is fundamental to our system. The Cabinet has to conduct its operations in the public view. It is subject to a constant stream of criticism, both within the House and without. Its problem is to be able to maintain the loyalty of its supporters despite the impact of this criticism upon them. That is not so easy as it appears. A Cabinet has to learn the direction of its supporters' minds. It has to recognize that in the making of every policy there are limits beyond which it may not go. A bad blunder may easily disturb the very foundations of its majority. A clear drift of electoral opinion away from its support may sow a spirit of rebellion in the House before which even a Government with a vast majority is impotent. Maintaining a majority is never a simple and straightforward matter; the discipline of followers is not the obedience of private soldiers to their commanders. There enter into its making a host of subtle psychological considerations the accurate measurement of which is vital to the Cabinet's life. It is dangerous to run the House on too tight a rein. Excessive secrecy, grave discourtesy, continuous threat of resignation or dissolution, inability to quell an angry public opinion outside, always breed revolt. A Cabinet maintains control in the degree that it is successful in not going too far beyond what the House approves. It must know when to yield; and it is important to yield gracefully. A Cabinet that tries to carry off its policy with too high a hand is almost always riding for a fall.

Cabinet control, this is to say, is subject to its ability to be sensitive to public opinion; and even a great majority will fail if it is supremely insensitive . . . An unpopular policy always creates the fear that it may lead to defeat at the next general election; and members are unwilling to serve under a Cabinet which does not recognize that it is leading them to defeat. 'There is the hard, ineluctable fact,' said Sir Samuel Hoare when he resigned, 'that I have not got the confidence of the great body of opinion in the country, and I feel that it is essential for the

Foreign Secretary, more than any other minister in the country, to have behind him the general approval of his fellow-countrymen.' Had Mr Baldwin refused to withdraw the Cabinet's proposals on Abyssinia, it is certain that a considerable part of his followers would have voted against him, and resignation or dissolution would have followed. The retirement of Sir Samuel Hoare was the propitiatory sacrifice he had to make.

28. WOULD A REDUCTION OF CABINET CONTROL LEAD TO BETTER GOVERNMENT

[H. J. Laski, *Parliamentary Government in England*, Allen and Unwin, 1938, pp. 167–169]

It must be emphasized that [any] enlargement [of the role of the House] ought not to interfere with the Cabinet's control of the main stream of parliamentary activity. Coherence of policy would at once be lost and with it the ability to place responsibility where it truly should lie. Indeed, it may be fairly said that the real success of our system lies precisely in the exact allocation of responsibility that it makes possible. It is an immense advantage always to know who is to blame when something goes wrong. Anyone who compares the American system with ours can see at once that this is the case. It is usually unfair to blame the President, for he could not get just the bill he wanted; he had to placate this interest and that, not seldom in a secret way that public opinion cannot adequately explore. It is not always fair to blame the Congress; it ceases, under the separation of powers, to remain a legislature if it accepts the position of the President's creature. Once the power of the Cabinet over the private member was relaxed we should have what is in fact government by public meeting. It is only because party leadership is vested in the Cabinet that the House does not present the spectacle of a mass of vested interests, each struggling to see that it is maintained and protected by the governmental process. Those who ask for the abrogation of any considerable measure of Cabinet control are in fact asking for what would be bound to develop into the destruction of ministerial responsibility.

I cannot believe that our system would benefit thereby.

The resultant legislation would not be built upon principle; it would be much more like the 'pork barrel' legislation of Congress. Ministers would be continually sacrificing this and that to one well-organized interest after another; they have, as it is, to sacrifice enough. It is, moreover, a bad thing to make any Government put forward and, later, administer measures in which it does not really believe, but which it has accepted under threat of defeat. Mr Ramsay Muir has argued that the result would be 'moderate' measures, because the diminution of Cabinet control would leave the private member free to be inventive in the general interest.

That is, I think, an excessively simple view. It wholly misconceives the nature of the House of Commons. For beneath the formal fact of territorial representation—for which no convenient substitute has so far been discovered—the House is essentially a vocational body. Members, no doubt, are elected for Devonport and Dover, London and Manningtree. But that does not conceal the fact that they are lawyers, business men, retired soldiers and sailors, bankers, railway directors, trade union officials and the like. Each of them cannot help watching the process of legislation in terms of the vocation to which he belongs. We all know that an owner of coal royalties would take a very different view of the purchase price in a scheme of nationalization to which he was entitled than a miner or even a cotton broker. We know that miners in the House will take a very different view of miners' hours of labour and their reasonable limits than, say, the members of the dockyard constituencies. The weaker Cabinet control is, the more we drift back to the system of which the Private Enclosure Acts of the eighteenth and nineteenth century are the supreme example. The American senator is independent of the executive power in the way some critics in this country think desirable. It is not, I think, unfair to say that it is exactly that independence which constitutes the power of those vocational 'lobbies' which are such a vicious feature of the American system.

29. THE ART OF MANAGING 'THE HOUSE'

[from Sir Ivor Jennings, *Cabinet Government*, C.U.P., 2nd Ed., 1951, pp. 442–443]

It does not follow, and it is not true, that a Government in possession of a majority forms a temporary dictatorship. It can, no doubt, press unpalatable measures upon the House, But, as Peel also said: 'Menaces of resignation if the House of Commons do not adopt certain measures are very unpalatable, and I think they should be reserved for very rare and very important occasion.' The Government's majority is its authority; that majority rests upon popular support. If either disappears, the Government, too, will disappear in due course. The member's most precious possession is his party label; but the label is valueless unless the electors give it a value. If he desires to maintain his majority, he must keep in close touch with his constituency. He will soon become aware that the tide of the Government's popularity is receding. He will become more and more obstreperous as his electoral support falls away. It has been said that Governments, like men, no sooner begin to live than they begin to die. But if they manage well, they may be a conscionable time a-dying; and if they manage ill they will die young. In this sense a party leader may say with Carlyle: 'I am their leader, therefore I must follow them.' A Government must perpetually look over its shoulder to see whether it is being followed. If it is not, it must alter direction. For in this sense, and in this sense only, is it true that a democracy is government of the people by the people.

It follows that a Government, even with an enormous majority, cannot neglect the feeling of the House. The temperature of the party is, in large measure, the temperature of the electorate. A minute Opposition, like the Labour Opposition of 1931–5, uses its opportunities to appeal to public opinion. The House is its platform, the newspapers are its microphones, and the people is its audience.

30. A CABINET DICTATORSHIP?

[from *House of Lords Debates*, 17th May, 1950; Official Report cc. 237–sq.q.]

VISCOUNT CECIL OF CHELWOOD rose to move to resolve, That the growing power of the Cabinet is a danger to the democratic constitution of the country. The noble Viscount said: . . . It seems to me that if this state of things goes on, we are bound to have an increasing concentration of power in the hands of the Administration—that is to say, the Cabinet—which will tend more and more to be an oligarchy consisting of individuals who, by political docility, have earned the approval of those who have control of the Party organisation. I know that any argument of the kind I have tried to present your Lordships is always answered by saying that, after all, the members of the House of Commons represent the electorate, and if the electorate disapprove of them and of their subservience to the Government they can be rejected. But is that proposition true? In practice, the electorate cannot just choose anyone; they must choose a candidate put forward by some organisation. Moreover, if they dislike the behaviour of their Member, they can do nothing until there is another General Election. The truth is that, under our present Constitution, when the Cabinet is once in power there is no way of effectively controlling it . . .

So the position really is this. The Cabinet, appointed by the Prime Minister, have dictatorial powers over the whole administrative functions of the Government, and the Prime Minister is answerable only to the majority of the House of Commons. Further, the membership of that majority owe their position to the political organisation of the Party of which the Prime Minister is the chief. If they show any disposition to take an independent line, intimation is conveyed to them that they will not be the Party candidates at the next Election. Even if any of them is supported by the local organisation which originally chose him, experience shows that that support will disappear under pressure from London . . .

THE LORD CHANCELLOR (VISCOUNT JOWITT) . . . As I conceive it, a democracy must provide the most adequate opportunities for discussion and for criticism, unlike an autocracy under which laws are imposed without the people being given a chance to discuss them. But if a democracy is going to mean mere discussion, if this House or the other place is to become a mere talking shop, then that would be one of the greatest dangers with which we could be confronted . . .

The complexity of modern life demands inevitably that more and more must the Government of the day interfere with the individual . . . In every country this has gone on, and in the complexity of life as it exists today it is inevitable that it should go on. The Cabinet is not cut off from contact with current opinion. Indeed, it is of the essence of the whole conception that the Cabinet should listen to what the House of Commons and the Members of the House of Commons are thinking and saying, and should listen to what the electorate are thinking and saying. It listens and it learns. In very truth, I may apply to such a body Carlyle's witty saying: 'I am their leader, therefore I must follow.'

Consider what control Parliament has in making its opinion felt. It has the admirable system of Parliamentary Questions. I am told that there are something like 15,000 to 16,000 Questions every year. There is the Adjournment debate, and there is the possibility of Motions on the Adjournment. It is quite unreal to suppose that the Cabinet shut themselves off from the current or prevalent opinions of the day. I suppose it is common knowledge that one of the most frequent visitors to the Cabinet in this and in all other Governments has been the Chief Whip, in order of course that the Cabinet and the House of Commons may be closely enmeshed. Sir David Maxwell-Fyfe wrote an interesting and thoughtful article in the *New English Review* in March of last year, and on this topic of the extent of control which the House of Commons exercises, he points out that although at that date the Government had lost only one by-election, twenty-three Ministers had come and gone . . .

I believe that the real danger to our system of democracy and freedom lies today in the possibility that it may not be prompt and swift in action. By all means let us provide in every way we can the fullest and most adequate discussion but . . . if we find that we have developed a system which is all talk and no action, then the minds of men will turn to some other system which does give them prompt action. The problem before democracy is to combine these two things. I believe that the secret of the successful working of our Constitution . . . consists in the steady confidence which is reposed by Parliament in the Cabinet. If that confidence were withdrawn, we should have a series of short and unstable Governments until we might find that we had prepared the ground for some sort of despotism . . .

VISCOUNT SIMON: . . . To my mind, the question is not one of Cabinet solidarity, or of the necessity of unity of decision in a Cabinet; it is a question of the extent to which in recent times a Cabinet once in office has felt sure that it can do what it likes without effective challenge; and it is a question as to whether there is no increased submissiveness in the ordinary Member of Parliament to those who are his leaders, with the result that in fact Ministers possess a greatly increased power compared with what they used to have . . . I wonder whether there is not a development—in my view, an exaggerated and distorted development—of the doctrine of electoral mandate. There is nothing we hear so frequently nowadays as: 'You may not like this, but the Government have a mandate from the electors to do it.' Subject to those who know more about our electoral history than I do, . . . I do not think the practice into which we have fallen of having at the beginning of every General Election an elaborate electoral programme, covering all sorts of topical subjects designed to attract the votes of different sections of the electorate—town and country, service people, officials, the poor voter, everybody—is of very ancient date. It is a comparative novelty . . .

The doctrine is now current . . . that once a Government is installed in power after a General Election, the Government has an absolute unquestioned authority in all circumstances to carry out by legislation every item in that listed programme, however casually it may appear in the manifesto . . . I think it is a mistake to treat the electorate, the sovereign power in this country, as though they acted on the day of a General Election in putting a particular Government into power, and that they then went to sleep until there is another General Election when they suddenly wake up and, as often as not, reverse the decision they gave before.

. . . [It] is not the case, that, on the true view, the electorate has put into power a Government which is authorised beyond all question to operate as it pleases until the next General Election comes along. That, to my mind, is the real question which is involved in what we are discussing . . .

It is not that anyone challenges the constitutional proposition of Cabinet unity. It is not that anybody seeks to deny the essential rule that the Cabinet must act together and stand together. That is elementary. The question is: to what extent can this united body act without any serious consideration of what critics may say, because they think: 'We are dead safe; we have enough people here to vote for us'? Their supporters may not have heard a word of the argument; they may not themselves think the Cabinet is right, but, after all, 'They vote for us, every vote counts, and that is all that matters.' . . .

. . . [The] point is, are we not in fact drifting into a position in which the Cabinet not only is a solid Cabinet of people who act together, as of course they always must do, but can count on a mechanical majority which in no circumstances will desert them whatever be the extravagance to which they propose to go? . . . I cannot help feeling that in earlier days the private Member in fact had much more influence behind the scenes, as well as in the voting Lobby, than the private Member has today . . . I do not at all deny that we must see developments, and it may be that in some ways the developments are good and necessary. There are a great many things which must, because of their nature, be governed by regulation, and which cannot be made the subject of express statutory enactment and amendment. The real question is: Have we not tended to drift into a situation in which the increasing subservience of the private Members of the House of Commons in effect threatens to turn our constitutional system into a system in which the Government feel no restraint at all upon what they propose to do? . . .

31. CABINET AND PARLIAMENT: A BALANCE OF POWER?

[from Lord Morrison of Lambeth, *Government and Parliament*, O.U.P., 1954, pp. 93–96]

In our country, unlike France, there is a delicate balance of power between the Cabinet and the House of Commons. The

Government, for the sake of itself and its party, cannot be indifferent to defeat in the House. It must do everything it can to avoid defeat. In France defeat is most unlikely to lead to the dissolution of Parliament and a General Election, or even necessarily to a change of policy: what happens is that one Government of mixed elements goes out and another Government (sometimes after serious delay) of the same or differently mixed elements comes in. But in the United Kingdom the defeat of the Government on other than trivial matters is serious. It will most probably involve the resignation of the Government, and unless it is possible to form another Government with a parliamentary majority, dissolution and a General Election will follow. I think that this is to the good and that it is to be preferred to the working of the French system of parliamentary government.

Some people think that the British practice puts too much power into the hands of the Government and its Whips. However, whilst it can be and sometimes is abused, generally speaking that is not so—particularly if we assume, as I think we should, that a Government of democratic strength is to be preferred to a minority or peacetime Coalition Government of wobble and weakness. Some price has to be paid to avoid confusion. If the House of Commons sets aside the policy or wishes of the Government, the Prime Minister can seek a dissolution from the Sovereign, and this is a deterrent to parliamentary revolt. But equally the Government must seek to retain the support of a parliamentary majority by persuasion, goodwill, mutual understanding, and, upon occasion, must make concessions, because the consequence to itself and to its electoral support are likely to be damaging if it goes to the country with its ranks divided. And it is essential that Governments should take parliamentary and public opinion into account. A Cabinet that proceeded to ride roughshod over the feelings of its supporters, relying on the Whips to enforce its will, would be asking for trouble; and it would not be long before it got it. It must be ready to take a firm line on essential matters of public interest, but a Government cannot hold its majority together unless it takes trouble to do so . . . Therefore, if Governments are often saved from parliamentary defeat by the back-benchers' fear of dissolution, it is no less true that Governments must treat their supporters with respect and understanding, because this is in accordance with the spirit of our parliamentary democracy and it is essential to the success and survival of the Government and its political party.

Indeed, we should go further than this. On many matters of policy the Government will resist the Opposition and the Opposition will fight the Government. This is natural and right. It breathes life and zest into our parliamentary proceedings and, let us hope, educates the nation. The duly elected majority must rule; but the Opposition has its rights and duties. The Opposition has been elected by its supporters to put their point of view in Parliament. And it is in accordance with the spirit of our parliamentary democracy that the Government should be prepared to listen to and to consider Opposition arguments and representations, for our belief in government by majority certainly does not mean that that majority should act in an arbitrary spirit. It is silly as well as intolerable if the Government, without considering the merits, assumes that every Opposition amendment to a Bill or opinion on policy is wrong and, therefore, to be rejected out of hand. Oppositions can be right and Governments can be wrong. Therefore, Ministers should fairly consider arguments seriously advanced from both sides of the House. It is also the duty of the Opposition fairly to consider arguments seriously advanced by the Government. It may be that these desiderata are somewhat idealistic, having regard to the hurly-burly of parliamentary life, and I know that there are and will be many occasions when they are not observed. I would, however, assure the reader that they are observed more often than many people think, and that there are many Acts of Parliament in which can be found words and ideas that have been suggested from both sides of the House. Administration is also affected—and rightly affected—by criticisms and suggestion from various quarters in the House.

Just as the Government has not, and ought not to have, absolute power, neither have nor ought the back-benchers to have absolute power. If back-benchers could freely do just as they liked according to their individual wishes or prejudices or even according to the moods they were in on some particular day—and believe me, there are moods of the day as well as Orders of the Day—we should have parliamentary chaos, and the orderliness and authority of government would be seriously impaired. It is not in the interest of good government, of parliament, or of our democratic institutions generally, that there should be no sense of coherence or collective responsibility on the back-benches. In France Governments are sometimes made and unmade every few weeks, largely because the power of the National Assembly is excessive as against the authority of the Government. The means of enforcing a real sense of responsibility are absent. So just as the British Government must be careful to win the respect and support of the House of Commons, it is also necessary that the Members of Parliament should be actuated by a proper sense of responsibility in casting or even not casting their votes in the House. Intelligence, a fair weighing up of the pros and cons, proper consideration of public opinion, a sense of loyalty and comradeship to one's political associates, consideration of the overall or longer-term interests of the country, as well as the merits of the immediate issue involved—all these are factors which are, or should be, in the mind of the back-bencher.

PART IV
The Role of the House of Commons

32. THE PARLIAMENTARY SPIRIT

[from Campion (ed.), *British Government since 1918*, Allen and Unwin, 1950, p. 18]

If a modern Government is omnipotent in the House of Commons, and if it owes its position to the blind party loyalty of its followers, why does it not take the step which leaders, animated solely by party spirit, have found to be logical in other countries—get rid of its opponents altogether and make its own party the sole party in the state? There is no legal impediment to this, nothing to prevent Parliament by a majority vote putting an end to legal opposition and introducing the single-party system.

The fact that this suggestion sounds fantastic to us proves, I think, that some factor has been left out of account. We do not regard the Government, any Government, as actuated purely by party spirit. We tacitly assume the existence of a counterbalancing factor—call it the 'parliamentary spirit.' 'Parliamentary spirit' is by no means incompatible with 'party spirit'—in our system it includes it. For centuries party has been the dynamic, and also the organizing, agency in Parliament, and without party Parliament would fall into impotence and anarchy. But the parliamentary spirit does put a limit to the indulgence of party spirit. In a parliamentary system no party can be completely self-centred. It instinctively avoids doing anything which would destroy the parliamentary system or seriously impede its working. It must at least tolerate the existence of other parties, let the electors vote for them if they wish, and leave them free to express their views in the country and in Parliament.

33. THE DOGS BARK IN PARLIAMENT

[from Sir Ivor Jennings, *Cabinet Government*, C.U.P., 2nd Ed., 1951, pp. 473–4]

Cromwell said that when he forcibly dissolved the Long Parliament 'not a dog barked'. Government can be carried on quite successfully without a Parliament. It is indeed a dilatory and inefficient talking machine. Yet speed and efficiency are not the only requirements of government. Justice is the supreme political virtue. Nor is ability to act first and think afterwards, if at all, a quality which commends itself. The British Governmental machine is, in spite of its many defects, one of the most efficient, if not the most efficient, constitutional structures of the world. It is reasonably efficient because it can be criticised. It is reasonably just because its actions are proclaimed to the people by those who have no cause to praise it. It is, in short, a good system because it rests upon Parliament and, through Parliament, upon the willing consent of those who are governed. The dogs bark *in* Parliament; if there were no Parliament, they might bite.

34. A FREE SOVEREIGN PARLIAMENT

[from Sir Winston Churchill, *Their Finest Hour* (Second World War, Vol. II) Cassell, 1949, p. 292]

A free sovereign Parliament, fairly chosen by universal suffrage, able to turn out the Government any day, but proud to uphold it in the darkest days was one of the points which were in dispute with the enemy—Parliament won.

I doubt whether any of the Dictators had as much effective power throughout his whole nation as the British War Cabinet. When we expressed our desires we were sustained by the people's representatives and cheerfully obeyed by all. Yet at no time was the right of criticism impaired. Nearly always the critics respected the national interest. When on occasions they challenged us the House voted them down by overwhelming majorities, and this, in contrast with totalitarian methods, without the slightest coercion, intervention, or use of the police or Secret Service. It was a proud thought that Parliamentary Democracy or whatever our British public life can be called, can endure, surmount, and survive all trials. Even the threat of annihilation did not daunt our Members, but this fortunately did not come to pass.

35. THE SIGNIFICANCE OF DEBATE

[from Walter Bagehot, *The English Constitution*, Fontana Library ed., 1963, pp. 72–73]

Cabinet government educates the nation; the Presidential does not educate it, and may corrupt it. It has been said that England invented the phrase, 'Her Majesty's Opposition'; that it was the first Government which made a criticism of administration as much a part of the policy as administration itself. This critical opposition is the consequence of Cabinet government. The great scene of debate, the great engine of popular instruction and political controversy, is the legislative assembly. A speech there by an eminent statesman, a party movement by a great political combination, are the best means yet known for arousing, enlivening, and teaching a people. The Cabinet system ensures such debates, for it makes them the means by which statesmen advertise themselves for future and confirm themselves in present Governments. It brings forward men eager to speak, and gives them occasions to speak. The deciding catastrophes of Cabinet governments are critical divisions preceded by fine discussions. Everything which is worth saying, everything which ought to be said, most certainly *will* be said. Conscientious men think they ought to persuade others; selfish men think they would like to obtrude themselves. The nation is forced to hear two sides—all the sides, perhaps of that which most concerns it. And it likes to hear—it is eager to know. Human nature despises long arguments which come to nothing—heavy speeches which precede no motion—abstract disquisitions which leave visible things where they were. But all men heed great results, and a change of Government is a great result. It has a hundred ramifications; it runs through society; it gives hope to many, and it takes away hope from many. It is one of those marked events which, by its magnitude and its melodrama, impress men even too much. And debates which have this catastrophe at the end of them—or may so have it—are sure to be listened to, and sure to sink deep into the national mind.

36. HAS THE HOUSE OF COMMONS DETERIORATED?

[from H. J. Laski, *Reflections on the Constitution*, Manchester U.P., 1951, pp. 10, 15–16, 36–37]

Severe judgments have been passed upon the effectiveness of the House of Commons not only by those who have observed it merely from without, but, hardly less, by many who have known it intimately from within. We have been asked to regard it as nothing but an organ of registration for the Cabinet, a body of miscellaneous amateurs, whose discussions do not count, whose criticism and investigations go unheeded, whose independence has been so impaired by the rigidity of party discipline that it has lost the high status it once enjoyed when the whole nation watched with passionate interest the epic contests in which men like Gladstone and Disraeli crossed swords in debate. We have been told that it has delegated so much of its power to Ministers and the officials of their Departments that it can no longer protect the freedom of citizens nor safeguard their property from the inexhaustible rapacity of a ruthless bureaucracy. We are urged to regard it as in need of reforms so massive that when it emerged from their acceptance it would no longer be recognisable as the classic institution to which so many admiring tributes were wont to be paid...

We are told by so experienced an observer as Mr Amery that Parliamentary government is already dead, and has been replaced by Cabinet government. The critics tell us that despite the wider social range from which members of the House of Commons are now drawn, compared, say, with the year 1832, the member of Parliament today is less able, less independent, and far less competent to form an opinion upon the matters upon which he votes than was his predecessor. Our attention is drawn to the fact that nearly all important legislation is government legislation and that those private members are few indeed who can hope to pilot a Bill of their own to the statute-book. Debates, it is argued, have become mere formalities, tolerated by the Government only because they do not affect the result in the division lobby. Far too many Bills are passed and far too few of them are debated with sufficient amplitude. Too many are sent upstairs to have their details settled in one of the Committees which now deal with all but the most vital legislation. There are bitter criticisms of the growth of delegated legislation, and of the consequential growth of administrative law—a growth predicted more than sixty years ago by Maitland—and it is insisted that the rule of Law and the freedom of the citizen are gravely menaced by these developments. Some argue that the House of Commons sits for too many months in the year. Mr Christopher Hollis has recently complained not only that it is useless to raise matters of debate on the adjournment, but even that question time is less significant than it used to be, and that, 'a great deal more often than not,' it is far easier to get a constituent's grievance remedied by a private letter to the Department concerned, than to raise it in the House, where the reluctance of a Minister and his officials to admit a mistake in public gets them on their dignity and makes them adamant rather than open-minded and rational. Many critics are irritated by the fact that Ministers refuse to answer questions on the day-to-day decisions taken by the Boards of nationalised industries. Others complain that the hours during which the House sits are far too long, and that the frequency of all night sittings is indefensible. If we add up all the complaints, and accept them at the face value they are given by those who put them forward, it would almost seem as though one might as well get rid of the House of Commons altogether. Yet I think that most of the critics whose good-will is not in doubt would, if pressed, admit the real alternative to the House of Commons is the concentration camp. Where a legislative assembly goes on discussing its business in the certain knowledge that in not more than five years from the first day of its first session it will have to submit its work to the free judgment of what is, I think, by far the most mature electorate in the world, I think there is real ground for saying that discussion does matter very seriously, and that the critics have set most of their complaints in a distorted historical perspective . . .

I see no reason to suppose that the status of the House of Commons has deteriorated in the last fifty years. In [no aspect] should I be prepared to admit the need of special remedies to meet a declining situation. It is the House which makes and unmakes Ministerial reputations. It is the House that watches with minute care the need for administration to be both just and reasonable. A Minister who persists in a policy against which the clear voice of the House has warned him will find, as a general rule, that his own Party will criticise him as bitterly as the Opposition. The House knows almost by intuition those well-known types, the careerist, the man who talks merely for the sake of hearing his own voice, the man with a special hobby who brings it up as Mr Dick brought up King Charles' head, and the crashing bore whose election to membership is a surprise, but whose re-election is something like a miracle. I think it is normally true that the House rises to the great occasion; and despite most complaints that every Opposition will make, it is usually true that from the passage of the second reading of a Bill to the stage where it is sent on to the House of Lords most things that need to be said both for and against it will in the course of debate be said. In general—Mr Attlee is a notable exception—most members from the two front benches tend to speak too long, less, I suspect, because of what they have to say than because they think it disrespectful both to the house and to their own positions, to occupy less than about forty minutes and upwards. It is of course, true that there is a good deal of repetition in the run of speeches in any debate; but this is true of all debating assemblies, and could only be avoided by confining discussion to one speech on either side. I should agree that, in many subjects, the speeches of members, and even of Ministers, reveal that they are not expert about them; but members of the House of Commons are not elected because they are expert and one of the most notable things in Parliamentary history is how rarely we find a really distinguished specialist successful in the kind of discussion for which the House of Commons is intended. After all, it is not a meeting of experts like, say, a gathering of members of the Chemical Society who have come to hear a paper on some aspect of chemical research, or of those members of the London Mathematical Society interested in the theory of numbers who have met in great excitement to hear someone of the calibre of the late Professor A. H. Hardy, or of the eminent Indian mathematician,

Ramanujan, describe a new approach to the solution of Fermat's theorem. They are essentially a group of representative men and women, mostly not inherently notable in themselves, but clothed with a representative capacity by the constituencies which have sent them to the House of Commons. With a small number of exceptions, they are not returned to Parliament for exceptional beauty of character, or distinction of mind; they have been returned there to support a party which their supporters hope will win enough seats to be able to form a government under the Premiership of its leader. The more fully we bear this in mind, the more clearly, I suggest, we shall understand what is the essential nature of the House of Commons.

37. THE MEMBER IN PARLIAMENT

[from Nigel Nicolson, *People and Parliament*, Weidenfeld and Nicolson, 1958, pp. 62–64]

It is historical continuity which has made Parliament greater than the sum of all its ephemeral members. Reading the reports of debates two hundred years old, it is possible to recapture exactly the mood of the House on that particular day. The forms of speech, the interruptions, the procedure, the very character of individual Members, are as authentically reproduced in our own time as the chimes of an eighteenth-century clock. But it is not only the antiquity of Parliament which cuts a man down in size. It is the terrible power to sum up character and detect fraud. Like a television camera, Parliament catches him at his weakest and most exposed. Even David Lloyd-George confessed that he could not rise to his feet at the dispatch box without his knees knocking together. It is in part due to the shape of the Chamber, which ensures that the speaker will have his back turned to his friends and face the concentrated glare of his opponents, but also to the knowledge that he only has an audience because all the other Members present are waiting for him to sit down so that they will have a chance to talk themselves. After trying for six hours to catch the Speaker's eye to deliver a speech already whittled down by the speeches of others, the Member begins to wonder why he exposes himself to the ordeal. The humiliating, enervating, revealing power of Parliament is in these moments at its most merciless.

Constituents, when they speak of Parliament as a talking shop ('Why don't you *do* something?'), can have little idea of the hypnotic power it exerts. All its members are linked by common experience of its disappointments, of how far achievement in debate lags behind intention. 'I do not think I know any bores in the House,' wrote Lord Wedgwood with some audacity, 'so well are we trained to confine self-advertisement to our constituencies . . . Inside the House, that bitterness of party strife outside, to which we have to conform in public, strikes us as somewhat vulgar.' It is one of the few places where the bore is forced to recognize himself as such, and one of the marks of a parliamentary bore is to allow his political attitude to affect his personal relationships. The violence of the controversy in the Chamber is at least in part a show. It will not be reproduced in any other quarter of the House, and the printed record of debates gives but the faintest hint of the underlying unity. Politicians, the creators of party, are often the most appalled by their own creation. All of them enjoy an occasional row and the dexterity with which the sabres are handled by their champions. But this is one of the manifestations of Parliament, not its object. Its greatest failure is not to have made the distinction evident to the world outside.

Parliament also teaches its Members, as it never can the public that government is immensely complex, and that a clear mind for administration is as important a qualification for membership as strong political conviction. Two-thirds of the time of Parliament is spent in discussing what is possible: the other third is spent in discussing what is desirable. In the constituencies the proportions are generally reversed. Constant, though indirect, contact with members of the civil service, who from their box under the gallery must so often regard their legislators in the same light as the legislators regard their constituents, gradually eliminates a man's contempt for careful forethought, teaches him the difference between an exception and a precedent, and warns him when a fire will burn itself out and when to call the fire-brigade. He soon begins to realize that decisions of government are usually right, even though most of his attention is concentrated on the occasions when they may be wrong.

He comes to admit to himself, though he may continue to say the opposite, that some grievances are incapable of solution except by creating other grievances ten times as bad.

38. THE STATUS OF PARLIAMENT

[from A. H. Birch, *Representative and Responsible Government*, Allen and Unwin, 1964, pp. 166–167]

In the Liberal language Parliament is a corporate entity wielding power. It possesses sovereignty, it holds ministers to account, it controls the executive. In the other language, which may for convenience be called 'the Whitehall language', Parliament is not a corporate entity so much as an arena or forum. In this arena individual Members air grievances and groups of Members carry on the party struggle. Ministers appear so that, in Morrison's term, Members can 'have a go' at them; debates on large issues are staged so that the opposition may present an alternative policy for the benefit of the electors. It is significant that Captain Harry Crookshank, a former Leader of the House, was shocked by the proposal that the Report Stage of legislation should be taken in committee. 'After all', he said, 'we are sent here to represent particular views, not to coalesce into a corporate body upstairs . . . Oppositions are not sent to make perfect bills out of the government measures'. It is also significant that in the debate on the Report of the Select Committee on Procedure of 1958-59 both the Leader of the House and the leading spokesman for the opposition made a point of reminding members that Parliament is the scene of a constant struggle for power between the parties.

As a language of description the Whitehall language is, up to a point, superior to the Liberal language. In general, Parliament occupies the role cast for it by Whitehall spokesmen. But this is by no means the whole story, and the British political system cannot be understood unless it is realized that in this sphere the Liberal language is the language of criticism, defining an ideal with which actual behaviour can be compared. Very occasionally the House of Commons lives up to this ideal and forces the government to acknowledge that (for the moment, at any rate) Parliamentary supremacy is more than a fiction.

This happened in 1935, when the House forced the Cabinet to disown the Hoare-Laval pact. It happened, as every one knows, in 1940, when Neville Chamberlain was forced to resign. It happened twice in 1959; first when the Obscene Publications Bill was drastically amended in committee, and later when the Government was forced to order a full-scale enquiry into an allegation that a policeman in a remote part of Scotland had struck an adolescent boy who had sworn at him. It happened again in July 1962, when the House forced the Home Secretary to revoke a deportation order made under the Commonwealth Immigration Act. Rare as such occasions may be, they are of crucial and continuing importance. The knowledge that, in the last resort, back-benchers can revolt leads ministers to pay more attention to back-bencher's opinions than they otherwise would. And the occasional spectacle of Parliament asserting its latent power almost certainly raises the status of M.P.s in the eyes of the general public.

Generally Parliament occupies a much more subservient role, even though its debates may make newspaper headlines. Then the Liberal language is used by those who wish to criticize the conduct of Parliamentary affairs. Thus, in 1960 the *Economist* lamented that Parliament was deprived 'of any function save that of running a Punch and Judy show on the front lawn to divert the people from looking through the windows of their government'. In 1957, a *Times* editorial painted an even gloomier picture of the Parliamentary performance:

> The cheap gibes, the incessant accusations and counter-accusations, the mocking 'Ministerial cheers' and the inane cries of 'Resign', the desperate fighting over things that do not matter, which probably hides from the participants themselves their poverty of ideas about those things that do matter are all part of the same picture.

39. THE PROPER FUNCTIONS OF REPRESENTATIVE BODIES

[from J. S. Mill, *Considerations on Representative Government*, Everyman's Edition, 1910, pp. 229–235, 239–241]

There is a radical distinction between controlling the business of government and actually doing it . . . It is one question, therefore, what a popular assembly should control another what it should itself do. It should, as we have already seen, control all the operations of government. But in order to determine through what channel this general control may most expediently be exercised, and what portion of the business of government the representative assembly should hold in its own hands, it is necessary to consider what kinds of business, a numerous body is competent to perform properly. That alone which it can do well it ought to take personally upon itself. With regard to the rest, its proper province is not to do it, but to take means for having it well done by others . . . In the first place, it is admitted in all countries in which the representative system is practically understood that numerous representative bodies ought not to administer. The maxim is grounded not only on the most essential principles of good government, but on those of the successful conduct of business of any description. No body of men, unless organised and under command, is fit for action, in the proper sense. Even a select board, composed of a few members, and these specially conversant with the business to be done, is always an inferior instrument to some one individual who could be found among them, and would be improved in character if that one person were made the chief, and all the others reduced to subordinates. What can be done better by a body than by any individual is deliberation. When it is necessary or important to secure hearing and consideration to many conflicting opinions, a deliberative body is indispensable . . .

But a popular assembly is still less fitted to administer, or to dictate in detail to those who have the charge of administration. Even when honestly meant, the interference is almost always injurious. Every branch of public administration is a skilled business, which has its own peculiar principles and traditional rules, many of them not even known, in any effectual way, except to those who have at some time had a hand in carrying on the business, and acquainted with the department. I do not mean that the transaction of public business has esoteric mysteries, only to be understood by the initiated. Its principles are all intelligible to any person of good sense, who has in his mind a true picture of the circumstances and conditions to be dealt with: but to have this he must know these circumstances and conditions; and the knowledge does not come by intuition . . . All these difficulties are sure to be ignored by a representative assembly which attempts to decide on special acts of administration. At its best, it is inexperience sitting in judgment on experience, ignorance on knowledge: ignorance which, never suspecting the existence of what it does not know, is equally careless and supercilious, making light of, if not resenting all pretensions to have a judgment better worth attending to than its own. Thus it is when no interested motives intervene: but when they do, the result is jobbery more unblushing and audacious than the worst corruption which can well take place in a public office under a government of publicity. It is not necessary that the interested bias should extend to the majority of the assembly. In any particular case it is often enough that it affects two or three of their number. Those two or three will have a greater interest in misleading the body than any other of its members are likely to have in putting it right. The bulk of the assembly may keep their hands clean, but they cannot keep their minds vigilant or their judgments discerning in matters which they know nothing about; and an indolent majority, like an indolent individual, belongs to the person who takes more pains with it . . .

The proper duty of a representative assembly in regard to matters of administration is not to decide them by its own vote, but to take care that the persons who have to decide them shall be the proper persons. Even this they cannot advantageously do by nominating the individuals. There is no act which more imperatively requires to be performed under a strong sense of individual responsibility than the nomination to employments. The experience of every person conversant with public affairs bears out the assertion, that there is scarcely any act respecting which the conscience of an average man is less sensitive; scarcely any case in which less consideration is paid to qualifications, partly because men do not know, and partly because they do not care for, the difference in qualifications between one person and another . . .

It has never been thought desirable that Parliament should itself nominate even the members of a Cabinet. It is enough that it virtually decides who shall be prime minister, or who shall be the two or three individuals from whom the prime minister shall be chosen. In doing this it merely recognises the fact that a certain person is the candidate of the party whose general policy commands its support. In reality, the only thing which Parliament decides is, which of two, or at most three, parties or bodies of men, shall furnish the executive government: the opinion of the party itself decides which of its members is fittest to be placed at the head. According to the existing practice of the British Constitution, these things seem to be on as good a footing as they can be. Parliament does not nominate any minister, but the Crown appoints the head of the administration in conformity to the general wishes and inclinations manifested by Parliament and the other ministers on the recommendation of the chief; while every minister has the undivided moral responsibility of appointing fit persons to the other offices of administration which are not permanent . . . To all these considerations, at least theoretically, I fully anticipate a general assent: though, practically, the tendency is strong in representative bodies to interfere more and more in the details of administration, by virtue of the general law, that whoever has the strongest power is more and more tempted to make an excessive use of it; and this is one of the practical dangers to which the futurity of representative governments will be exposed . . .

Instead of the function of governing, for which it is radically unfit, the proper office of a representative assembly is to watch and control the government: to throw the light of publicity on its acts: to compel a fully exposition and justification of all of them which any one considers questionable; to censure them if found condemnable, and, if the men who compose the government abuse their trust, or fulfil it in a manner which conflicts with the deliberate sense of the nation, to expel them from office, and either expressly or virtually appoint their successors. This is surely ample power, and security enough for the liberty of the nation. In addition to this, the Parliament has an office, not inferior even to this in importance: to be at once the nation's Committee of Grievances, and its Congress of Opinions; an arena in which not only the general opinion of the nation, but that of every section of it, and as far as possible of every eminent individual whom it contains, can produce itself in full light and challenge discussion; where every person in the country may count upon finding somebody who speaks his mind, as well or better than he could speak it himself—not to friends and partisans exclusively but in the face of opponents, to be tested by adverse controversy; where those whose opinion is overruled, feel satisfied that it is heard, and set aside not by a mere act of will, but for what are thought superior reasons, and commend themselves as such to the representatives of the majority of the nation; where every party or opinion in the country can muster its strength, and be cured of any illusion concerning the number or power of its adherents; where the opinion which prevails in the nation makes itself manifest as prevailing, and marshals its hosts in the presence of the government, which is thus enabled and compelled to give way to it on the mere manifestation, without the actual employment, of its strength; where statesmen can assure themselves, far more certainly than by any other signs, what elements of opinion and power are growing, and what declining, and are enabled to shape their measures with some regard not solely to present exigencies, but to tendencies in progress. Representative assemblies are often taunted by their enemies with being places of mere talk and *bavardage*. There has seldom been more misplaced derision. I know not how a representative assembly can more usefully employ itself than in talk, when the subject of talk is the great public interests of the country, and every sentence of it represents the opinion either of some important body of persons in the nation, or of an individual in whom some such body have reposed their confidence. A place where every interest and shade of opinion in the country can have its cause even passionately pleaded, in the face of the government and of all other interests and opinions, can compel them to listen, and either comply, or state clearly why they do not, is in itself, if it answered no other purpose, one of the most important political institutions that can exist anywhere, and one of the foremost benefits of free government. Such 'talking' would never be looked upon with disparagement if it were not allowed to stop 'doing'; which it never would, if assemblies knew and acknowledged that talking and discussion are their proper business, while *doing*, as the result of discussion, is the task not of a miscellaneous body, but of individuals specially trained to it; that the fit office of an assembly is to see that those individuals are honestly and intelligently chosen, and to interfere no further with them, except by unlimited latitude of suggestion and criticism, and by applying or withholding the final seal of national assent. It is for want of this judicious reserve that popular assemblies attempt to do what they cannot do well—govern and legislate—and provide no machinery but their own for much of it, when of course every hour spent in talk is an hour withdrawn from actual business. But the very fact which most unfits such bodies for a Council of Legislation qualifies them the more for their other office—namely, that they are not a selection of the greatest political minds in the country, from whose opinions little could with certainty be inferred concerning those of the nation, but are, when properly constituted, a fair sample of every grade of intellect among the people which is at all entitled to a voice in public affairs. Their part is to indicate wants, to be an organ for popular demands, and a place of adverse discussion for all opinions relating to public matters, both great and small and, along with this, to check by criticism, and eventually by withdrawing their support, those high public officers who really conduct the public business, or who appoint those by whom it is conducted. Nothing but the restriction of the function of representative bodies within these rational limits will enable the benefits of popular control to be enjoyed in conjunction with the no less important requisites (growing ever more important as human affairs increase in scale and in complex) of skilled legislation and administration. There are no means of combining these benefits except by separating the functions which guarantee the one from those which essentially require the other; by disjoining the office of control and criticism from the actual conduct of affairs, and devolving the former on the representatives of the Many, while securing for the latter, under strict responsibility to the nation, the acquired knowledge and practised intelligence of a specially trained and experienced Few.

40. THE FUNCTIONS OF THE HOUSE OF COMMONS

[from Walter Bagehot, *The English Constitution*, Fontana Library ed., 1963, pp. 150–154]

The main function of the House of Commons is one which we know quite well, though our common constitutional speech does not recognise it. The House of Commons is an electoral chamber; it is the assembly which chooses our president. Washington and his fellow-politicians contrived an electoral college, to be composed (as was hoped) of the wisest people in the nation, which, after due deliberation, was to choose for president the wisest man in the nation. But the college is sham; it has no independence and no life. No one knows, or cares to know, who its members are. They never discuss, and never deliberate. They were chosen to vote that Mr Lincoln be President, or that Mr Breckenridge be President; they do so vote, and they go home. But our House of Commons is a real choosing body; it elects the people it likes. And it dismisses whom it likes too. No matter that a few months since it was chosen to support Lord Aberdeen or Lord Palmerson; upon a sudden occasion it ousts the statesman to whom it at first adhered, and selects an opposite statesman whom it at first rejected. Doubtless in such cases there is a tacit reference to probable public opinion; but certainly also there is much free will in the judgment of the Commons. The House only goes where it thinks in the end the nation will follow; but it takes its chance of the nation following or not following; it assumes the initiative, and acts upon its discretion or its caprice.

When the American nation has chosen its President, its virtue goes out of it, and out of the Transmissive College through which it chooses. But because the House of Commons has the power of dismissal in addition to the power of election, its relations to the Premier are incessant. They guide him and he leads them. He is to them what they are to the nation. He only goes where he believes they will go after him. But he has to take the lead; he must choose his direction, and begin the journey. Nor must he flinch. A good horse likes to feel the rider's bit; and a great deliberative assembly likes to feel that it is under worthy guidance. A Minister who succumbs to the House,—who ostentatiously seeks its pleasure,—who does not try to regulate it,—who will not boldly point out plain errors to it, seldom thrives. The great leaders of Parliament have varied much, but they have all had a certain firmness. A great assembly is as soon spoiled by over-indulgence as a little child. The whole life of English politics is the action and reaction between the Ministry and the Parliament. The appointees strive to guide, and the appointers surge under the guidance.

The elective is now the most important function of the House of Commons. It is most desirable to insist, and be tedious, on this, because our tradition ignores it. At the end of half the sessions of Parliament, you will read in the newspapers, and you will hear even from those who have looked close at the matter and should know better, 'Parliament has done nothing this session. Some things were promised in the Queens' speech, but they were only little things; and most of them have not passed.' Lord Lyndhurst used for years to recount the small outcomings of legislative achievement; and yet those were the days of the first Whig Governments, who had more to do in Legislation, and did more, than any Government. The true answer to such harangues as Lord Lyndhurst's by a Minister should have been in the first person. He should have said firmly 'Parliament has maintained ME, and that was its greatest duty; Parliament has carried on what, in the language of traditional respect, we call the Queen's Government; it has maintained what wisely or unwisely it deemed the best executive of the English nation'.

The second function of the House of Commons is what I may call an expressive function. It is its office to express the mind of the English people on all matters which come before it. Whether it does so well or ill I shall discuss presently.

The third function of Parliament is what I may call—preserving a sort of technicality even in familiar matters for the sake of distinctness—the teaching function. A great and open council of considerable men cannot be placed in the middle of a society without altering that society. It ought to alter it for the better. It ought to teach the nation what it does not know. How far the House of Commons can so teach, and how far it does so teach, are matters for subsequent discussion.

Fourthly, the House of Commons has what may be called an informing function—a function which though in its present form quite modern is singularly analogous to a mediaeval function. In old times one office of the House of Commons was to inform the sovereign what was wrong. It laid before the Crown the grievances and complaints of particular interests. Since the publication of the Parliamentary debates a corresponding office of Parliament is to lay these same grievances, these same complaints, before the nation, which is the present sovereign. The nation needs it quite as much as the King ever needed it. A free people is indeed mostly fair, liberty practises men in a give-and-take, which is the rough essence of justice. The English people, possibly even above other free nations, is fair. But a free nation rarely can be—and the English nation is not—quick of apprehension. It only comprehends what is familiar to it—what comes into its own experience, what squares with its own thought. 'I never heard of such a thing in my life,' the middle-class Englishman says, and he thinks he so refutes an argument. The common disputant cannot say in reply that his experience is but limited, and that the assertion may be true, though he had never met with anything at all like it. But a great debate in Parliament *does* bring home something of this feeling. Any notion, any creed, any feeling, any grievance which can get a decent number of English members to stand up for it, is felt by almost all Englishmen to be perhaps a false and pernicious opinion, but at any rate possible—an opinion within the intellectual sphere an opinion to be reckoned with. And it is an immense achievement. Practical diplomatists say that a free Government is harder to deal with than a despotic Government; you may be able to get the despot to hear the other side; his Ministers, men of trained intelligence, will be sure to know what makes against them; and they *may* tell him. But a free nation never hears any side save its own. The newspapers only repeat the side their purchasers like: the favourable arguments are set out, elaborated, illustrated, the adverse arguments maimed, misstated, confused. The worst judge, they say, is a deaf judge; the most dull Government is a free Government on matters its ruling classes will not hear. I am disposed to reckon it as the second function of Parliament in point of importance, that to some extent it makes us hear what otherwise we should not.

Lastly, there is the function of legislation of which of course it would be preposterous to deny the great importance, and which I only deny to be *as* important as the executive management of the whole State, or the political education given by Parliament to the whole nation. There are, I allow, seasons when legislation is more important than either of these. The nation may be misfitted with its laws, and need to change them: some particular corn law may hurt all industry, and it may be worth a thousand administrative blunders to get rid of it. But generally the laws of a nation suit its life; special adaptations of them are but subordinate; the administration and conduct of that life is the matter which presses most. Nevertheless, the statute-book of every great nation yearly contains many important new laws, and the English statute-book does so above any. An immense mass, indeed, of the legislation is not, in the proper language of jurisprudence, legislation at all. A law is a general command applicable to many cases. The 'special acts' which crowd the statute-book and weary Parliamentary committees are applicable to one case only. They do not lay down rules according to which railways shall be made, they enact that such a railway shall be made from this place to that place, and they have no bearing upon any other transaction. But after every deduction and abatement, the annual legislation of Parliament is a result of singular importance; were it not so, it could not be, as it often is considered, the sole result of its annual assembling.

41. IS PARLIAMENT A LEGISLATURE?

[from L. S. Amery, *Thoughts on the Constitution*, O.U.P., 1947, pp. 11–12]

Parliament is not, and never has been, a legislature, in the sense of a body specially and primarily empowered to make laws. The function of legislation, while shared between 'King, Lords and Commons in Parliament assembled', has always been predominantly exercised by Government which, indeed, has never allowed Parliament as such to take any initiative in one of its most important fields, that of finance. The main task of Parliament is still what it was when first summoned, not to legislate or govern, but to secure full discussion and ventilation of all matters, legislative or administrative, as the condition of giving its assent to Bills whether introduced by the Government or by private members, or its supports to Ministers.

42. ANOTHER VIEW OF THE FUNCTIONS OF PARLIAMENT

[from H. J. Laski, *Parliamentary Government in England*, Allen and Unwin, 1938, pp. 144, 149–150, 158–161]

I

To make a Government then, with the initiative in legislation is the first task of the House. How it performs that task I shall discuss when I come to deal with the problem of Cabinet-making. If we assume that a Government is in being, what are the functions the House must perform? There is the ventilation of grievance. There is the extraction of information. There is the business of debate, with the attempt, through debate, to sustain public interest, and to educate it, in the significance of what is being done. There is what we usually term the selective function of the House—by which is meant that subtle psychological process by which one member makes a reputation and another fails to make one, with its consequential repercussions on the personnel of Governments. There is, lastly, the question of what place, if any, the private member as such is to occupy in the direction of the Commons' business. Each of these matters requires separate consideration.

II

The power to ventilate grievance means the power to compel attention to grievance. A Government that is compelled to explain itself under cross-examination will do its best to avoid the grounds of complaint. Nothing makes responsible government so sure. Where this power is absent, the room for tyranny is always wide; for nothing so develops inertia in a people as the inability to formulate grievance, and to see that its redress is pressed upon the central source of power. This, at least, the House of Commons secures; and, upon big occasions, it secures it in a background of dramatic emphasis which concentrates wide attention upon the issue involved. The Savidge case was what the journalists call 'front page news' until the Government had given assurance of remedy for the complaint. Can anyone imagine a Berlin stenographer receiving similar treatment if she had complained to a Reichstag Deputy about the unwelcome attentions of the German Gestapo?

III

The selective function of the House of Commons is the most mysterious of all its habits; and it is far easier to describe the mysterious alchemy it expresses than to explain it. The making of a reputation in the House is not a direct function of ability; many men of first-rate intelligence. Sir George Jessel, for instance, were failures in the House of Commons. It is not accessible to oratorical talent or debating power merely; it was never, for instance, moved by Brougham whose importance was almost wholly derived from outside the House of Commons. A reputation for character may give a member great standing in the chamber even when it is not allied to any exceptional mental power; Lord Althorp and Mr Walter Long are both examples of this prestige. The House will admire without respect; and no one can watch the interplay of its proceedings without observing how carefully it draws a distinction between these. It will listen with far greater attention to a bad speaker who in a halting way is trying to say something he feels deeply, or to convey information which it believes to be significant, than to a facile debater who is obviously speaking, however well, merely to bring his name before the public. It tends to distrust the clever man who tries to score points. It dislikes the pontifical type who appears to be instructing members for their own good. It is a very difficult assembly to bully, even from the Front Benches. It will accord little but suspicion to a reputation brought into the chamber from outside unless its possessor assumes that he must, *ab initio*, win the goodwill of members. It hates the member who uses invective as a speciality; yet there is nobody so sympathetic to one the intensity of whose attack is measured by some deeply-felt experience which lies behind it.

The easy thing, of course, to say of all this is that the House of Commons is an attractive club, with all the habits that pertain to this special institution. There is, no doubt, a real truth in this; men who have to live together and work together for years on end can hardly, even amid the modern conditions of party warfare, help developing between one another the habits of good fellowship; these, moreover, are important and valuable, because they tend, within limits, to create the atmosphere necessary to that art of successful compromise which is of the essence of parliamentary government. If the Government side stood to the Opposition in the posture of gladiators determined to draw blood it is clear that debate would be at least difficult and understanding impossible.

But, in fact, these habits serve another purpose of immense importance. The impact of a member upon the House is a very good way (though it is not the only way) of testing his availability for ministerial position. A man who is to rule a Department well must have the qualities which enable him to be acceptable to the House of Commons. That he is so acceptable does not mean that he will be a good minister; but not to be so acceptable does probably mean that he is not likely to be an effective one. It is not merely true, as the old Greek proverb has it, that office shows the man; it is still more true that ability to win the attention of the House is a proof of fitness, at least in some degree, for power. It is a part of that art of managing men which is the pivot of leadership. It brings out qualities by tests which go to the root of character. A Government that is not subject to criticism may pick its members as it will; any fool, as Napoleon said, can govern in a state of siege. But a Government the members of which are constantly under the fire of criticism, who have before it to maintain the appearance of reasonableness, to refrain from losing their tempers, to show courtesy and restraint as their normal temper, who have to recognize that there is a point at which neither rhetoric nor reiteration is an answer to argument, a Government schooled to this discipline is at least likely to keep its head in any but the gravest times.

Broadly, I think, it is true to say that the House enables this kind of quality to be made available for office through the kind of reputation it gives to its members. No doubt it makes mistakes, but it does not often make bad mistakes. Those whom it finds interesting or persuasive are very likely to be interesting or persuasive; and such men are moved to make the effort to display these qualities because the rewards of their recognition in our system are so obviously great. The House, in a word is able by its atmosphere to draw out the best from a man of the qualities that are important for ruling in a party system. That has been remarkably demonstrated in our own time by Lord Baldwin. The qualities which gave him his peculiar hold over the House were the qualities that, a little later gave him his peculiar hold over the nation. It is, I think, certain that so delicate an affair as the abdication of Edward VIII could not have been carried out so successfully without that hold. It is impossible to do more than hint at its secret; but I believe that the centre of its mystery lies in the power to evoke a sense of trust which transcends the division of parties. That is the quality Lord Althorp had; it is the quality also that explains why, without any very notable intelligence, Sir Edward Grey exercised so remarkable an authority over members. And it should, I think, be added that the trust, in its turn, depends upon the intuitive sense of the House that the minister concerned respects it and, through it, the great, if impalpable assumptions upon which it rests. The Parliament of 1918–22 was a bad Parliament because there was lacking any abiding sense of that trust, and similarly the Parliament of 1931 was a bad Parliament because the circumstances in which the election which preceded it had been fought rendered it impossible for that trust to be asked for and given.

43. PARLIAMENT AND THE EXECUTIVE

[from F. A. Ogg, *English Government and Politics*, Macmillan, 2nd ed. 1936, pp. 452, 457–459]

What of Parliament's relation to the executive and administrative work of the government? Here less startling changes are to be recorded, because at no time in the past has Parliament either actually or theoretically wielded such direct control as in the domain of legislation. Even in this field, however, the tendency has been in the same direction. Most cabinet members are principal officers in the great executive departments. As ministers, their business is to supervise the work carried on in and through these departments; and ever since the cabinet system assumed its matured form, their direct and full responsibility to the House of Commons for all their executive actions has been accepted as axiomatic. The theory is that the ministers are responsible to the elected chamber for all that they do, singly in small or isolated matters, collectively in more important ones; that their acts are constantly subject to inquiry and criticism; and that the great powers which they wield can be stripped from them, at any time by the simple withholding of support. There are, furthermore, several recognized methods by which this responsibility can be asserted and enforced.

(Here Professor Ogg lists such methods as questions, adjournment motions, supply days, etc.)

In such ways are the ministers, in their executive capacity, held to their presumed responsibility. It does not follow, however, that the House of Commons actually participates in, or even habitually interferes with, the ministers' administrative work. On the contrary, the British executive is more free from legislative control than is either the president of the United States or the ministry in France. Never, save when the Long Parliament, in the Cromwellian era, drew to itself the executive power and bestowed it upon committees which it appointed, has Parliament as a whole or the House of Commons in particular manifested a disposition to take part in any direct way in the exercise of that power. It provides the money required for administrative purposes by authorizing taxation; it appropriates, with more or less particularity, the purposes to which the money so provided is to be applied; it criticizes the mode in which money is spent and in which public affairs are administered; its support is indispensable to those who are responsible for administration; but it does not administer. Nor does it often seek to regulate administration except in the most general way. It does not attempt to say how the departments shall be organized, how large their staffs shall be, what the civil servants shall be paid, or how reports shall be prepared. It does not expect any appointments of officials, high or low, to come before it for confirmation. It keeps hands off the executive and administrative machinery in a fashion quite unknown to the American Congress, which, notwithstanding our supposed respect for separation of powers, insists on reaching over into the executive and administrative spheres and regulating even the matter of salaries down to the last detail.

The thing that Parliament (that is to say, the House of Commons) is supposed to do is to furnish the inquiry and criticism that will keep the ministers and their subordinates up to the mark—not to issue orders in advance as to what they shall do, but to survey the things that they have already done and hold them to account therefore. A strong executive government, tempered and controlled by constant, vigilant, and representative criticism, is the objective. The point to be impressed, however, is that, on the executive side equally with the legislative, the tendency in later years has been toward a considerably less direct and effective responsibility of the ministers than, for example, when Bagehot wrote. Experiences during the World War had something to do with it, but the change was going on earlier, and the causes are to be found to some extent in the same general shift of conditions that has rendered Parliament less independent of the electorate in the field of legislation. Here, too, the major fact is the closer contact between London and the provinces, produced by the railroad, the telegraph, the telephone, the newspaper, the motor-car, the aeroplane, and radio broadcasting, enabling the ministers to keep the country informed and to receive back the people's impressions and reaction in a fashion undreamt of even a generation ago. This means that the ministers now take their cue more largely from what seems to be public opinion, and that, so long as they feel that they have backing from this source, they are relatively indifferent to what is said or done at Westminster. Criticisms are taken lightly; rebuffs which formerly would have caused a political sensation, perhaps a cabinet crisis, are ignored or explained away. Other factors, however, enter in. The growing volume of business in the House of Commons makes it impossible to scrutinize the work of the government even as closely as was formerly done, which of course means just so much more freedom of action in the great offices in Whitehall. Parliament, furthermore, has suffered a decline in prestige which has caused people to look more hopefully to the executive agencies, and this has tended still further to induce the ministers to tie up their political fortunes rather with public sentiment than with parliamentary debates and votes. The truth is that scarcely a ministry in fifty years has been turned out of office by a hostile Parliament because of its executive acts; and the chances of such a thing happening have of late been steadily diminishing.

44. SAFEGUARDS AGAINST EXECUTIVE POWER

[*Committee on Ministers' Powers, 1932.* Extracts from evidence of Sir Maurice L. Gwyer, Procurator-General and Treasury Solicitor]

The Committee will, I hope, permit me in conclusion to suggest that the subject matter of their investigation is not merely one of the scope of Departmental powers at the present time. It goes far deeper and involves the whole philosophy and technique of modern government. The greater the complexity of our civilisation and the wider the range of our legislation, the more difficult it is for a popularly elected legislature to exercise complete control over administrative policy. The utmost under present conditions that it can do in fact is to secure that competent administrators are chosen and to enforce strictly the principle of administrative responsibility; and fundamental change would imply the adoption of a new theory of government . . .

Questioned by Sir Warren Fisher

Assuming that as individuals we do not want to be subject to the arbitrary discretion of the Executive . . . do you really think we have at the present moment as individuals effective safeguards against executive tyranny?— . . . I do not think the control of Parliament over the details of administrative action is always as effective as it was fifty years ago in this country, but what the remedy may be, I should be sorry to say.

From the parliamentary point of view you would agree that the existence of question time *in terrorem* is about the only safeguard we have?—That is as effective as anything . . .

45. WHAT *is* THE REAL JOB OF THE HOUSE OF COMMONS?

[*Select Committee on Procedure*, H.C. 161 of 1931. Extracts from evidence of Lord Eustace Percy]

The proper business of the House of Commons may be defined roughly as follows: to focus public attention on the important issues of the day, to grant taxation limited to the immediate needs of the Executive, to appropriate the public revenues to particular services, to press the Executive (in return for the taxes granted) for the redress of popular grievances, and to grant the Executive such additional legal powers as may be necessary for the efficient conduct of public administration.

The critic may object that this definition is an old-fashioned one. The reply to that objection is that, whether we like it or not, the House of Commons has never succeeded in extending its effective action much beyond the field where it had established itself two hundred years ago, after it had asserted its legitimate rights against the Crown. It does not, and cannot, itself govern the country, and many of its present defects probably arise from the recent 'democratic' tendency to convert it into a sovereign parliamentary assembly on the Continental model, governing the country through a committee of ministers. In our constitutional practice, the distinction between Executive and Legislature is, in essence more clearly drawn than in the written constitutions of countries which have nominally adopted the principle of the 'separation of powers.' The King's Ministers are responsible to Parliament, but they are responsible for the discharge of duties which Parliament is radically unfitted to discharge for itself. It is not even the business of the House of Commons to 'control' the King's Ministers, if by that is meant to control the detail of their administration or even of their expenditure. It controls Ministers most effectively by forming a broad general opinion as to their personal reliability, and treating them accordingly, but it never has been, and never will be, able to offer them authoritative guidance in the efficient and economical management of their departments . . .

46. HOW THE HOUSE CONTROLS POLICY AND ADMINISTRATION

[*Select Committee on Procedure*, Third Report, H.C. 189 of 1946. Extracts from Memorandum from the Clerk to the House]

Control of policy and administration occupies on an average about forty per cent of the time of the House—an allocation which on the face of it appears adequate. But the classification is misleading. The line between policy and administration may be difficult to draw, and it is not possible to distinguish forms of procedure which are used for the specific control of one or the other. Nevertheless the control of policy and the control of administration are two broadly distinct functions, and if the several forms of procedure which together fall under this head are examined, it will be seen that by far the greater part of them is used for the discussion of questions of broad policy rather than of administrative detail. Thus the Debate on the King's speech (5·8 days per session) is used to discuss the broad outlines of the Government programme. Adjournment motions (5·9 days) lend themselves to discussion of administrative points, but are often used for raising questions of policy; and substantive motions (14·2 days) are used to raise larger subjects. Above all, the business of Supply, which accounts for the largest amount of time under this head (32·3 days), has in recent years tended more and more to provide opportunities for debates on policy. The debates on the various stages of the Consolidated Fund Bills tend to be taken up with full-day discussions on general policy rather than with details of administration. The Estimates themselves, which in theory provide the occasion *par excellence* for the raising of grievances against administration, have of late years tended to be used for the discussion of major issues of policy. An analysis of the Departments selected for discussion on Supply days bears out this impression. Out of 202 days allotted to Supply in ten sessions in the period 1921 to 1937-38, 24¼ were used for the discussion of the Defence Services, 21½ for Scottish Departments, twenty for the Foreign Office and 16½ for the Ministry of Labour. If it be admitted that the debates on the 21½ days spent on Scottish Departments may have been largely administrative in character, it is fair to assume that the larger part of the time ostensibly given to the discussion of the

Fighting Services, the Foreign Office and the Ministry of Labour, was actually used to discuss national issues of defence, foreign policy and economic problems. In fine, the amount of time devoted to really administrative points, so far from tending to increase with the growth of administrative activity has greatly diminished.

47. 'GOVERNMENTS GOVERN, PARLIAMENTS CRITICISE'

[from Sir Ivor Jennings, *Cabinet Government*, C.U.P., 2nd ed., 1951, pp. 449–450]

It is, in short, the function of the Government to govern and of the House of Commons to criticise; but there are limits to the scope of criticism; and if the Government asserts that discussion is not in the public interest the House can do no more than accept the decision. Even where publication of information is not inimical, the powers of the House are limited in fact. It is a deliberative assembly, not a governing body.

At the same time, few would be disposed to agree with Sir James Graham's statement: 'The House of Commons, although a good judge of the merits of an Administration and of their merits as a whole, is bewildered in a labyrinth of details and miscarries in its judgment when it attempts to deal with minute particulars. It is safer and easier to displace a Ministry than to change and direct its policy by the active intervention of Parliament.' A Government will not give way on a major question of policy. Parliamentary criticism of details compels the Government, by an appeal to public opinion, and its reaction in the House, to modify its attitude, and to qualify the application of its principles, without overthrowing the principles themselves. It is only by an attack on details that 'concessions' can be secured.

48. WHAT DO WE MEAN BY CONTROL?

[from Bernard Crick, *The Reform of Parliament*, Weidenfeld and Nicolson, 1964, pp. 77–78]

Thus the phrase 'Parliamentary control', and talk about the 'decline of Parliamentary control', should not mislead anyone into asking for a situation in which Governments can have their legislation changed or defeated, or their life terminated (except in the most desperate emergency when normal politics will in any case break down, as in Chamberlain's 'defeat' in 1940). Control means *influence*, not direct power; *advice*, not command; *criticism*, not obstruction, *scrutiny*, not initiation, and *publicity*, not secrecy. Here is a very realistic sense of Parliamentary control which *does* affect any Government. The Government will make decisions, whether by existing powers or by bringing in new legislation, in the knowledge that these decisions, sooner or later, will find their way to debate on the Floor of one of the Houses of Parliament. The type of scrutiny they will get will obviously affect, in purely political terms, the type of actions undertaken. And the Civil Service will administer with the knowledge that it too may be called upon to justify perhaps even the most minute actions.

Governments are virile and adult; they are beyond the strict parental control of Parliament. But they are likely to be deeply influenced by well put home truths from the family, if only (or above all) because this may be some sort of clue to their public reputation; and also because, after all, they have to share the same overcrowded house. Defeating the Government or having the whips withdrawn represent, like calling in the police, the breakdown, not the assertion, of normal control.

Governments deserve praise in so far as they expose themselves, willingly and helpfully, to influence, advice, criticism, scrutiny and publicity; and they deserve blame in so far as they try to hide from unpleasant discussions and to keep their reasons and actions secret. Parliaments deserve praise or blame as to whether or not they can develop institutions whose control is powerful in terms of General Elections and not of Governmental instability. This 'praise' and 'blame' is not moralistic: it is prudential. A Government subject to such controls is not likely to get too far out of touch with public opinion; it may not, even in Bagehot's sense, attempt to 'teach' public opinion, but it will not destroy it. So Parliamentary control is not the stop switch, it is the tuning, the tone and the amplifier of a system of communication which tells governments what the electorate want (rightly or wrongly) and what they will stand for (rightly or wrongly), and tells the electorate what is possible within the resources available (however much opinions will vary on what is possible).

It is in this sense of control that we must now examine the main ways by which Parliament attempts to control (influence, advise, criticise, scrutinise and publicise) the Executive. But one preliminary comment: it follows from this that it is possible to exaggerate what many see as the 'all important' aspect of financial control. Certainly the history of Parliament was the history of the power of the purse over the Crown. But now that 'the Crown' is a Party Ministry, control is nothing if it is not influence over the policy of Governments. It is politically impossible to separate out economic from political factors. It is procedurally worthless to look at the form of legislation or of estimates without being able to consider the content. And the fact that Parliament scrutinises financial legislation in a less and less detailed manner is not the cause of the general decline of Parliamentary influence, but is the effect; therefore it cannot sensibly be regarded as the unique lever, or even the first priority, in any attempt to restore or create a true reciprocity between government and consent. The problem is of a general lack of development, or in some cases of the decline, of devices for informing and communicating authoritatively.

PART V
The Role of the Opposition

49. OPPOSITION AND GOVERNMENT

[from Sir Ivor Jennings, *Cabinet Government*, C.U.P., 2nd ed., 1951, p. 439]

It is not untrue to say that the most important part of Parliament is the Opposition in the House of Commons. The function of Parliament is not to govern but to criticise. Its criticism, too, is directed not so much towards a fundamental modification of the Government's policy as towards the education of public opinion. The Government's majority exists to support the Government. The function of the Opposition is to secure a majority against the Government at the next general election and thus to replace the Government. This does not imply that a Government may not be defeated in the House of Commons. Nor does it imply that parliamentary criticism may not persuade the Government to modify, or even to withdraw, its proposals. These qualifications are important; but they do not destroy the truth of the principle that the Government governs and the Opposition criticises. Failure to understand this simple principle if one of the causes of the failure of so many of the progeny of the Mother of Parliaments and of the supersession of parliamentary government by dictatorships.

50. THE GRAND INQUEST OF THE NATION

[from Lawrence Lowell, *The Government of England*, Macmillan, 1908, Vol. I, p. 355]

The system of a responsible ministry can develop in a normal and healthy way only in case the legislative body is divided into two parties, and under those conditions it is the inevitable consequence of the system that Parliament cannot support the cabinet on one question and oppose it on another. The programme of the ministers must be accepted or rejected as a whole, and hence the power of initiative, both legislative and executive, must rest entirely with them. This is clearly the tendency in Parliament at the present day. The House of Commons is finding more and more difficulty in passing any effective vote, except a vote of censure. It tends to lose all powers except the power to criticise and the power to sentence to death. Parliament has been called the great inquest of the nation, and for that purpose its functions have of late been rather enlarged than impaired. Nor are the inquisitors confined to any one section of the House, for while that part is played chiefly by the Opposition, the government often receives a caution from its own supporters also. If the parliamentary system has made the cabinet of the day autocratic, it is an autocracy exerted with the utmost publicity, under a constant fire of criticism; and tempered by the force of public opinion, the risk of a vote of want of confidence, and the prospects of the next election.

51. 'HER MAJESTY'S OPPOSITION'

[from Campion (ed.), *Parliament: a survey*, Allen and Unwin, 1952, pp. 29–31]

The growth of party organization and discipline, which has so greatly strengthened the hands of the modern Ministry, has contributed something by way of compensation towards the maintenance of the parliamentary system. It has consolidated the forces and enhanced the importance of the Opposition in the House of Commons. The need of a check on executive power is deeply ingrained in the parliamentary tradition. In the seventeenth century opposition had been the function of Parliament, as a body. When the selection of Ministers from the largest party in the House of Commons made it clear that consistent criticism could not be expected from the majority of the House, this function passed to the minority. 'His Majesty's Opposition' acquired a recognized official status as an indispensible element in the constitution. There may be several parties in opposition, but *the* Opposition means the second main party, temporarily in a minority, with leaders experienced in office, who are ready, when the time arises, to form an alternative government. This affords a guarantee that its criticism will be directed by a consistent policy and conducted with responsibility—not in a spirit calculated to ruin the game for the sake of the prize.

The 'Official Opposition' is a standing proof of the British genius for inventing political machinery. It has been adopted in all the Dominion Parliaments; the lack of it is the chief weakness of most of the Continental systems. It derives, of course, from the two-Party system; but in its developed form it represents a happy fusion of the parliamentary spirit of toleration with the democratic tendency to exalt party organization. The system involves the discouragement of individual initiative almost as much on the Opposition back benches as on those of the Government Party, for party organization seems more adapted to frontal attack in mass formation than to individual sniping. While admitting the loss to parliamentary life resulting from the sacrifice of the independent private Member, it cannot be denied that under modern conditions the concerted action of the Opposition is the best means of controlling a Government—by criticizing defects in administration loudly enough for the public to take notice. This is not a particularly pleasant, if salutary, experience for Ministers; and it is only natural that they should be tempted to think both that the Opposition abuse their opportunities and that their opportunities are unnecessarily ample. The facilities which the Opposition enjoy for initiating criticism on subjects of their own selection are dependent on technical forms and parliamentary conventions which it would be out of place to explain here. But the share of the time of the House which the Government (who nominally control the disposal of time and are always short of time for their own business) put at the disposal of a body whose *raison d'etre* is to show up the mistakes of Ministers and eventually to turn them out of office—this share of time, which during the last fifty years has not fallen below a quarter of the effective days of the session, is worth more interest than it usually receives. The least that can be said is that, since it is only through the Opposition that some measure of parliamentary control survives, the uninterrupted respect for the rights of the Opposition which contemporary Governments have shown should be accepted as *prima facie* evidence of the soundness of their parliamentary faith.

52. PARLIAMENTARY PROCEDURE AND THE OPPOSITION

[from Campion, ed., *British Government since 1918*, Allen and Unwin, 1950, pp. 20–21, 30]

The practice of the House of Commons emphasizes the importance of the official Opposition in every possible way. This is right because under modern conditions it has fallen to the Opposition to discharge what was regarded before the institution of Cabinet Government as the primary function of the House as a whole—the control by criticism of the executive. Its leader is paid a salary out of the Consolidated Fund, and is thus beyond the reach of majority vote without formal legislation. It is organized like the government party, with a 'shadow' Cabinet and Whips of its own. It has its own rights over the time of the House. A word is necessary to show how time is provided for the Opposition. Apart from being consulted as to the length of time required for the discussion of the various stages of Government measures, the Opposition has by a convention of about fifty years standing the right to choose the subjects to be debated on the days allotted to the consideration of the Estimates and the bills by which they are finally authorised. According to modern practice this means that the Opposition has the right to initiate discussion of any branch of administration on about thirty-two days in each session. In addition the Government is morally bound to grant a day for the discussion of any vote of censure which the Opposition wish to move. The Opposition leaders also have the right to choose the subjects to be debated on certain items of business of a very general kind (in which the procedure of the House abounds) such as the Address in reply to the King's Speech, motions for the adjournment of the House, and even certain stages of the Budget. The average amount of time each session which the Opposition controls in this way is very substantial. On the whole it is fair to say that the initiative in criticism which is enjoyed by the Opposition is by far the most important modern element in freedom of debate, and that its preservation is something which the country should value as a guarantee against any form of totalitarianism—as a real check on the further growth of ministerial autocracy in Parliament. It would be the clearest proof of the triumph of party spirit over parliamentary spirit if any government set out to whittle away the rights of the Opposition . . .

That the government of the day (Conservative or Labour) which is nominally in entire control of the time of the House should find itself bound to restrict itself for its own business to an allotment of time which works out on the average to about forty three per cent of the whole time of the session (thirty nine per cent for its own programme of legislation) while surrendering over thirty per cent to the Opposition for choosing subjects on which to criticise the Government—that no Government has felt prepared to defy the rules and conventions which established these proportions (though it has full legal power to do so)—these facts seem to afford sufficient proof not only of the fairness of the rules and conventions but also of the persistence of the parliamentary spirit which established them, and which remains the best check on the dominance of a single party.

53. 'AS THOU DRAWEST, SWEAR HORRIBLE'

[from Jennings, *Cabinet Government*, C.U.P., 2nd ed., 1951, pp. 464–465]

Attacks upon the Government and upon individual ministers are the function of the Opposition. The duty of the Opposition is to oppose. It adopts Sir Toby's advice, 'So soon as ever thou seest him draw; and, as thou drawest, swear horrible.' That duty is the major check which the Constitution provides upon corruption and defective administration. It is, too the means by which individual injustices are prevented. The House of Commons is at its best when it debates those individual acts of oppression or bad faith which can never completely be overcome in a system of government which places responsibility in such minor officials as police officers. It is the public duty of the Opposition to raise such questions. It is a duty hardly less important than that of government. 'His Majesty's Opposition' is second in importance to 'His Majesty's Government'. The apparent absurdity that the Opposition asks for parliamentary time to be set aside by the Government in order that the Opposition may censure the Government, or that the Government is asked to move a vote of supplies for the Ministry of Labour in order that the Opposition may attack the Minister of Labour is not an absurdity at all. It is the recognition by both sides of the House that the Government governs openly and honestly and that it is prepared to meet criticism not by secret police and concentration camps but by rational argument.

In fact, opposition and government are carried on alike by agreement. The minority agrees that the majority must govern, and the majority agrees that the minority should criticise. The process of parliamentary government would break down if there were not mutual forbearance. The most important elements in parliamentary procedure are the discussions 'behind the Speaker's Chair' or 'through the usual channels'. The Prime Minister meets the convenience of the leader of the Opposition and the leader of the Opposition meets the convenience of the Government. The respective Whips, in consultation with the respective leaders, settle the subjects to be debated, the time to be allowed and, sometimes, the information to be provided and the line of attack. The Government agrees that a vote of censure be moved on Monday provided that a Bill be given a second reading on Tuesday. The Opposition assents to its inevitable defeat at 6.30 p.m. in order that it may move a resolution for the rest of the evening and suffer its inevitable defeat at 10 p.m.

54. IS THE OPPOSITION TOO POWERFUL?

[*Select Committee on Procedure*, H.C. 161 of 1931. Extracts from evidence of Right Hon. J. Ramsay Macdonald, M.P., The Prime Minister, paras. 9, 10, 29]

Do you consider the procedure of Parliament unduly handicaps the Government in getting its business through?—On the whole, yes.

So any reforms you would suggest would be in the direction

of making it easier for the Government to get its business through, and consequently putting more spokes in the wheels of the Opposition, whose object it is to prevent and delay business? —If the business of the Opposition is to delay, then I am perfectly willing to put spokes in their wheel. If the business of the Opposition is to secure adequate examination, I do not propose to put any spokes in their wheel. Members disagree as to where the line between the two is to be drawn...

...—This fundamental question comes. Really, what is the House of Commons itself? It consists not only of a Government but of an Opposition, and they have both got functions and rights. The great right of the Opposition is the full discussion of measures proposed by the Government. It is there, I think, that our fundamental weakness lies. There is a doctrine that it is the function of the Opposition to oppose. I have always regarded that as a crime against the State. It is not the function of the opposition to oppose, it is the function of the Opposition to oppose Second Reading, but once the Second Reading has been accepted, the only function of the Opposition is to improve in its own direction within the scope of the Vote that has been registered, that is, that it should have full liberty to examine on Committee and Report, and then to say its final word of opposition on the Third Reading of the Bill. The Opposition has no right to obstruct in the sense of making Parliament barren or unproductive...

55. PARLIAMENTARY OBSTRUCTION

[from Lord Morrison of Lambeth, *Government and Parliament*, O.U.P., 1954, pp. 96–98]

Obstruction in the House of Commons has a long history. Its greatest practitioners were the Irish Nationalist Members. Their sole mission in life being the achievement of Home Rule for Ireland, they were not called upon to expound any settled political philosophy. They could vote in the House with either Liberals or Conservatives according to what was, in their view, expedient for the moment for Home Rule or the achievement of changes such as Irish land reform. It was a matter of indifference to them whether the British parliamentary system worked or not; indeed, their bias was in favour of stopping it from working, for the greater the nuisance they could make of themselves the sooner might come the day when the British would be glad to be rid of them by conceding Home Rule.

The Conservatives and Liberals and the Labour Party have practised obstruction, the art of using up parliamentary time with the object of preventing the Government from getting its controversial measures through, or of upsetting the Government's parliamentary timetable. I think there has been a change for the better in the feeling of most M.P.s about obstruction, except perhaps when great measures of an acutely controversial character are before the House. In earlier years obstruction—even though often annoying and boring—was accepted as a more or less legitimate form of parliamentary activity or amusement. There was, and still is, in some quarters an impression that to accuse a party or a Member of obstruction is unparliamentary, but this is not so, for it has been ruled that it is a legitimate parliamentary allegation.

There was, of course, obstruction by Conservatives in the Parliaments of 1924 and 1929–31 against the minority Labour Governments. At that time there was no time-limit on the discussion of supplementary estimates. Consequently, even if the amounts were negligible, it was easy for the Conservative Opposition to keep debate going for quite a long time, seeking further information and charging the Government with having failed to estimate properly. On legislation there were many time-wasting speeches. We who were members of the Labour Party and supporters of the Government naturally found all this not only boring but irritating, though allowance must be made for our not unnatural bias. I personally felt, in addition, that what I described in my own mind as 'this playing the fool' was humiliating to the parliamentary institution itself and not calculated to bring credit to the House of Commons as a whole.

I think that things are materially better now and that this has been brought about not only by changes in parliamentary procedure, but also because there is a general feeling in the House that the obstruction of business which is not really disputed, and the spinning out of needless and rather boring speeches (even if at times they are clever) is not conducive to that public respect for the House of Commons which we all desire. In the Parliament of 1945–50, which had a large Labour majority, there was not much silly obstruction, though the Guillotine had to be used on three Bills. In the 1950–1 Parliament, with a Labour majority of only six, obstruction was practised by putting down Prayers against Orders to keep Ministers and their supporters up late but with no real intention of opposing the Order or dividing in favour of its annulment. This experiment of the Opposition did not go well. It was really unpopular inside and outside the House, and when the Government was driven to retaliate by adjourning the House before Prayers were reached the protest was nominal rather than real and agreement was soon reached whereby abuse was avoided. There has been some obstruction in the Parliament elected in 1951, but not as heavy or persistent as in earlier years. I, personally, am very pleased at the tendency for purposeless and needless obstruction to be dropped. Hard fighting against the measures which arouse really genuine and strong feeling is another matter. But obstruction, even brilliant obstruction which is merely playing the fool, is not a good thing.

Of course, if a Government with a very small majority brings in highly controversial legislation which is not urgent in the public interest, it is asking for trouble. The logical deduction from a close election result is that the electorate has 'put the brakes on' for the time being and that there is little or no mandate for exciting things. And if the Opposition is genuinely convinced that the Government has no mandate for controversial measures and that they are not urgent, it has a moral justification for sustained opposition.

Even if a Government has a working majority there is a duty upon it to avoid highly controversial legislation or administrative policies for which it has no proper mandate from the people, unless circumstances have arisen which make action necessary in the public interest. If the Opposition is to be given no moral case for obstruction, the Government must 'play the game' and respect the principles of parliamentary democracy, otherwise representative government will be endangered. However, the public interest comes first, and if action is necessary to protect it, action must be taken.

56. THE DUTY TO OPPOSE

[from Rt. Hon. Earl Winterton, *Orders of the Day*, Cassell, 1952, pp. 210–211, 317–319]

I

Equally it is the duty of an Opposition to use every legitimate method, by prolonged discussion where necessary, of supporting their own principles and attacking those of their opponents. The process can naturally be carried too far, but critics of the British parliamentary system who regard such tactics as childish, unworthy and unpatriotic should realise that the logical alternative is that which has prevailed in the legislative assemblies of totalitarian countries in the last quarter of a century. Certainly, in the years about which I am writing, we of the Opposition carried out our duty, of which the following extract from my diary furnishes an example, very fully.

THURSDAY, 21ST MARCH, 1907

> Army Annual Bill; this year it affords more opportunities for criticism than usual and Bob Cecil, Helmsley, Claude Hay, Rutherford, Wilfred Ashley, Hunt, myself and several others, kept the ball rolling so well that we managed to sit right on until six o'clock in the afternoon. There were the usual all-night sitting scenes. Jerry McVeagh remarked, as Bull and Hunt came up the Floor of the House as tellers, 'Here comes the Prodigal Son and the Fatted Calf'[1]. The value of the sitting lies in the fact that the Government will have to sit on Saturday.

II

The quality of Mr Churchill's speeches was of great benefit to the Conservatives in opposition, but the leader of a Party in opposition needs to have other qualities than that of the gift of oratory; he should learn to endure boredom without showing

[1] This was a good example of the particular type of wit which appeals to M.P.s. Mr Rowland Hunt, who was nicknamed 'Boadicea', on account of a remarkable maiden speech mainly devoted to the British Queen in question, had recently had his 'whip' restored to him. It had been temporarily taken from him because of an attack in a speech of his upon Mr Balfour. Sir William Bull, Member for Hammersmith, was a fat, florid man who closely resembled the legendary 'John Bull'.

how hard the ordeal is, and he should watch and wait in the Chamber itself or be at hand in his room for instant recall by the Chief Whip during dull, ordinary debates. For no one can tell when a situation may arise which he alone, with his authority, can handle satisfactorily. A Minister, by an unguarded statement, may make a serious slip, to the embarrassment of his Party, or the ex-Minister in charge of the Opposition front Bench, may make a similar mistake. Excitement rises in the House, the Chamber begins to fill. Journalists flock into the Press Gallery, for this may be an incident which will mean headline news. If the Leader of the Opposition is not there, he cannot exploit the first of those situations nor mitigate the harm done to his Party's interests by the second. Moreover, his absence will be noticed by thousands of his supporters next day when the Press report appears. For reasons with which one can sympathise, Mr Churchill, unlike most of his predecessors, was not a regular attendant at unimportant debates in the 1945 or 1950 Parliaments. There was an immense call for his services outside the House; he prepared his speeches most carefully after much meditation and reflection; he was writing a book; he was leading world opinion on international relationships. Yet the fact remains that he was sometimes not in the House when his presence would have been invaluable.

There were other reasons for the failure of the Opposition to perform its functions. The younger members of the Conservative Party, have, in recent years, become imbued with the belief that they can best serve the interests of the Party and advance the prospects of their own careers by becoming immersed in the affairs of the numerous committees and sub-committees of the Party which meet, during the sittings of the House, in a committee room. They are in the Chamber itself only when they want to speak or are interested in the particular subject. So, all too often in the 1945 and 1950 Parliaments, the Opposition back benches were sparsely filled by a handful of M.P.s too engrossed in thinking out what they were going to say, if they were fortunate enough to be 'called', to encourage by cheers those of their own side who were actually speaking. No impression of unity or enthusiasm was created. Old Hands, like myself, could get over this tepidity by deliberately picking a quarrel with the Government spokesman which almost invariably produces cheers, counter-cheers, and an exhilarating excitement.

But the Party methods were hard on a young, capable, but nervous new member of it. He got too little encouragement. I have referred in earlier chapters of this book to the help which Mr Balfour gave, in the 1906 Parliament, to those of us who were then young and told how he would come to our rescue when in difficulties and enthusiastically applaud our most jejune efforts by loud 'hear, hears'. To some, the view I present may seem old-fashioned. They would argue that fantastically inadequate Press reports of its proceedings have reduced the value of constant attendance in, and attention to, the Chamber. They would contend that a good party speech over the wireless is worth in votes a dozen exploitations of a situation in the House by a keen Opposition in full attendance and out for blood. I hope and think they are wrong, for, if they are right, the certain decline of the House of Commons is inevitable. I am encouraged in the belief that I am right by the fact that, again and again, whilst writing this book, former colleagues of mine in the Commons have told me that the Labour Opposition since the 1951 election have been far more successful than we were when in a similar position. Again and again, the statement has been made to me: 'You see, the Socialists are always there ready to seize on any situation to their advantage'. My friends usually add that the Labour Party is very unscrupulous in opposition; this is a charge always brought by supporters of any Government against any Opposition which is effective. If my friends are right and if a Party, so split over 'Bevanism' as the Labour Party are, is more effective than we were when we sat on the left of Mr Speaker, this constitutes a reflection upon Conservative methods in the Commons between 1945 and 1951.

57. OPPOSITION TODAY

[from R. H. Crossman, Introduction to Bagehot's *The English Constitution*, Fontana Library ed., 1963, pp. 42–43]

Theoretically, the task of checking and controlling the executive, which previously belonged in a real sense to the House as a whole, has now passed to the Opposition. But the Opposition is incapable of adequately fulfilling it. For with good management and even a moderate sized majority, any modern government can survive, whatever the Opposition may do, until the Prime Minister decides to dissolve. Modern Oppositions are often accused of ineffectiveness, and rebuked for shadow boxing. But this is all they can do—unless they are willing over a period of months to obstruct legislation and so halt the process of government. But by taking opposition to this level, an Opposition lays itself open to the charge of extremism and irresponsibility, and may well lose the support of that mass of floating voters which it must hope to win in order to turn out the government. Hence the tendency of the modern Opposition to play safe.

PART VI
Party and Parliament

58. PARTY IS OF THE ESSENCE OF PARLIAMENT

[from Walter Bagehot, *The English Constitution*, Fontana Library ed., 1963, pp. 158–161]

The moment, indeed, that we distinctly conceive that the House of Commons is mainly and above all things an elective assembly, we at once perceive that party is of its essence. There never was an election without a party. You cannot get a child into an asylum without a combination. At such places you may see 'Vote for orphan A' upon a placard, and 'Vote for orphan B (also an idiot!!!)' upon a banner, and the party of each is busy about its placard and banner. What is true at such minor and momentary elections must be much more true in a great and constant election of rulers. The House of Commons lives in a state of perpetual potential choice; at any moment it can choose a ruler and dismiss a ruler. And therefore party is inherent in it, is bone of its bone, and breath of its breath.

Secondly, though the leaders of party no longer have the vast patronage of the last century with which to bribe, they can coerce by a threat far more potent than any allurement—they can dissolve. This is the secret which keeps parties together. Mr Cobden most unjustly said: 'He had never been able to discover what was the proper moment, according to members of Parliament, for a dissolution. He had heard them say they were ready to vote for everything else, but he had never heard them say they were ready to vote for that.' Efficiency in an assembly requires a solid mass of steady votes; and these are *collected* by a deferential attachment to particular men, or by a belief in the principles those men represent, and they are *maintained* by a fear of those men—by the fear that if you vote against them, you may yourself soon not have a vote at all.

Thirdly, it may seem odd to say so, just after inculcating that party organisation is the vital principle of representative government, but that organisation is permanently efficient, because it is not composed of warm partisans. The body is eager, but the atoms are cool. If it were otherwise, Parliamentary government would become the worst of governments—a sectarian government. The party in power would go all the lengths their orators proposed—all that their formulae enjoined, as far as they have ever said they would go. But the partisans of the English Parliament are not of such a temper. They are Whigs, or Radicals, or Tories, but they are much else too. They are common Englishmen, and, as Father Newman complains, 'hard to be worked up to the dogmatic level'. They are not eager to press the tenets of their party to impossible conclusions. On the contrary, the way to lead them—the best and acknowledged way—is to affect a studied and illogical moderation. You may hear men say 'Without committing myself to the tenet that 3 + 2 make 5, though I am free to admit that the honourable member for Bradford has advanced very grave arguments on behalf of it, I think I may, with permission of the Committee, assume that 2 + 3 do not make 4, which will be a sufficient basis for the important propositions which I shall venture to submit on the present occasion.' This language is very suitable to the greater part of the House of Commons. Most men of business love a sort of twilight. They have lived all their lives in an atmosphere of probabilities and of doubt, where nothing is very clear, where there are some chances for many events, where there is much to be said for several courses, where nevertheless one course must be determinedly chosen and fixedly adhered to. They like to hear arguments suited to this intellectual haze. So far from caution or hesitation in the statement of the argument striking them as an indication of imbecility, it seems to them a sign of practicality. They got rich themselves by transactions of which they could not have stated the argumentative ground—and all they ask for is a distinct though moderate conclusion, that they can repeat when asked; something which they feel *not* to be abstract argument, but abstract argument diluted and dissolved in real life. 'There seem to me,' an impatient young man once said, 'to be no stay in Peel's arguments.' And that was why Sir Robert Peel was the best leader of the Commons in our time; we like to have the rigidity taken out of an argument, and the substance left.

Nor indeed, under our system of government, are the leaders themselves of the House of Commons, for the most part, eager to carry party conclusions too far. They are in contact with reality. An Opposition, on coming into power, is often like a speculative merchant whose bills become due. Ministers have to make good their promises, and they find a difficulty in so doing. They have said the state of things is so and so, and if you give us the power we will do thus and thus. But when they come to handle the official documents, to converse with the permanent under-secretary—familiar with disagreeable facts, and though in manner most respectful, yet most imperturbable in opinion—very soon doubts intervene. Of course, something must be done; the speculative merchant cannot forget his bills; the late Opposition cannot, in office, forget those sentences which terrible admirers in the country still quote. But just as the merchant asks his debtor, 'Could you not take a bill at four months?' so the new Minister says to the permanent under-secretary, 'Could you not suggest a middle course? I am of course not bound by mere sentences used in debate; I have never been accused of letting a false ambition of consistency warp my conduct; but,' etc., etc. And the end always is that a middle course is devised which *looks* as much as possible like what was suggested in opposition, but which *is* as much as possible what patent facts—facts which seem to live in the office, so teasing and unceasing are they—prove ought to be done.

Of all modes of enforcing moderation on a party, the best is to contrive that the members of that party shall be intrinsically moderate, careful, and almost shrinking men; and the next best to contrive that the leaders of the party, who have protested most on its behalf, shall be placed in the closest contact with the actual world. Our English system contains both contrivances; it makes party government permanent and possible in the sole way in which it can be so, by making it mild.

But these expedients, though they sufficiently remove the defects which make a common club or quarter-sessions impotent, would not enable the House of Commons to govern England.

A representative public meeting is subject to a defect over and above those of other public meetings. It may not be independent. The Constituencies may not let it alone. But if they do not, all the checks which have been enumerated upon the evils of a party organisation would be futile. The feeling of a constituency is the feeling of a dominant party, and that feeling is elicited, stimulated, sometimes even manufactured by the local political agent. Such an opinion could not be moderate; could not be subject to effectual discussion; could not be in close contact with pressing facts; could not be framed under a chastening sense of near responsibility; could not be formed as those form their opinions who have to act upon them. Constituency government is the precise opposite of Parliamentary government. It is the government of immoderate persons far from the scene of action, instead of the government of moderate persons close to the scene of action; it is the judgment of persons judging in the last resort and without penalty, in lieu of persons judging in fear of a dissolution, and ever conscious that they are subject to an appeal.

59. THE FEAR OF PARTY DOMINATION

[from A. H. Birch, *Representative and Responsible Government*, Allen and Unwin, 1964, pp. 74–76]

I

Liberals had always assumed that the extension of the franchise would extend the popular basis of Parliament without otherwise changing its nature, and it was perhaps natural for them to be slow to realize that this was not to be the case. In practice the second Reform Act led to a growth of party organizations in the country and the development of the means by which party leaders could discipline their back-bench supporters. Members had to secure the votes of an electorate too numerous to be canvassed personally by the candidates, who therefore became dependent on the endorsement and support of a party organization. This might have led to the growth of local party machines and bosses, as in the United States. In fact, for a number of reasons which need not be discussed here, it was the national party leaders rather than the local party branches who gained most from this development in Britain. The consequence was that the members of the government were able to put pressure on their own back-benchers by threatening that if the latter voted against the government in Parliament they might find themselves in the uncomfortable position of having to fight the next election without the support of the party. The sanction was rarely imposed but the threat of it diminished the independence of Parliament both as a legislature and as a body that made and unmade ministries.

II

In his monumental study of *Democracy and the Organization of Political Parties*, Ostrogorski painted an alarming picture of the consequences of the growth of caucuses. They were beginning to dominate Parliament, destroy the independence of back-benchers, convert Parliamentary leaders into party dictators, and act as an arbiter 'between Parliament and outside opinion',[1] As a result, the delicate equilibrium of cabinet government was being 'destroyed in favour of the leaders. Formerly . . . the leader of the party was only *primus inter pares*; now he is a general in command of an army . . . Raised above the levelled crowd of M.P.s, the leaders now lean directly on the great mass of voters, whose feelings of loyalty go straight to the leaders over the heads of the Members . . . This being so, the elections have assumed the character of personal plebiscites, each constituency voting not so much for this or that candidate as for Mr Gladstone or against Lord Beaconsfield or Lord Salisbury'.[2]

Similar views were expressed by Goldwin Smith, the Liberal writer who emigrated to Canada, Sidney Low, the English historian, and A. L. Lowell, the President of Harvard University. Goldwin Smith went so far as to say that 'the caucus is enthroned on the ruins of the old British constitution'.[3] Low observed that in recent years the cabinet had grown in power, and tended to be 'amenable to the control of the constituent bodies themselves rather than to that of their elected representatives'[4].

[1] *Democracy and the Organization of Political Parties*, London, 1902, vol.1., pp. 215–16.

[2] Ibid., pp. 607–8.

[3] *See A Trip to England*, London, 1892, p. 120. Quoted in Ostrogorski, op. cit., p. 618.

[4] *The Governance of England*, London, 1904, p. 54.

Criticizing the [views of] the Duke of Devonshire, Low pointed out that the real power of the House of Commons was declining. 'Much of its efficiency has passed to other agents. Its supremacy is qualified by the growth of rival jurisdictions. Its own servants have become for some purposes, its masters. The cabinet is more powerful, and has drawn to itself many attributes which the Commons are still imagined to possess. The electorate, more conscious of its own existence under an extended franchise, wields a direct instead of a delegated authority.'[5]

60. PARTY AND MINISTERIAL RESPONSIBILITY

[from Marshall and Moodie, *Some Problems of the Constitution*, Hutchinson, 1959, pp. 77–78]

The development of party solidarity poses then a delicate question about the convention of responsibility. The convention states, in its original form, the conditions upon which a government may hold and forfeit office. Yet everyone knows that when governments nowadays go out of office, it is not the operation of the convention which brings this about, but the decision of the party in power to submit itself to a general election—an apt illustration of the way in which changes in the number and nature of the political parties, may transform the operation of a conventional rule. The sanction envisaged in the principle of accountability—namely the House of Commons as an entity withdrawing its confidence from Ministers accordingly as it approves or disapproves of their proposals—is for all practical purposes simply not in operation. Its existence is a kind of limbo-existence. Yet some reflection is cast into the world of political reality, since the Government customarily behaves in a way which would be quite mystifying to an observer who knew only that the majority party was in possession of the right to use the legislative machinery of the Commons. Both Ministers and back-benchers make frequent references to 'the House', as an entity; the Government sometimes genuinely defers to 'the feeling of the House' (admittedly with an appreciation of potential dissident feeling on the ministerial benches); and there always remains the possibility that there may be further changes

[5] Ibid., pp. 58–9.

in the party situation or that some catastrophic issue may throw party divisions into confusion and revive the traditional sanction. But are these good enough reasons for using the traditional language of governmental accountability in the present situation?

61. THE MENACE OF PARTY

[from L. S. Amery, *Thoughts on the Constitution*, O.U.P., 1947, pp. 43–47]

The most important change, however, in the last half-century, and the most serious political menace to our whole system of parliamentary government, lies in the enormous development of the power of the party machine. 'Party', to quote Burke, 'is a body of men united for promoting by their joint endeavours the national interest upon some particular principle upon which they are all agreed.' It affords the natural means of organizing public opinion for the promotion of a new set of ideas striving to win acceptance, or for the defence of existing ideas whose permanent validity it wishes to uphold. By ensuring that the case for neither side is neglected it serves an important function in educating public opinion. In Parliament it gives stability and cohesion to the majority upon whose support any system of responsible government must rely, as well as to the minority whose responsible criticism is not less essential a part of the work of that institution. In the country it serves between elections to maintain contact between the public on the one hand and Parliament and Government on the other, and, at election times, to define and concentrate the issues. With us . . . the two-party system has been the normal type to which, after occasional interludes, we have regularly reverted, for the very reason that it has always centred round the business of maintaining a majority in Parliament for a Government or securing its displacement by another Government. Our parties have been primarily parliamentary institutions looking for public support for their work in Parliament.

The progressive enlargement of the electorate has involved an ever increasing need for political organization. Long departed are the days when it was thought sufficient for some local solicitor to see to it that the small percentage of the population qualified to vote were actually on the register, and when a rudimentary nucleus of party committees could be mobilized for action on the eve of an election. Whole-time professional agents work, year in year out, at keeping alive an elaborate network of committees in every constituency, not only to maintain enthusiasm but, above all, to build up a body of canvassers who, when the election comes, will sally forth to argue with the doubtful, but even more to persuade their sympathizers to take the trouble to walk or drive round to the neighbouring polling station. Above these are the district and regional organizers, and above these again the central office of the party with its head agent and its staff of interviewers, speakers, research workers, and propaganda writers. Parallel to this official structure there is also the more democratic structure of regional and national unions of constituency representatives, culminating in a national union or conference which meets periodically to voice its views and to come into direct contact with the leader of the party in Parliament. All this is a natural healthy and, indeed, indispensable feature of modern political life.

The danger lies in the growth of the notion that such an organization, instead of being a useful and, indeed, indispensable adjunct to the work of the party system in Parliament, should in effect supersede it, directing government from outside Parliament and using Parliament merely as an instrument for carrying through policies shaped without reference to it. This danger of by-passing Parliament arises, not so much from party organization in itself, as from the same misconceptions as to the nature of our system of government and as to the meaning of majority rule which have wrecked the imitations of our Constitution in other countries. The first of these misconceptions is that our system of government is based on the initiative of the voter and on delegation from below. If that really were the case, then it would always be open to argue that the voter's party organization embodies his definite and final conclusions, his 'mandate', on all subjects and is, in fact, entitled on his behalf to prescribe the policy of the Government which he has created. Once that argument is accepted the party executive becomes the master and not the servant of the Government. Parliament becomes a mere instrument for registering its decrees. The personal character and quality of members no longer matters and debates lose all real significance. Policy is shaped, not in the light of full and free discussion, nor even in that contact with realities and with that sense of national responsibility and continuity which influences a Cabinet, but by an irresponsible partisan caucus, thinking only in terms of party aims or party interests. The danger of irresponsible power is even greater when an outside body, like the Trade Union Congress, primarily existing for industrial purposes, attempts to use its influence in party organization and finance in order to direct the general policy of a government.

The second and kindred misconception concerns the meaning of majority decision and majority rule. Decision by majority is not an absolute and unquestionable principle. Our Constitution, to use Burke's phrase, 'is something more than a problem in arithmetic'. There is no divine right of a mere numerical majority, of x/2 plus 1, any more than of kings. Majority decision is a measure of convenience essential to the dispatch of business 'the result', to quote Burke again, 'of a very particular and special convention, confirmed by long habits of obedience'. Thanks to that convention Government is carried on with the acquiescence of the minority. When it comes to legislation it is of the very essence of our conception of the Reign of Law that it should not be regarded as a mere emanation of the will of the Government, but as something accepted by the nation as a whole. That requisite of consent for changing the law, or at least of acceptance when changed, is the root from which sprang our whole parliamentary system with its representation of the various interests and elements in the national life and with its elaborate provisions for full discussion. The idea that a majority just because it is a majority, is entitled to pass without full discussion what legislation it pleases, regardless of the extent of the changes involved or of the intensity of the opposition to them—the idea, in fact, that majority edicts are the same things as laws—is wholly alien to the spirit of our Constitution.

It is not unnatural, perhaps, that this doctrine of the unqualified right of a party majority and the concomitant theory of ultimate control by a party executive should in the past have exercised so strong a hold over the Socialist party. Unlike the older historic parties it originated outside Parliament, more concerned for many years with organization in the country and with dissemination of its principles than with the tasks of government which, indeed, it has tended to conceive as primarily, if not exclusively, concerned with translating those principles into legislation. The Party Executive was in its case anterior to any Cabinet or 'Shadow Cabinet' and still maintains its separate existence and authority. In Australia, indeed, Labour party executives have insisted on settling in detail both appointments to, and distribution of, offices in the Cabinet and have even gone to the length of demanding from Ministers signed, but undated, resignations enabling them to be recalled at any moment.

62. IS PARLIAMENT THREATENED?

[from H. J. Laski, *Reflections on the Constitution*, Manchester U.P., 1951, pp. 92–93]

On the House of Commons as an institution I would like to add this final word. With all the changes that have taken place in it during this last half century, I see no decline in its greatness, nor any ultimate danger that it should be by-passed in its fundamental purposes, above all in the most fundamental of all its purposes, the duty to see that the conditions are maintained which protect the freedom of the ordinary citizen. I do not accept Mr Amery's view that Parliament is threatened either by bodies like a party's executive committee, or by outside organisations like the Federation of British Industries or the Trade Union Congress. I do not accept, either, his fear that majority rule will be abused, and the historic traditions of our constitution broken by the use of angry misconceptions of what those traditions imply. On the contrary, I should argue that, in the years since 1945, public respect for the House of Commons has grown swiftly, and is much deeper today than it was either in 1925 or in 1935. Mr Amery himself has noted that it is equally accepted by Labour Ministers as by Conservatives, and that a Labour Party Conference is permeated by the characteristics of what is best in the Parliamentary system no less than the conferences of the older parties. I see no danger to the supremacy of the House of Commons in the new phase of its long life upon which it has entered. If there is a danger ahead, it seems to me to lie in the use of great financial and industrial power to prevent the will of the electorate being made effective by the government of its choice. That is a risk to which Mr Herbert Morrison has recently and vigorously drawn attention. In a period of rapid social change, it is a risk that might easily become a grave one; for it represents the effort of men who though small in numbers, have the immense powers great wealth confers, to challenge, by means outside the ordinary conventions of Parliamentary life, the right of the House of Commons to support the Government of the day, and put its measures upon the Statute Book. That is the method which invites all parties to a disrespect for constitutional tradition. If we can overcome this risk we may be able to make the social and economic changes our national life requires while retaining the unity of a commonwealth that can live at peace with itself. In the light of history it is difficult to imagine a more splendid achievement.

63. PARTIES WITHIN PARTIES

[from R. Rose, 'Parties and tendencies in Britain, *Political Studies*, XII, No. 1 (1964), pp. 43–44]

The existence of varied, unstable policy parties within the formally united governing party maintains and strengthens a number of restraints upon the exercise of power by the Cabinet, which today is secure against defeat in the House of Commons because of the acceptance of the discipline of the two-party system by M.P.s and electors.

Policy parties act as a counterweight against pressure groups. The co-operation of pressure groups is important for the success of a government. But because pressure group allegiances have not been demonstrated to be strong enough to affect voting behaviour significantly organized group leaders can rarely succeed in punishing a recalcitrant government at the polls. But members of policy parties opposed to particular pressure groups may create trouble in Cabinet, in speeches leaked from private party meetings and on the floor of the Commons itself. For instance, the Attlee Government's nationalization of the steel industry was persevered in against the wishes of affected pressure groups and of important Cabinet members because of the strength of the left-wing tendency on this issue, including several ministers who had jumped outside their usual factional positions.

A united Cabinet can fend off criticism from the opposition party indefinitely. (Concessions are more likely to be made to disaffected potential voters than to partisan opponents: witness the announcement of the repeal of the Schedule A tax on home-ownership following the Liberal victory at Orpington in 1962.) But the protest of a policy party within the governing party is immediately felt, especially if it involves sharp divisions during the private deliberations of the Cabinet. In at least four cases in this century—1905, 1923, 1931 and 1951—policy divisions have been notable as major causes in a government in office defaulting, and going down to electoral defeat shortly thereafter. The possibility is always present, as the lobbying within the Conservative Party, including the Cabinet, showed in the week before the division in the Profumo debate of 17th June, 1963. The threat to expel a group of several dozen M.P.s who vote against a party whip is meaningless, because such an expulsion would hurt the electoral party by making more clear cut divisions within the ranks.

By voting together in Parliament, M.P.s in different policy parties reaffirm their common identification with a single electoral party. Voting together shows a degree of cohesion which political parties in many countries lack. But it does not provide continuously cohesive support for a party leader. Rather, the division lobbies represent only one phase in a lengthy process, a phase far distant in time from the one in which the most substantial decisions will be made about a problem. When problems arise salient to factions ministers can anticipate to a considerable extent the nature of support and opposition to alternative policies under consideration. But lacking factional guide-lines, ministers can only note the tendencies associated with policy alternatives, without being able to estimate so well the numbers of M.P.s who will associate themselves with the several tendencies. Only after the front bench takes a line can it find out whether the hints and threats of M.P.s lobbying them are in fact accurate predictions of opposition or part of the complicated game of bluff involved in situations of political uncertainty. Because public dispute within an electoral party can harm both sides in the dispute, a high premium is placed upon accurate information which can be used to anticipate and forestall policy disputes. This accounts for the importance of party whips; they provide the two-way flow of information between the party leader and back bench M.P.s. Individual Ministers have parliamentary private secretaries to warn them of impending difficulties. The object of this communication, from the point of view of a nominally impregnable leadership, is to keep the leadership informed about possible sources of discontent, and threats of factions forming around tendencies opposed to those prevailing among the dominant leadership group. In this way, the appearance of unity can be maintained by aborting public controversy. This was, for instance, the technique that Clement Attlee used when informal collections of M.P.s began discussing his replacement, by Sir Stafford Cripps in the Cabinet. It was essential at this point in order to forestall the conversion of a left-wing tendency into a strong Left faction with a potential Prime Minister at its head. More recently, Harold Macmillan has demonstrated in successive Cabinet changes since the 1959 general election an awareness of the importance of keeping his political associates divided and balanced against one another by the distribution of Cabinet posts.

64. PRIVILEGE AND PARTY MEETINGS

[*Committee of Privileges*, H.C. 138 of 1947. Extract from Report]

In modern times the practice of holding private meetings in the precincts of the Palace of Westminster of different parties has become well established and, in the view of Your Committee, it must now be taken to form a normal and everyday incident of parliamentary procedure, without which the business of Parliament could not conveniently be conducted. Thus, meetings held within the precincts of the Palace of Westminster during the parliamentary session are normally attended only by Members as such, and the information which is given at such meetings is, in Your Committee's view, given to those attending them in their capacity as Members. Your Committee therefore conclude on this matter that attendance of Members at a private party meeting held in the precincts of the Palace of Westminster during the parliamentary session, to discuss parliamentary matters connected with the current or future proceedings of Parliament, is attendance in their capacity of Members of Parliament. It does not, of course, follow that this conclusion attracts to such meetings all the privileges which are attached to the transactions of Parliament as a whole . . .

It follows that an unfounded imputation in regard to such meetings involves an affront to the House as such. Your Committee consider that an unjustified allegation that Members regularly betray the confidence of private party meetings either for payment or whilst their discretion has been undermined by drink is a serious contempt.

65. MEMBERS AND PARTY

[from Nigel Nicolson, *People and Parliament*, Weidenfeld and Nicolson, 1958, pp. 78–79]

Even in normal conditions, however, a Minister cannot state in detail the proposals of the Government before he has stated them to the House. One notable exception to the rule, recorded by Mr Morrison, was when the Labour Government gave advance notice to the Parliamentary Labour Party of their intention to introduce peacetime conscription, 'since it was not in the party programme and was likely to come as a shock'. But a Minister will normally give the committee no more than an idea of the considerations which are in his mind as he approaches a decision and of the alternatives open to him, and then sit back to listen to the ideas of his back-benchers. For example, the Minister of Agriculture might state to the Agricultural Committee the arguments for and against the deliberate spreading of myxamatosis; or the Leader of the House might open in general terms at the 1922 Committee a discussion on Member's pay. It is difficult to imagine that either of them would deliberately flout the majority feeling of the committee; and if they did so, those who had spoken strongly would feel that they had given all the advance notice required by convention before expressing their dissent in public.

On the other hand, it would be rare for a Committee to force a Minister to reverse a major aspect of policy previously declared. At the most, policy might be changed in response to back-bench pressure, by crablike movements tending in the same general direction but slipping gently sideways to meet the criticisms expressed. An example is the amendment to the Landlord and Tenant Act in the spring of 1958, to mitigate the hardships caused by the Rent Act. It was public knowledge that a group of Conservative back-bench Members had confronted the Minister of Housing with examples of hardship in their own constituencies, and his own information had led him to anticipate the trouble. By agreement the change was made in a manner least likely to tamper with the main purpose of the Rent Act or to damage the Government's prestige.

The criticism has been made that the committee system prevents the public from knowing the genuine opinions of their representatives, and that a measure would often be defeated in the House if Members continued to act in accordance with the views they expressed in private. 'The sheep escape from the fold,' wrote Sir Ivor Jennings, with typical contempt for the back-bench Member, 'and assemble in flocks of their own choosing, but they can always be called back by the division bell.' There are three answers to that: first, any back-bench criticisms are anticipated by Ministers from views previously expressed in committee ('the party wouldn't stand for it'); secondly, draft Bills or administrative proposals are often altered as a result of what the Minister hears in private before they even reach the public eye; and thirdly, everyday experience shows that when pushed too far, a recalcitrant Member will have no hesitation in carrying his dissent to the open Chamber. But it is true that in Committee Members fly kites which they would not fly in public. They feel less reticence in expressing points of view based on rumour or chance examples. And in moments of crisis for the party they will temper their public criticism, unless impelled by a strength of feeling which cannot be concealed. The committee system does not so much whittle down dissent, as divert it at a preliminary stage into channels where it is all the more effective for being private.

PART VII

The Role of the Private Member: Free Votes

66. 'AN M.P. IS NOT A PUPPET'

[from Sir Courtenay Ilbert, *Parliament*, Home Univ. Lib., 1948, pp. 165]

In the common talk about party tyranny, and about the despotism exercised by cabinets or whips, there is, to speak plainly, much nonsense and much cant. A member of Parliament is not a puppet, but a human being, very human, influenced by the same kind of considerations and actuated by the same kind of motives as his fellow mortals outside the walls of the House . . . no one knows better than a political leader what arts of persuasion, what tactics of conciliation and compromise, are required to keep a party together. He knows that too severe a strain must not be put on party allegiance, that diversity of opinions within the party ranks must be recognised, and that on many points the lines of division between different opinions by no means coincide with the lines of division between different political parties. And leaders and followers alike are aware that they cannot afford to disregard public opinion outside Parliament, that they must watch its variations and fluctuations, and guide their actions accordingly.

67. 'NO CRACK OF THE PARTY WHIP'

[from Rt. Hon. Earl Winterton, *Orders of the Day*, 1953, p. 277]

I know that many readers of these words who are not in political life will violently dissent from my views on this subject, but, in fact, a Chief Whip must exercise a considerable measure of discipline over the members of his Party unless it is to disintegrate. Of all the boring and dangerous 'bromides' of the opponents of the British parliamentary system, the phrase 'voting at the crack of the Party Whip' is the worst. Those who use it should study some Continental legislatures where the doctrine they preach is practised. In these countries, with their absence of large organised political parties and the existence of a large number of small groups who form, dissolve and reform, there is no 'crack of the Party Whip'. So members vote as they please, or as they think will please their constituents, whatever the interests of the country may be. This results in the average life of governments being a few weeks. 'Oldfashioned Liberal', 'Pro Bono Publico' and others who, in the correspondence columns of the Press, advocate either proportional representation or the destruction of the British Party System as it exists today, should be compelled to spend a year in France studying French electoral and political conditions. It would do them as much good as it would any British supporter of the Communist cause to spend a year in a Siberian Labour camp. A complete reversal of view would likely to result in each case.

68. WHIPS AND M.P.S A 'TWO-WAY TRAFFIC'

[from Morrison, *Government and Parliament*, O.U.P., 1954, pp. 104–105; 166–168]

I

It is a widespread belief that the Whips have no other duty than to bully and coerce Members against their will into voting in the party lobby and speaking in accordance with the 'party line'. This is an inaccurate and incomplete picture of the functions of the Whips. It is persuasion rather than bullying that is the rule; it is reasoning with a recalcitrant Member rather than coercion that is the general practice. The good Whip seeks to avoid a situation in which the troubled or troublesome Member is driven to choose between forced, humiliating conformity, and flagrant revolt which may raise all the difficult problems of official disciplinary action. There are extreme cases from time to time which may justify and, indeed, necessitate straight speaking, but peaceful persuasion, friendly reasoning, and argument based on the need for keeping the party together, are far more normal and effective.

Moreover, the Whips' Office conducts a two-way traffic. During the nearly six years that I was Leader of the House of Commons I impressed upon the Labour M.P.s and the Whips that the Whips had just as much a duty to convey to me and to other Ministers the anxieties, worries, and unhappiness of back-benchers as they had to convey to the back-benchers the wishes of the Government. I would myself see troubled—or troublesome—M.P.s if necessary. Such interviews were normally pleasant and helpful. This part of the Whips' functions was fully discharged. They were the ears and eyes not only of the Government but of the back-benchers. Indeed, they would be incompetent Whips who did not warn Ministers when in power, or the Front Bench when in Opposition, of potential trouble, though they would not be frightened too easily. Frequently, the Chief Whip is asked by Government or party leaders, 'What is the feeling in the party about this?', or 'Is there likely to be trouble about that?' Clearly, it would be impossible for the Chief Whip to give an intelligent answer unless he and his colleagues not only took steps to be in touch with the back-benchers, but had such a good relationship with them that the back-benchers did not hesitate to pour out their anxieties and troubles.

II

It may be asked whether I have not exaggerated the responsiveness of Ministers and the Cabinet to back-bench opinion and that of the House as a whole. Do the Ministers not get away with most things, in the short run at least? With most things, yes; but there have been noticeable exceptions. In the course of parliamentary history there have been a number of instances of Ministers making concessions or changes in policy following upon pressure in Parliament. Some examples occur to me. There was the case . . . of the free vote on the proposal to suspend capital punishment in the Criminal Justice Bill. The fall of the Chamberlain Government in 1940 was the result of back-bench revolt. The Milk Industry Bill of December 1938 was not proceeded with in view of the objections which were raised in many quarters, being postponed for further discussion and re-examination. The Judges' Remuneration Bill did not pass in the Session of 1952–3 owing to parliamentary objections to the 'tax-free' element in the Bill. The Hoare-Laval Pact in connexion with Mussolini's aggression against Abyssinia led to a parliamentary storm and Sir Samuel Hoare had to resign as Foreign Secretary.

The reader may wonder why the list is not very much longer, but he must take into account a very important consideration. That is—as has been amply shown—that there exist many channels through which Ministers are made aware of their own back-bench opinion, through debates on the Address and on other occasions. Speeches in the country and articles in newspapers and periodicals opposed to the Government provide extensive opportunities for the Opposition to make its views known. In considering projected legislation or policy a sensible Government will take all opinions into account before becoming committed, and so it is likely that modifications will have been made before the publication of Bills. This may be described as the process of concession in advance of parliamentary proceedings, though sometimes Ministers may prefer to save up concessions until Parliament is dealing with the Matter. To the extent that the Government in shaping its policy has anticipated back-bench and Opposition criticisms, Ministers are entitled to the credit. Such concessions of course cannot very well be recorded in the columns of Hansard. They do, however, tend to limit the number of publicly known occasions on which concessions have been made . . .

69. THE PRIVATE MEMBER: DECLINE IN STATUS?

[from H. J. Laski, *Parliamentary Government in England*, Allen and Unwin, 1938, pp. 142–143, 165–167]

I

The life of the House of Commons depends upon its representation only of such predominant strands of general public opinion as will, normally, enable a Government to be formed behind which there is an effective majority. Thereby that Government is able to inject a stream of continuous tendency into affairs. The business of making a Government and providing it, or refusing to provide it, with the formal authority for carrying on the public business is the pivotal function of the House of Commons upon which all other functions turn.

It means, of course, that the life of the House of Commons is necessarily lived in terms of the party system. Parties are the basis upon which the organization of the House for coherency is made possible; and the member of the House of Commons must with very few exceptions, be a good party man if it is to do its work adequately. The philosopher in his study may repine at this necessity. He may insist that this involves the sacrifice of individual conscience to party allegiance. He may argue that it leads members blindly into the division-lobbies on matters about which they have not even heard the debate in the chamber. He may write angrily . . . about Cabinet dictation in the House. The facts are quite different from these closet abstractions. The number of times when an average member feels inclined to vote against his party, especially when it is in office, is pretty small; and the evidence seems to show that when the impulse so to vote is an urgent one, he obeys it. It is foolish to imagine that, in matters of debate, a member must make up his mind upon each separate item the House decides. The House is a body for getting business done; the member's task is to be aware of large tendencies and to be on hand to support those the general direction of which he broadly approves. If he has so nice a conscience that a scrupulous examination of mostly technical minutiae is the necessary preamble to his vote, the proper comment upon this attitude is that he is not by temperament suited to be a member of a legislative assembly.

II

The last of the general questions which I must here discuss is the place of the private member in the organization of the House. It is fashionble nowadays for critics of the present position to lament almost with tears over the decline of his status. He is bound hand and foot, we are told, to the party machine. He can ask questions, he can debate, he can introduce his little bills and his private members' motions, so long as it is understood that no consequence will follow from them. But party has made the Cabinet the master; and if he does not obey the party whip he will soon find himself cast into the outer darkness. A Conservative constituency will not adopt again as candidate a member who repeatedly votes against his party; and the control of the Labour machine is, it is pointed out, even more rigorous. Its standing orders permit a member to refrain from voting where his conscience is engaged; but he may not go into the division-lobby against a party-decision without risking his right to continue as a member of the party. For all serious purposes, therefore, we are asked to regard the private member as a mere unit in a division-list, with no effective sphere of independent action of his own.

The lament, I suggest, is wholly misconceived. It mistakes the functions the modern House of Commons has to perform; it mistakes the purposes of parties in the modern State; it is an anachronistic legacy of a dead period in our history when politics was a gentleman's amusement, and the sphere of governmental activity was so small that an atomistic House of Commons was possible. The only way to restore to the private member the kind of position he occupied eighty, or even fifty years ago, is to go back to the historic conditions which made that position possible. History does not permit us to indulge in such luxuries.

The problem of modern government is a problem of time; this is the basic reason why the initiative in legislation has passed from the private member. In general if a matter is important enough to be embodied in a bill, it is desirable that the responsibility for its passage should rest with the Government. It cannot, in any case, hope for time unless the Government approves of it; and if it is a matter upon which it does not feel keenly enough to introduce it the chances are strongly against it being worthwhile spending the time of the House on its passage. I do not think this conclusion is invalidated by the fact that a private member, Mr A. P. Herbert, has by his zeal and energy secured a small instalment of divorce law reform. For, because his bill was not a Government bill, he was compelled to accept drastic amendments which narrowed its scope in a high degree; and the truncated measure which resulted will probably prevent the serious rationalization of the marriage laws for many years to come. If anything, Mr Herbert's experience shows plainly that when any big theme requires legislative action, only the Government has the requisite authority to deal with it on an ample scale.

If, therefore, we assume that the general function of legislation ought essentially to be initiated by Government, what remains for the private member? The ventilation of grievance; the extraction of information; the criticism of the administrative process; what contribution he can make to debate. In addition to these, he can raise, in private members' motions, the discussion of large principles which test the movement of public opinion. He can serve on committees of enquiry. I do not myself think that this can be regarded as a small field of action. But I should agree that, especially for members on the Government side of the House, it is not an adequate field for an active-minded man. The problem, I therefore suggest, is to enlarge that field without treading on the essential right of Government to initiate legislation. This can, I believe, be done without any such invasion if we once assume that the real function of the House is to watch the process of administration as the safeguard of the private citizen. In the proper scrutiny of delegated legislation, in the improvement by analysis, by criticism, by suggestion, of departmental work, in the enlargement of the place of the Select Committee of enquiry in our system, there is a wide range of service awaiting the private member of which we do not, in the present organization of the House, take anything like full advantage.

70. A WORKING-MAN IN THE HOUSE

[from Aneurin Bevan, *In place of fear*, Heinemann, 1952, pp. 5–7]

The function of parliamentary democracy, under universal franchise, historically considered, is to expose wealth-privilege to the attack of the people. It is a sword pointed at the heart of property-power. The arena where the issues are joined is Parliament.

The atmosphere of Parliament, its physical arrangements, its procedure, its semi-ecclesiastical ritual, are therefore worth careful study. They are all profoundly intimidating for the products of a board school system who are the bearers of a fiery message from the great industrial constituencies. The first essential in the pioneers of a new social order is a big bump of irreverence.

'The past lies like an Alp upon the human mind.' The House of Commons is a whole range of mountains. If the new Member gets there too late in life he is already trailing a pretty considerable past of his own, making him heavy-footed and cautious. When to this is added the visible penumbra of six centuries of receding legislators, he feels weighed to the ground. Often he never gets to his feet again.

His first impressions is that he is in church. The vaulted roofs and stained-glass windows, the rows of statues of great statesmen of the past, the echoing halls, the soft-footed attendants and the whispered conversation, contrast depressingly with the crowded meetings and the clang and clash of hot opinions he has just left behind in his election campaign. Here he is, a tribune of the people, coming to make his voice heard in the seats of power. Instead, it seems he is expected to worship; and the most conservative of all religions—ancestor worship.

The first thing he should bear in mind is that these were not his ancestors. His forbears had no part in the past, the accumulated dust of which now muffles his own footfalls. His forefathers were tending sheep or ploughing the land, or serving the statesmen whose names he sees written on the walls around him, or whose portraits look down upon him in the long corridors. It is not the past of his people that extends in colourful pageantry before his eyes. They were shut out from all this; were forbidden to take part in the dramatic scenes depicted in these frescoes. In him his people are there for the first time and the history he will make will not be merely an episode in the story he is now reading. It must be wholly different: as different as is the social status which he now brings with him.

To preserve the keen edge of his critical judgment he will find that he must adopt an attitude of scepticism amounting almost to cynicism, for Parliamentary procedure neglects nothing which might soften the acerbities of his class feelings. In one sense the House of Commons is the most unrepresentative of representative assemblies. It is an elaborate conspiracy to prevent the real clash of opinion which exists outside from finding an appropriate echo within its walls. It is a social shock-absorber placed between privilege and the pressure of popular discontent.

The new Member's first experience of this is when he learns that passionate feelings must never find expression in forth-right speech. His first speech teaches him that. Having come straight from contact with his constituents, he is full of their grievances and his own resentment, and naturally, he does his best to shock his listeners into some realisation of it.

He delivers himself therefore with great force and, he hopes and fears, with considerable provocativeness. When his opponent arises to reply he expects to hear an equally strong and uncompromising answer. His opponent does nothing of the sort. In strict conformity with Parliamentary tradition, he congratulates the new Member upon a most successful maiden speech and expresses the urbane hope that the House will have frequent opportunities of hearing him in the future. The Members present endorse this quite insincere sentiment with murmurs of approval. With that, his opponent pays no more attention to him but goes on to deliver the speech he had intended to make. After remaining in his seat a little longer, the new Member crawls out of the House with feelings of deep relief at having got it over, mingled with a paralysing sense of frustration.

I would not have bothered to describe this typical experience of a working man speaking in the House of Commons for the first time were it not characteristic of the whole atmosphere. The classic Parliamentary style of speech is understatement. It is a style unsuited to the representative of working people because it slurs and mutes the deep antagonisms which exist in society.

71. WHIPS AND M.P.S TRUST AND MUTUAL RESPECT

[from Nigel Nicolson, *People and Parliament*, Weidenfeld and Nicolson, 1958, pp. 74–77]

Pressure is exerted in two directions, by back-bench Members on party-leaders, and by Whips on back-benchers. It would be wrong to think of them in a state of permanent combat, yet almost no week passes in his parliamentary life when a Member of the Government party does not try to persuade a Minister to do something which the Minister does not wish to do, or when the Member is not himself under some degree of suspicion in the Whip's office. Those who accuse Members of Parliament of sheepish inactivity would be surprised to discover with what energy most of them struggle in the pen. What other purpose have they in being there at all, except to use their influence on behalf of their constituents or their own ideas? There is no sense in repeating that Members are shackled by their Whips, when the newspapers carry an almost daily story of some 'revolt'—back-bench Conservative pressure on the Minister of Housing to amend the Rent Act, or on the Chancellor of the Exchequer to exclude retrospective legislation from the Finance Bill; socialist dissatisfaction with the party's policy on nuclear weapons, or murmurs of protest against its new proposals to control private industry. Few of these reports are baseless, and their frequency is a measure of the amount of flexibility left within the parliamentary parties.

There is no barrier between front and back-benches, except that imposed by shyness, inexperience, or diffidence in troubling an important and busy man. Most back-bench Members have served on terms of equality with their leading spokesmen before their promotion, or have themselves been Ministers in the past. Friendship is not killed by disagreement, nor by the conferment of distinction on one man and not on another. A Minister does not easily forget the temptations to dissent and the pangs of doubt which he, too, was subject on the back benches. They are all Members of Parliament. Disagreement is a staple part of their existence. 'Loyalty' is a word heard far less at Westminster than outside, because it is a quality open to such different interpretations and reservations, that it ceases to have much meaning. Is a back-bench Member disloyal to his Minister if he tells him privately that he thinks the Minister has made an error of judgment? Or only if he says so in public? In both cases, the Minister's job is made no easier, but it would not occur to him to resent it. All he would ask is that such disagreement should first be expressed privately, to give him a chance to explain the motives and implications of his policy which cannot be publicly stated, and to modify it, perhaps, to meet the Member's point-of-view before their disagreement leads to an open row.

The Whips' function is not to stifle genuine dissent, but to canalize it as far as possible along channels hidden from the public gaze. The notion that a Whip stands over a rebellious Member expostulating against his disloyalty and threatening him with the loss of all chance of future office, is remote from the truth. Apart from their thankless duty as janitors to save the Government from chance defeat in the division lobbies, they must act as a two-way Intelligence service, to warn Ministers of trouble stirring on the back benches, and to warn Members of the consequences of carrying disagreement to extreme lengths. 'It is persuasion rather than bullying that is the rule.' Mr Herbert Morrison has written; 'it is reasoning with a recalcitrant Member rather than coercion'. Bullying would do no good, because the Member has the final word. A threat to his political prospects would make no sense, with a front-bench of Ministers daily on view, each one of whom has at some period of his career flouted the Whips on a major issue. 'If you must, you must,' is their method of approach to a potential rebel. 'But I beg you to think it over. See the Minister first. Think of his difficulties, and the boost you will be giving to the Opposition. And at least don't vote against the Government. Surely it would be enough for you merely to abstain?'

Nobody who has had experience of one of these interviews can have come away with a feeling of outrage or disgust. One's indignation is often the less afterwards than before. So subtle is their relationship, that a Member will, for instance, deliberately warn his Whip that he intends to move an amendment against the Government on a Standing Committee, and add, 'Do you think you can get enough of our people together to defeat it?' To an outsider it must seem as incomprehensible that a Member should thus help to organize the rejection of his own motion as that a painter should canvass the Hanging Committee of the Royal Academy to reject his picture. But the Member knows very well that his warning has created confidence in the Whip's mind that he is not the sort of man to gain his object by trickiness. If his motion has any validity, it will be more likely to find acceptance with the Government or its purpose met in another way, than if he had tried to carry his point by storm and surprise. If it has not, he has at least been able to put his argument and drive it to its conclusion in a vote.

Trust and mutual respect are the motive power of this curious back-stage mechanism of politics. Trust that a Member will not defy his party on a sudden whim, or for purposes of self-advertisement; trust that the Whips will not blight his reputation or deny him the few privileges in their gift because of an isolated act of insubordination; trust that the Minister will give due weight to a serious objection moderately presented, even when it causes him embarrassment. This attitude extends outside the Whips' office to the whole of Parliament. The standing of a Member with the Opposition as well as with his own party depends largely on his method of dissent. To curry favour with his opponents by attacking his own side is as contemptible as to conceal his profoundest disagreement in the hope of gaining favour with the Whips. There are turns of phrase in parliamentary speaking which carry the same sort of double meaning as the language of diplomacy. A Labour Member will say to a Minister of the present Government: 'It is utterly disgraceful that the Minister should treat these poor people so callously.' A Conservative would say: 'While I am glad that my Right Honourable Friend has been able to do so much for them, I would like to suggest for his consideration two further steps which his Ministry might take.' Both speakers mean exactly the same thing, one much less, the other much more, than he actually says. Hypocrisy? I do not think it can be described as such, when the whole House recognizes the nuances of the words used. If the Conservative had spoken like the Socialist, there would have been a hoot of approval from the Opposition, but a hoot of derision too.

72. WHAT CAN THE PRIVATE MEMBER DO?

[from A. H. Birch, *Representative and Responsible Government*, Allen and Unwin, 1964, pp. 151–153, 196–200]

I

The truth is that it is not one factor but a whole range of factors, reinforcing each other, which produce a situation in which Parliamentary criticism of the administration is generally poorly informed and largely ineffective. In the first place, back-benchers do not have much time to devote to the acquisition of specialized information about administrative matters. They are busy with the internal politics of their own parties; they constantly travel to and from their constituencies, making speeches, attending social functions, and meeting electors; they attend to a large correspondence with (in general) inadequate secretarial help, and take up innumerable grievances on behalf of constituents; in many cases they also carry on part-time careers as lawyers, journalists, or business men.

Secondly, as a class back-benchers do not have much incentive to become experts on a wide range of topics. Those who are ambitious may take the advice Lord Woolton gave when he was Chairman of the Conservative Party and specialize on one subject, so that the Whips may get to know that they are reliable people to put up when the subject is debated. But many M.P.s do not feel it is necessary to do this, and of those who do a high proportion on the government side of the House will be sterilized as critics by being offered posts in the administration . . .

A third factor is the greatly increased tendency of interest groups to negotiate directly with the administration . . . One effect of this is to reduce still further the incentive for back-benchers to acquire specialized knowledge of the affairs with which these groups are concerned. For instance, any M.P. with a general interest in agriculture knows that agricultural policy is determined, within limits set by the cabinet, by direct negotiations between the National Farmers Union and the Ministry. If the negotiations break down at any stage, the subsequent Parliamentary debate is dominated by Government spokesmen on the one hand and spokesmen briefed by the Union on the other. In these circumstances it is not surprising that few M.P.s are inclined to spend much time making an independent study of agricultural affairs.

A fourth factor is that defence and foreign affairs, which loom larger in government policy and government expenditure than ever before in peacetime, are wrapped in a veil of secrecy and discretion. This is only partly a matter of the Official Secrets Act, for Winston Churchill showed in the 1930's that this need not prevent effective criticism of defence policy. Much more important than this is the existence of a tradition of secrecy and discretion which the leading members of both main parties generally respect. The government's problems at any time are apt to be broadly similar to those which the leaders of the opposition experienced when they were last in power and which they expect to experience again when they are next in power; as a result observance of this tradition is not only good form but is also usually good tactics.

All these factors impose a more severe limitation on Parliamentary control than does the growth of party discipline. John Stuart Mill said that Parliament's functions were 'to watch and control the government: to throw the light of publicity on its acts: to compel a full exposition and justification of all of them which anyone considers questionable: to censure them if found condemnable'. If M.P.s were well informed about all the government's activities Parliament could perform the first three of these functions, even if party solidarity prevented it performing the fourth. But if M.P.s do not know exactly what the government is doing they cannot perform any of these functions effectively. It was awareness of this that led one Member to observe that 'the House of Commons is in great danger of becoming the administration's pekinese, able maybe to snarl and snap a bit after the event but never possessed of that current knowledge which is so essential if we are to have any chance of performing the function of watchdog'.

II

A citizen who has a grievance against the government has the right to take the matter up with his Member of Parliament and can expect that the M.P. will do something about it unless the grievance is clearly unjustified. The M.P. will normally write or speak to the minister concerned: he may in some circumstances take the matter up at Question Time. In this way complaints which would otherwise have got no further than a junior official are brought to the attention of those in positions of higher authority. Moreover, by acting constantly on behalf of their constituents in this fashion M.P.s come to know better than most people what aspects of government policy or administration are becoming unpopular or causing hardship. They pass this information on to the party whips if they are on the government side; they exploit it in speeches and debates if they are in opposition. In this way M.P.s play an important part in the process by which those in power are made aware of the impact of their decisions on the man-in-the-street.

Such action by M.P.s sometimes has a direct effect on government policy. In 1957, for instance, the debates on the proposed Rent Act were marked by confident and mutually incompatible generalizations by politicians about the degree of hardship that the Act was likely to cause. After the first stages of the Act came into effect M.P.s were able to assess the hardship directly by considering the specific cases put to them by constituents. It quickly became clear that in many areas the Act would make little difference, in some it would work fairly smoothly, but in some (mainly in Greater London) it would cause appreciable hardship to tenants unless its full implementation were delayed. After hearing representations by M.P.s the Minister concerned introduced an amending bill which enabled tenants threatened with eviction orders to appeal to the courts for a suspension of the orders.

In cases like this the M.P.'s behaviour is not greatly affected by party politics: his political allegiance may determine to whom he passes on the information but it is not likely to distort the message appreciably. When it is a matter of transmitting opinions rather than one of reporting grievances the allegiance and personal attitudes of the M.P. are apt to be more important. A Conservative Member possessing a large majority in an agricultural constituency is unlikely to pay much attention to the opposition of some of his constituents to the system of tied cottages. A Nonconformist Member is more likely than a Roman Catholic to take serious notice of complaints about the establishment of betting shops. And if a Labour Member from an industrial town tells the House that his constituents are all up in arms about a proposal to charge differential rents for municipal houses, it is fair to assume that he has given more weight to the views of the tenants than to the views of the owner-occupiers in the area.

Since Members normally feel that they have to take note of letters from constituents, pressure groups often urge members and sympathizers to write to their local M.P. Uniform letters are generally discounted by M.P.s, but if constituents write in their own words and are clearly expressing their personal feelings M.P.s are inclined to take notice of the correspondence, even though its timing may indicate that it has been stimulated by a pressure group. In 1956 a barrage of letters from school-teachers to M.P.s formed part of the successful campaign waged by the National Union of Teachers to prevent the immediate increase in the rate of teachers' superannuation contributions that was provided for in the Bill then before Parliament. In 1961 a large number of letters from motor-cyclists to M.P.s apparently helped to persuade back-benchers not to support the Private Member's Bill which proposed that motor-cyclists should be compelled to take out insurance to cover injuries to passengers. This correspondence appears to have been stimulated not by one of the motoring organizations but simply by articles in the motor-cycling press.

These are two cases in which the lobbying of M.P.s appears to have had clear results, and it would not be very difficult to find other examples. But the effect of lobbying is not to be assessed simply on the basis of such cases, for it is a continuous process which has a continuous influence, in a variety of ways, on parliamentary opinion. There are spontaneous letters from individuals to M.P.s; there are letters organized or stimulated by others, whether they be established pressure groups or not; there are interviews with M.P.s in their constituencies or in the lobby at Westminster; there are petitions which M.P.s are asked to present to Parliament or to a minister; there are direct approaches by pressure groups to M.P.s both by post and by personal contact. The Political Correspondent of *The Times* estimates that in each day's mail the average M.P. is 'pursued by at least fifteen different causes, campaigns, companies, or cliques'. Many or most of these appeals go straight into the waste-paper basket, but some of them must have some effect on Members' attitudes. And, of course, most pressure groups try to develop and maintain personal contacts with Members. All the more important groups have regular Parliamentary spokesmen, while the great majority of M.P.s. have one or two interests and causes on whose behalf they are prepared to speak.

Although back-benchers have less power now than in the nineteenth century, they are by no means without influence. Their support is a necessary, though not a sufficient, condition for the success of Private Members' Bills: such a bill will die a speedy death unless it gets a good measure of back-bench support, but if it does there is some chance that the government of the day will find time for it. Back-benchers often persuade the government to accept amendments to bills at the committee stage, which, indeed, is rarely effective except when there is a discussion between one set of experts speaking through the Minister and other experts speaking through various back-bench M.P.s. Very occasionally back-benchers secure amendments at the committee stage despite the government's opposition. In 1959, for instance, the Obscene Publications Bill was transformed in committee by the addition of a section which enabled publishers to establish literary merit as at least a partial defence against the allegation of obscenity. And questions and debates on the floor of the House clearly influence ministers on occasions, even though the government's majority is not in danger.

These forms of influence are visible to the casual observer. More important still are the constant contacts of back-benchers with whips and ministers 'upstairs', and the work of the Parliamentary committees of the parties. On occasion back-bench influence upstairs is clearly discernible, as when the Labour Government of 1945–51 was under pressure from its left-wing supporters, or when Sir Thomas Dugdale decided to resign after criticism in the Conservative Party's Agricultural Committee. More recently, in 1961 it was evident that a group of Conservative back-benchers who were worried about the pace of developments in Northern Rhodesia, and who had doubtless been briefed by Sir Roy Welensky's supporters, were doing all they could to persuade the Government not to accede to African demands. In February, 1961 while talks on constitutional reform in Northern Rhodesia were in progress, the Colonial Secretary was questioned by the Conservative Colonial Committee. He was pressed to give an assurance that any new constitution would ensure the continuance of a European majority on the Legislative Council, and he was apparently indefinite on this point. On the following day his critics tabled a motion in the House calling on the Government to adhere to the principles of 1958 White Paper on Northern Rhodesia, and by that evening sixty-five Conservative back-benchers had signed it. No debate on this motion was held or intended; it was tabled simply as a demonstration of back-bench opinion.

A similar step was taken in July, 1961, by a group of Conservative Members who wished to warn the Prime Minister of the scale of back-bench opposition to the proposal that Britain should enter the Common Market before securing acceptable guarantees about agricultural protection and Commonwealth trade: on this occasion the motion was signed by thirty-two back-benchers.

It is unnecessary to multiply examples. There is a continuous process by which party leaders are made aware of the views of their Parliamentary supporters, and it is fair to assume that the influence of the latter is also continuous. It is this, rather than the ritual of Parliamentary debates which makes the Member of Parliament so important a channel of communication between the public and the Government.

73. DOES THE PRIVATE MEMBER WANT MORE FREE VOTES?

[from Nigel Nicolson, *People and Parliament*, Weidenfeld and Nicolson, 1958, pp. 71–74]

Let us first consider the instances where party discipline is deliberately lifted by allowing a free vote of the House and exposing the Member to the full play of external pressures.

There are more free votes than is often realized. During the last six years the totals have been: 1952, thirteen; 1953, thirteen; 1954, eight; 1955, nine; 1956, thirty-one (many of them connected with the Death Penalty Abolition Bill); 1957, fourteen. Several of these were votes on Private Bills promoted by local authorities. Though the principle of allowing an untrammelled expression of opinion on such occasions is a sound one, the practice is often absurd. Say the Rochester Corporation Bill is under discussion. In theory, Members crowd the Chamber to listen to the arguments for and against the Bill, and are led to their decision in much the same way as a jury in a murder trial. In fact, only a small proportion of those who will ultimately decide the fate of Rochester listen to the arguments at all. They are busy elsewhere. The division bells ring, and Members arrive from all quarters of the House expecting to find a Whip standing at the entrance to the appropriate lobby. There is no Whip; it is a free vote. Aghast, the Member tries to discover from his nearest neighbours whether Rochester should be allowed its Bill or not, while the Town Clerk of Rochester gnaws his finger-nails in his seat under the gallery. It may be so slight a consideration as that the Member himself represents a county borough like Rochester which will decide him in its favour; or a chance reminder that the Bill includes a clause to permit municipal trading which may decide him against it. It is fair to add that such Bills usually receive their Second Reading, and are passed for more serious examination to a Committee; but the absurdity of the process illustrates the advantages of whipped voting. It is impossible for Members to keep abreast of all matters which come before Parliament and form a balanced opinion on each of them.

That is an exceptional case. Usually free votes are awarded on occasions when considerable public interest has already been aroused, and national organizations have been stimulated to a frenzy of lobbying by the knowledge that no Member can shelter behind the dictation of his party. Often the cry is raised outside that a proposal should be decided by a free vote, simply because Government policy is known to be luke-warm or hostile. This is the almost annual practice of the National Federation of Old Age Pensioners, who naturally hope that enough Members will surrender to constituency pressure if a free vote is allowed. The same person will often insist that a matter should be 'taken out of party politics', and simultaneously promise to vote for any party which includes it in its election programme, without noticing the contradiction. Or the Opposition, in order to embarrass the Government, may call for a free vote on an issue which unites their own side and splits their opponents. These tactics rarely succeed, for the House has come to agree, within narrow limits, on the occasions when a free vote is justified: It cannot be on a topic which involves a large segment of Government policy, or heavy expenditure. It cannot be used simply as an excuse to save the Cabinet from coming to a decision. The issue must be one which arouses strong moral or religious feelings, and where genuine doubt is already known to exist in the House or in the country. Thus the subjects for free votes choose themselves: horror-comics; Kosher killing; Sunday Observance; stag-hunting; revision of the prayer-book. In other words, subjects on which there are known to be strong differences of opinion on both sides of the House, where a Government's prestige and general policy will not be affected whichever way the vote goes, and where majority opinion in the country is not clear but constituencies are deeply interested.

Members of Parliament are less fond of free votes than is supposed. They know that whichever way they use their unaccustomed freedom, they are likely to offend half of their constituents. It may be a subject on which the Member holds no strong views of his own; but if it is one on which he holds opposite views to those of a majority of his local supporters, he he is bound to ask himself whether the removal of the Whip at Westminster means that it can immediately be re-imposed by the party in his constituency. Is he obliged to do his best to discover the majority view of his electors, and speak and vote in accordance with it, whether he agrees with it or not? If so, should he be guided by the views of those who voted for him and threaten not to vote for him again if he ignores their wishes, more than by the views of his electorate as a whole? Is he speaking for himself, in the expectation that other speakers in the debate will reflect the views of a majority of his constituents when he does not share them just as he will be speaking on behalf of unknown millions in the country who agree with him? And if, during the course of the debate, a spokesman from the front bench expresses strongly the Government's own view of the matter, to what extent is that a limitation on a back-bench Member's complete freedom to disagree with it? . . . In theory the answer to [these questions] was given by Mr R. A. Butler in the debate on the Festival of Britain (Sunday opening) Bill, when he said, 'I trust that all votes will be given according to the prickings of conscience, and not under pressure of post-cards'. But it is not so simple.

74. WHAT JUSTIFICATION FOR FREE VOTES?

[from Morrison, *Government and Parliament*, O.U.P., 1954, pp. 162–164]

I

It is sometimes argued that there should be more frequent occasions when Members are free to vote as they wish, with the

Whips off, particularly during the Committee Stage of Bills. Those who hold this view urge that it would give Members a better opportunity to express their opinions and feelings in the division Lobby and would indeed help them to feel a greater sense of personal responsibility for what Parliament was doing; that it is unreasonable that the Whips should systematically be put on in respect of Government Business on matters of detail or even where high moral principles of a non-party character are involved. I well understand this point of view and have been a party to taking the Whips off on a certain number of occasions. In 1930, on the Road Traffic Bill which I had introduced as Minister of Transport, the Whips were taken off in respect of a Government proposal to abolish the speed limit; and abolition was carried on the Floor of the House on a free vote. As Home Secretary in the war I brought forward, with the support of the Coalition Government, a proposal for the opening of theatres on Sundays under the same conditions as cinemas for the benefit of troops who were away from home. Nevertheless, I successfully urged the Government to take the Whips off. In this case we were defeated by eight votes—we would certainly have won if the Whips had been on. In the chapter on the House of Lords I recount the free vote which was accorded to the House of Commons on the question of capital punishment. Those favouring its suspension won in the division Lobby, but it is very doubtful whether a majority of public opinion was behind them; the subject had not been mentioned in the election programme of either party and in the end the Commons had to submit to the decision of the House of Lords to leave the subject out of the Criminal Justice Bill. On all these occasions some of the Members would have been happier if they could have had official assistance from the Whips in making up their minds. However, I hope I have shown that I am not the inveterate enemy of free voting. I must add, however, that many Ministers and parliamentarians of long experience are doubtful about its virtues and are of opinion that it should be resorted to only on Private Members' Business and otherwise on very rare occasions.

If it were left to Members to decide whether there should be a free vote of the House, parliamentary difficulty and confusion of an awkward character would in all probability arise. The merits of the question would become confused with a desire on the part of many Members for a free vote. Moreover, there could be much argument about what should or should not be eligible for a free vote. What may appear to be an issue of detail to back-benchers may not be so much a matter of detail or may at any rate involve serious repercussions which Ministers can see but which back-benchers cannot so readily understand. For example, during the consideration of the Education Bill in 1944 there was a revolt against the Government (not on a free vote) and an amendment was carried in favour of equal pay for men and women teachers. Was this a matter of detail? It could be so argued. It could be argued that women teachers have a stronger case on grounds of equal work than a good many other employed women. Alternatively, it could have been argued that here was a great matter of principle on which the House of Commons should be free to express itself and decide. Nevertheless, Mr Churchill subsequently went to the House of Commons and made it reverse its decision as an issue of confidence, or at any rate persuaded it to do so. The Coalition Government took the view that this was certainly a matter where there would have been considerable repercussions in the Civil Service, the local government services, and, quite possibly, in private industry; and that if the principle was to be established in legislation, it should not be for one calling only, but after comprehensive consideration. I am not arguing the merits in this case; I mention it as an illustration of the difficulty in separating matters of detail from matters of broad public policy. And an Act of Parliament has to stand up as a coherent whole, or administrative and possibly legal trouble may well follow.

In Standing Committee upstairs, at any rate when there is a Government with a working majority, Members assert their independence with slightly more freedom than on the floor, even though it is officially discouraged. However, the Government is then in a stronger position because if fifty Members in Standing Committee upstairs out of over 600 M.P.s reach a decision opposed by Ministers the Government can, without much loss of face, accept it if it is not too great a matter of difficulty or, as often happens, it can have the decision reversed on the Floor of the House at Report Stage.

75. FREE VOTES AND GOVERNMENT RESPONSIBILITY

[from Marshall and Moodie's, *Some Problems of the Constitution*, Hutchinson, 1959, pp. 74–77]

Free votes suggest some further questions about the nature of the Government's collective responsibility to Parliament. Is the nature of responsibility to the Commons affected by the fact that the House is voting, when the Whips are off, as a collection of individuals rather than as the organized forum of party views? Moreover, what is the nature of the Government's responsibility when a decision reached in the Commons in this way is opposed to the majority view of the upper House? Both these questions emerged in 1956 when the House of Lords rejected the proposed abolition of the death penalty after it had been carried on a free vote in the Commons. It was strongly urged by Members supporting abolition that the Government's constitutional duty was to prefer the opinion of the lower House and to afford facilities for that view to prevail by carrying it against the Lord's opposition, under the procedure provided by the Parliament Act. This view was not accepted by the Government or by those who opposed abolition. An intractable deadlock between the two Houses had not, it was argued, been reached, and the conditions under which the Parliament Acts had previously been invoked—namely a dead-lock between an elected Government and the Commons on the one hand, and the Lords on the other—did not in this case exist. The Government was not as a government committed to, or in favour of, the course indicated by the Commons' vote. Some general arguments in support of this view were advanced in the editorial columns of *The Times*. The use of the Parliament Acts was not required, *The Times* argued, by any constitutional convention, and any such use would be adopting those Acts for a purpose quite foreign to the intention with which they were passed. The legislative authority in Great Britain was not vested in a single chamber or even two. It belonged to Queen, Lords, and Commons and the Constitution required every effort to be made to bring all three into harmony before emergency measures to give preference to one were applied. The Government, it was added, were the umpires and should make up their own minds.

Here is a problem generated by the informal and debatable nature of British constitutional conventions. From these general principles arguments could be marshalled on both sides. In the event, since they were backed by the Government, the views of those who supported the thesis advanced by *The Times* prevailed. The argument, nonetheless, deserves some scrutiny in isolation from the details of the capital punishment controversy. The view is often advanced, for example, that a government has the right to take an independent umpire's stance and to lead and influence opinion as against the electorate (though perhaps this is more than an umpire might be expected to do). This in turn may be defended on the ground that the Government consists of Members of Parliament who are not delegates but elected to govern in ways which as men of known party principles may seem best to them. It may be obviously true that when a government carries with it the support of a majority of the Commons as in all normal cases, its authority must prevail as against any contrary view. But these are different propositions from that which asserts that the government without a majority in the Commons preserves the right and duty of independent judgment, on a matter committed to a free vote of the House, as against a majority of the Commons as a whole. In what sense does such a view manifest the principle of ministerial responsibility to Parliament?

The Times ventured, in addition, on an argument which seems even more disputable. The Government's responsibility for finding a way out of the disagreement could be based, it was suggested, upon the fact that the Commons had voted according to their individual consciences and not as representatives of their constituents. It followed, *The Times* argued, that 'Lords and Members of Parliament are on an equal footing as so many individuals'. This seems a surprising doctrine. In the first place, the co-ordinate status of the three elements of the legislature is legally undeniable, but since the conventions of the constitution are, as Dicey declared, directed towards securing a supremacy of the will of the elected element, it is far from clear that the Lords are entitled as a matter of constitutional principle to be counted as politically co-ordinate legislative elements along with the Commons and Crown (whose entitlement is more remote still). But more important: in what sense can a vote of the

Commons be regarded as possessing less authority by reason of being a free vote? It is not necessary to invoke the Burkeian view that the exercise of individual conscience adds rather than detracts from the moral authority of the Common's vote. But *vis-à-vis* the Lords at least its authority can hardly be less than that of a vote of Members holding their individual consciences in abeyance.

If these objections have any force they provide a reason for suggesting that a government which holds itself totally absolved from following a course indicated by a free vote in the House is evading a constitutional responsibility to the Commons. Could it be urged in reply that responsibility was preserved in the present instance since the majority which found itself at odds with Ministers could have brought the Government down by opposing their subsequent measures and in fact refrained from doing so? This is certainly true, but it is true in practically every conceivable situation. If it were admitted in exculpation it would seem to follow that a government whilst it remained the government never could be convicted of evading responsibility on a particular issue, and that no meaning could be attached to the suggestion. For Members do not express disapproval by defeating their leaders except on the most fundamental issue (and possibly not even then). Perhaps therefore, we should say that the only responsibility of Ministers is to hold their party together. But this, whatever its soundness as a maxim of political strategy, sounds decidedly odd as a constitutional convention.

PART VIII

Legislation (including delegated legislation)

76. THE ASSEMBLY AND LEGISLATION

[from J. S. Mill, *Representative Government*, Everyman's Edition, 1910, pp. 235–237]

But it is equally true, though only of late and slowly beginning to be acknowledged, that a numerous assembly is as little fitted for the direct business of legislation as for that of administration. There is hardly any kind of intellectual work which so much needs to be done, not only by experienced and exercised minds, but by minds trained to the task through long and laborious study, as the business of making laws. This is a sufficient reason were there no other, why they can never be well made but by a committee of very few persons. A reason no less conclusive is, that every provision of a law requires to be framed with the most accurate and long-sighted perception of its effect on all the other provisions; and the law when made should be capable of fitting into a consistent whole with the previous existing laws. It is impossible that these conditions should be in any degree fulfilled when laws are voted clause by clause in a miscellaneous assembly. The incongruity of such a mode of legislating would strike all minds, were it not that our laws are already, as to form and construction, such a chaos, that the confusion and contradiction seem incapable of being made greater by any addition to the mass. Yet even now, the utter unfitness of our legislative machinery for its purpose is making itself practically felt every year more and more. The mere time necessarily occupied in getting through Bills renders Parliament more and more incapable of passing any, except on detached and narrow points. If a Bill is prepared which even attempts to deal with the whole of any subject (and it is impossible to legislate properly on any part without having the whole present to the mind), it hangs over from session to session through sheer impossibility of finding time to dispose of it. It matters not though the Bill may have been deliberately drawn up by the authority deemed best qualified, with all appliances and means to boot; or by a select commission, chosen for their conversancy with the subject, and having employed years in considering and digesting the particular measure; it cannot be passed, because the House of Commons will not forego the precious privilege of tinkering with it with their clumsy hands. The custom has of late been to some extent introduced when the principle of a Bill has been affirmed on the second reading, of referring it for consideration in detail to a Select Committee: but it has not been found that this practice causes much less time to be lost afterwards in carrying it through the Committee of the whole House: the opinions or private crotchets which have been overruled by knowledge, always insist on giving themselves a second chance before the tribunal of ignorance . . . And when a Bill of many clauses does succeed in getting itself discussed in detail, what can depict the state in which it comes out of Committee! Clauses omitted, which are essential to the working of the rest; incongruous ones inserted to conciliate some private interest, or some crotchety member who threatens to delay the Bill; articles foisted in on the motion of some sciolist with a mere smattering of the subject, leading to consequences which the member who introduced or those who supported the Bill did not at the moment foresee and which need an amending Act in the next session to correct their mischiefs. It is one of the evils of the present mode of managing these things, that the explaining and defending of a Bill, and of its various provisions, is scarcely ever performed by the person from whose mind they emanated, who probably has not a seat in the House. Their defence rests upon some minister or member of Parliament who did not frame them, who is dependent on cramming for all his arguments but those which are perfectly obvious, who does not know the full strength of his case, nor the best reasons by which to support it, and is wholly incapable of meeting unforeseen objections. This evil, as far as Government bills are concerned, admits of remedy, and has been remedied in some representative constitutions, by allowing the Government to be represented in either House by persons in its confidence, having a right to speak, though not to vote.

If that, as yet considerable, majority of the House of Commons who never desire to move an amendment or make speech would leave the whole regulation of business to those who do; if they would bethink themselves that better qualifications for legislation exist, and may be found if sought for, than a fluent tongue and the faculty of getting elected by a constituency; it would soon be recognised that, in legislation as well as administration, the only task to which a representative assembly can possibly be competent is not that of doing the work, but of causing it to be done; of determining to whom or to what sort of people it shall be confided, and giving or withholding the national sanction to it when performed . . .

77. EXHIBITIONS OF HELPLESS INGENUITY

[from Walter Bagehot, *The English Constitution*, Fontana Library ed., 1963, pp. 133–136]

At present the chance majorities on minor questions in the House of Commons are subject to no effectual control. The nation never attends to any but the principal matters of policy and State. Upon these it forms that rude, rough, ruling judgment which we call public opinion. But upon other things it does not think at all, and it would be useless for it to think. It has not the materials for forming a judgment: the detail of bills, the instrumental part of policy, the latent part of legislation, are wholly out of its way. It knows nothing about them, and could not find time or labour for the careful investigation by which alone they can be apprehended. A casual majority of the House of Commons has therefore dominant power: it can legislate as it wishes. And though the whole House of Commons upon great subjects very fairly represents public opinion, and though its judgment upon minor questions is, from some secret excellencies in its composition, remarkably sound and good; yet, like all similar assemblies, it is subject to the sudden action [of any number of interested members] . . . If, (say), 200 choose to combine on a point which the public does not care for, and which they care for because it affects their purse, they are absolute. A formidable sinister interest may always obtain the complete command of a dominant assembly by some chance and for a moment . . .

Every large assembly, is moreover, a fluctuating body; it is not one house, so to say, but a set of houses; it is one set of men to-night and another to-morrow night. A certain unity is doubtless preserved by the duty which the executive is supposed to undertake, and does undertake, of keeping a house; a constant element is so provided about which all sorts of variables accumulate and pass away. But even after due allowance for the full weight of this protective machinery, our House of Commons is, as all such chambers must be, subject to sudden turns and bursts of feeling, because the members who compose it change from time to time. The pernicious result is perpetual in our legislation; many Acts of Parliament are medleys of different motives, because the majority which passed one set of its clauses is different from that which passed another set.

But the greatest defect of the House of Commons is that it has no leisure. The life of the House is the worst of all lives—a life of distracting routine. It has an amount of business brought before it such as no similar assembly ever has had. The British Empire is a miscellaneous aggregate, and each bit of the aggregate brings its bit of business to the House of Commons. It is India one day and Jamaica the next; then again China, and then Schleswig-Holstein. Our legislation touches on all subjects, because our country contains all ingredients. The mere questions which are asked of the Ministers run over half human affairs; the Private Bill Acts, the mere *privilegia* of our Government—subordinate as they ought to be—probably give the House of Commons more absolute work than the whole business, both national and private, of any other assembly which has ever sat. The whole scene is so encumbered with changing business, that it is hard to keep your head in it.

Whatever, too, may be the case hereafter, when a better system has been struck out, at present the House does all the work of legislation, all the detail, and all the clauses itself. One of the most helpless exhibitions of helpless ingenuity and wasted mind is a committee of the whole House on a bill of many clauses which eager enemies are trying to spoil, and various friends are trying to mend. An Act of Parliament is at least as complex as a marriage settlement; and it is made much as a settlement would be if it were left to the vote and settled by the major part of persons concerned, including the unborn children. There is an advocate for every interest, and every interest clamours for every advantage. The executive Government by means of its disciplined forces, and the few invaluable members who sit and think, preserves some sort of unity. But the result is very imperfect. The best test of a machine is the work it turns out. Let any one who knows what legal documents ought to be, read first a will he has just been making and then an Act of Parliament; he will certainly say, 'I would have dismissed my attorney if he had done my business as the legislature has done the nation's business.'

78. THE EXECUTIVE THE TRUE SOURCE OF LEGISLATION

[from Sir Henry Maine, *Popular Government*, Murray, 1885, pp. 235–240]

The procedure of the American House of Representatives, both in respect of the origination of bills and of the interrogation of Ministers, is that of a political body which considers that its proper functions are not executive, but legislative. The British House of Commons, on the other hand, which the greatest part of the world regards as a legislative assembly (though it never quite answered to that description), has, since 1789, taken under its supervision and control the entire Executive government of Great Britain, and much of the government of her colonies and dependencies.

All legislative proposals which have any serious chance of becoming law, proceed in the United States from Committees of the Senate or of the House of Representatives. Where are we to place the birth of an English legislative measure? He who will give his mind to this question will find it one of the obscurest which ever perplexed the political observer. Some Bills undoubtedly have their origin in the Executive Departments, where vices of existing laws or systems have been disclosed in the process of actual administration. Others may be said to be conceived in the House of Commons, having for their embryo either the Report of a Committee of the House or of a resolution passed by it which, according to a modern practice, suggested no doubt by the difficulties of legislation, has taken the place of the private member's Bill. But if we may trust the experience of 1883, by far the most important measures, measures fraught with the gravest consequence to the whole future of the nation, have a much more remarkable beginning. One of the great English political parties, and naturally the party supporting the Government in power, holds a Conference of gentlemen, to whom I hope I may without offence apply the American name 'wire-pullers,' and this Conference dictates to the Government, not only the legislation which it is to submit to the House of Commons, but the order in which it is to be submitted. Here we are introduced to the great modern paradox of the British Constitution. While the House of Commons has assumed the supervision of the whole Executive Government, it has turned over to the Executive Government, the most important part of the business of legislation. For it is in the Cabinet that the effective work of legislation begins. The Ministers, hardly recuperated from the now very serious fatigues of a Session which lasts all but to the commencement of September, assemble in Cabinet in November, and in the course of a series of meetings, extending over rather more than a fortnight, determine what legislative proposals are to be submitted to Parliament. These proposals, sketched, we may believe, in not more than outline, are then placed in the hands of the Government draftsman; and, so much is there in all legislation which consists in the manipulation of detail and in the adaptation of vaguely conceived novelties to pre-existing law, that we should not probably go far wrong if we attributed four-fifths of every legislative enactment to the accomplished lawyer who puts into shape the Government Bills. From the measures which come from his hand, the tale of Bills to be announced in the Queen's Speech is made up, and at this point English legislation enters upon another stage.

The American political parties of course support and oppose particular legislative measures. They are elated at the success of a particular Bill, and disappointed by its failure. But no particular consequences beyond disappointment follow the rejection of a Bill. The Government of the country goes on as before. In England it is otherwise. Every Bill introduced into

Parliament by the Ministry (and we have seen that all the really important Bills are thus introduced) must be carried through the House of Commons without substantial alteration, or the Ministers will resign, and consequences of the gravest kind may follow in the remotest parts of an empire extending to the ends of the earth. Thus a Government Bill has to be forced through the House of Commons with the whole strength of party organisation, and in a shape very closely resembling that which the Executive Government gave to it. It should then in strictness pass through a searching discussion in the House of Lords; but this stage of English legislation is becoming merely nominal, and the judgment on it of the Crown has long since become a form. It is therefore the Executive Government which should be credited with the authorship of English legislation. We have thus an extraordinary result. The nation whose constitutional practice suggested to Montesquieu his memorable maxim concerning the Executive, Legislative, and Judicial powers, has in the course of a century falsified it. The formal Executive is the true source of legislation; the formal Legislature is incessantly concerned with Executive Government.

After its first birth, nothing can be more equable and nothing can be more plain to observation than the course of an American legislative measure. A Bill, both in the House of Representatives and the Senate, goes through an identical number of stages of about equal length. When it has passed both Houses, it must still commend itself to the President of the United States, who has a veto on it which, though qualified, is constantly used, and is very difficult to overcome. An English Bill begins in petty rivulets or stagnant pools. Then it runs underground for most of its course, withdrawn from the eye by the secrecy of the Cabinet. Emerging into the House of Commons, it can no more escape from its embankments than the water of a canal; but once dismissed from that House, it overcomes all remaining obstacles with the rush of a cataract, and mixes with the trackless ocean of British institutions.

79. THE DECLINING POWER OF THE HOUSE

[from Sir Sidney Low, *The Governance of England*, Longmans, 1904, pp. 76–80]

The declining power of the House of Commons in respect [of legislation] receives less attention than it deserves, though it has been admitted, sometimes with reluctance, sometimes with a certain satisfaction, by some keen observers. The late Lord Salisbury occasionally noticed the phenomenon, as in his speech at Edinburgh on October 30, 1894, when he said: 'There is an enormous change in the House of Commons as I recollect it, and the evolution is going on still; and we have reached this point—that discussion of a measure is possible in the Cabinet, but for any effective or useful purpose, it is rapidly, becoming an impossibility in the House of Commons.' Lord Salisbury, though he regarded the change with his customary philosophical and scientific detachment, did not consider that it was one to be applauded. Private members of the House sometimes raised their voices against it in angry or plaintive remonstrance. 'Were they prepared,' said one of these oppressed legislators[1] indignantly, in the debates on the Closure resolutions by which it was proposed to expedite proceedings on the Licensing Bill—

> Were they prepared to declare that as a body the House was unfitted to frame its measures, and that when a Bill passed into Committee, if time was short, or if the measure was controversial, or if any elements of complication arose, it was to be taken, not in the form in which Parliament has settled it, but in the form in which the Government draftsmen had framed it, and in which the Cabinet had chosen to adopt it? The Constitution had undergone a serious change. It had ceased to be government by Parliament; it had become government by Cabinet; and an even later development, they were told, had taken place, and it was now government by Prime Minister in Cabinet, little distinguishable from the autocracies into which the democracies of the past had degenerated . . . There was no tribunal by which legislation could be reviewed and criticised. The only security given was in the discussion and deliberation of Parliament, and if they came to the conclusion that this deliberation and discussion could not be expended

[1] Mr Lawson Walton in the House of Commons, July 1, 1904.

upon their measures, then they were abandoning one of the most important functions which the House had hitherto exercised.

No doubt a member's views as to the growing encroachments of the Government on the right of discussion are apt to be coloured by his own relations to it. The extinguished Opposition orator may writhe beneath the closure like a toad under the harrow. To the minister, anxious to push his Bill through, the harrow may seem only a useful implement of agriculture. But, aside from all party spirit, there must be many members of the House who regard their own powerlessness with misgiving and dissatisfaction. One of them puts the case strongly but temperately in these words:—

> There is no doubt as to the facts of recent Parliamentary history. In the last few years the powers of the Government have been greatly increased, those of private members have greatly declined—not merely powers of talking, for that is little, but of doing useful work. Each step in the process looks small, but the cumulative result is very considerable. For instance, the closure used to be occasionally refused. Even Mr W. H. Smith, who sat more continuously in the House watching its proceedings than any Leader of recent years, was refused the closure. The Government is practically never refused this closure, now. Then the rules are much more stringently applied in a more technical or quasi-legal manner than formerly, whether as regards questions, amendments, instructions, or points of order. Again, it was practically impossible, till the greater stringency of administering the rules of these later years, to pass Bills, as was done during the late Parliament, without an amendment of a single word.
>
> It is supposed to save time; but what effect does it have on private members, on both sides of the House, to be told that no contribution they can give, no argument they can make in the direction of improvement, is of the slightest use? The Government says it knows how to draw a Bill which is absolutely perfect, and all suggestions about the Bill are made to appear waste of time. If this be so, what is the use of a deliberative Assembly?[2]

It must be remembered that the situation of the ministerialist member outside the Ministry itself is not much better than that

[2] The quotation is from an excellent letter by 'an Old Member of the House of Commons' in the *Westminster Gazette*, March 19, 1901.

of his rival on the opposite benches. He, also, is only in a limited sense a legislator; he has scarcely any power to make new laws or to prevent them being made, or to amend old ones. He is not consulted, any more than the members of the Opposition, on Bills which ministers propose to introduce; he sees them only when they come from the printers; and then he knows that, whether he likes them or not, he will be expected to support them by his vote in the lobbies.

On the other hand this suppression of 'the liberty of unlicensed debate,' as Milton might have called it, and the regulation of desultory, half-instructed opinion, has found its advocates, and even its enthusiastic eulogists. Against the doubting words of Lord Salisbury, may be set the exultant language of Lord Salisbury's son, a brilliant young representative of the newer school of Toryism. Speaking in the House of Commons in March, 1901, in ardent defence of the revised rules of procedure brought forward by the Government, Lord Hugh Cecil uttered these remarkable sentences:—

> We hear often of the infringements of the rights of private members, and it cannot be denied that a transfer of political power from the House of Commons to the Cabinet is going on... Why is it that nobody cares, outside these walls, about the rights of private members? Because there is a deep-seated feeling that the House is an institution which has ceased to have much authority or much repute, and that when a better institution, the Cabinet, encroaches upon the rights of a worse one, it is a matter of small concern to the country.

Such language, as Mr Bernard Holland observes in that penetrating study of our method of Government entitled *Imperium et Libertas*, has hardly been heard within the precincts of the Palace of Westminster since the days of Charles I.[3] In 1791, Reeves, the author of the *History of English Law*, anxious to exalt the royal prerogative, used somewhat similar language

[3] Mr Holland adds: 'The theoretical and practical deduction from this doctrine is that the House of Commons is to become a mere body for registering the decrees of a secret committee, largely consisting of men in the House of Lords who never come near it. How long in that case will the House of Commons continue to attract the services of able men? It is felt already that, for a man who desires not so much honorary distinction as real and practical work, the London County Council offers satisfactions, which Parliament is powerless to bestow.' *Imperium et Libertas*, p. 257.

about the House of Commons, contending that the chambers of Parliament were but branches on our constitutional tree, which might be lopped off without seriously damaging the trunk. The House was deeply indignant, and compelled the Government to prosecute Reeves for sedition.[4] Nobody however, proposed to prosecute, or even to reprimand, Lord Hugh Cecil, for his open aspersion of the dignity and authority of the House of Commons. Perhaps it was felt that there was undeniable truth in his statement of the facts, whatever might be thought of his verdict on the merits of the two 'institutions,' which were the objects of his audacious comparison.

80. DOES PARLIAMENT INITIATE—OR MERELY REVIEW?

[from F. A. Ogg, *English Government and Politics*, Macmillan, 2nd ed. 1936, pp. 450–452]

Take first the matter of legislation. A hundred years ago, the cabinet as such had relatively little to do with the processes of law-making. Even then, the ministers were, with few exceptions, members of Parliament. But their duties were chiefly executive, and they bore no disproportionate share in the legislative activities of the houses. Now, all is different. They write the Speech from the Throne which lays down the legislative program for a session; they decide what subjects shall occupy the attention of the houses, prepare the bills on these subjects (with no opportunity for non-ministerial members to participate in preliminary discussions), introduce them, explain and defend them, push them to enactment, take full responsibility for them both before and after they are passed, and throw upon the House of Commons the onus of upsetting the government and very likely precipitating a general election if any weighty measure on which they continue to insist is defeated. They demand, and obtain, most of the time of the houses—all of it in the House of Commons after a certain stage of the session is reached—for the consideration of the measures in which they are interested. They crack the whip of party loyalty over the heads of their supporters on the benches and make it next to impossible for even the ablest and most spirited among

[4] *State Trials*, xxxvi. pp. 530–534.

them to question publicly, much less to vote against, the proposals upon which Whitehall has resolved.

The upshot is both obvious and significant. 'To say,' remarks the American writer who has made the closest study of the subject, 'that at present the cabinet legislates with the advice and consent of Parliament would hardly be an exaggeration; and it is only the right of private members to bring in a few motions and bills of their own, and to criticize government measures, or propose measures, or propose amendments to them, freely, that prevents legislation from being the work of a mere automatic majority. It does not follow that the action of the cabinet is arbitrary . . . The cabinet has its finger always on the pulse of the House of Commons, and especially of its own majority there; and it is ever on the watch for expressions of public feeling outside. Its function is in large part to sum up and formulate the desires of its supporters, but the majority must accept its conclusions, and in carrying them out becomes well-nigh automatic'[5] Law-making, as another writer observes, has been 'annexed by the government.' To be sure, the houses still have a good deal of opportunity to discuss larger phases of public policy, to bring public opinion to bear upon them, and indeed to help form such public opinion; and it is at this point that they nowadays do their best work. Yet even here the cabinet ordinarily has the great advantage of formulating the problems and setting the stage for debate; sometimes it has so far committed the country to a given course of action that there can be no backing down without stultification; and since questions of policy are almost invariably considered on party lines, the ministers usually have only to convince and satisfy their own pledged supporters. Like most legislatures in cabinet-government countries today, Parliament does not initiate or create, but merely reviews, and usually accepts and registers, policy; 'government by discussion' which Bagehot so fondly described has almost disappeared.

[5] A. L. Lowell, *The Government of England*, Macmillan, 1908. I, 326.

81. THE VOLUME OF LEGISLATION

[*Select Committee on Procedure*. Third Report, H.C. 189 of 1946. Extracts from Memorandum by the Clerk to the House, paras 6–9]

. . . legislation takes up more of the time of the House than either of the other two main functions. Over the last forty years it has on the average occupied not quite half the total time available, and the proportion has remained remarkably constant during the period. In the first part of the period, 1906-13, when the average length of the session was 149 days, 75·7 days were spent on legislation; in the second part of the period, 1919-29, when sessions tended to be shorter (139·9 days on the average) the amount of time spent on legislation fell proportionally to 62·8 days; and in the last part of the period, 1929–38, when sessions became longer again (157·7 days on the average), the average time spent on legislation rose to 79·7 days.

Although the *proportion* of the session spent on legislation remained constant, . . . the volume of legislation per session rose steadily throughout the whole period. In the first part of the period, the average number of pages in the sessional volume of the statute book was 355; in the second part of the period, in spite of shorter sessions and fewer days spent on legislation, an average of 64·8 pages of statutes were passed per session; and in the last part of the period the average rose to 99·5 pages. In other words, the speed of legislation has increased from 4·9 pages per legislation day to 13·5 pages. Thus the volume of legislation increased nearly two and three-quarter times, and this result was possible without increasing the number of days spent on legislation because the speed of legislating increased in the same proportion.

Various causes may have contributed to this result, but so far as procedure is concerned the saving of time has been brought about by extending the use of standing committees and by intensifying such methods of curtailing debate as selection of amendments, the allocation of time (the 'guillotine'), and the closure, though the last-named was used sparingly in the last part of the period.

. . . Sir Gilbert Campion infers that it is hardly possible to save any more of the time of the House by any of the existing methods, and, if more time is to be saved, some radical reform of procedure is necessary.

82. STANDING COMMITTEES AND LEGISLATION

[from K. C. Wheare, *Government by Committee*, Oxford, 1955, pp. 121–122, 128, 129, 132, 135, 153–155]

The standing committees do not receive a bill until the House has decided in favour of its principles by giving it a second reading. The committee is limited in its consideration, therefore, to matters within the principles already decided upon by the House. It is important to bear this restriction in mind. It distinguishes the function of standing committees of the House of Commons in the legislative process in Britain from that permitted to committees in other parliaments, such for example as the American Congress or the French Parliament or indeed of most parliaments on the Continent of Europe. In the United States... and in continental legislatures on the French model, a bill is submitted to a committee of the Parliament for consideration before it has been considered, much less approved of, by the Parliament as a whole. As a result the committee may consider everything in the bill and may propose amendments of principle as well as of detail . . . With the exception of the Scottish Standing Committee—and that is not a substantial exception, for as few as ten members can prevent the bill going to the Scottish Committee at the second-reading stage—the share of committees in the legislative process of the House of Commons is confined to that stage in the process where the principles of the bill have been determined and lie outside the ambit of the committee...

Although officials are present in the committee room they are technically not on the floor of the committee. They do not speak nor may they be questioned by members of the committee. Standing committees have no witnesses. What officials have to say in defence of a bill must be said to the Minister; he must translate or trasmit it to the committee. Similarly, such views about the bill as other experts may hold cannot be placed directly before the committee. They must approach the Minister or the members of the committee individually. This procedure is in contrast not only to the procedure of select committees of inquiry in the House of Commons or of other committees to inquire or to advise in Britain, but also to the procedure of committees to legislate in the United States and in many continental countries, such as France. There it is accepted as an essential part of a committee's consideration of a bill that the views not only of the Minister and his department should be heard but also of others who wish to express an opinion. Considerable time is given over to 'hearings' when experts for and against the measure attempt to influence the committee in evidence. No such procedure is permitted in the standing-committee stage of legislation in Britain.

It may be said to begin with that the standing committees are not specialised committees. That is to say that, unlike the French or American committees, they are not set up at the beginning of a session to deal with specific subjects such as commerce, trade and industry, health, education, foreign relations, and so on. In this respect, too, they differ from the select committees on public accounts, estimates, and statutory instruments, and from the committees set up by local authorities in Britain. Members of a standing committee therefore lack the opportunity to make a continuous study, extending perhaps from one session to another, of a particular branch of policy, as do the members of the select committees just mentioned. Although proposals have been made from time to time that standing committees should have a specialized field allotted to each of them—and a notable suggestion to this end was put forward by the Clerk of the House of Commons, Sir Horace Dawkins, before the Select Committee on Procedure in 1931—the plan has not been adopted. It is interesting to notice, also, that before 1907 the standing committees of the House, and the Grand Committees which preceded them, had always been appointed on a specialist basis. Since that date, however, the procedure is to appoint as many standing committees as are necessary to deal with bills, and to allot bills to them when they are free to take them. The 'lay' or 'neutral' nature of the committees is emphasized or illustrated perhaps, by the fact that committees are distinguished from each other by letters of the alphabet and are known as Committees A, B, C, D, E, and so on . . .

The standing committees of the House of Commons, then,

are not specialized committees in the sense of being committees set up to deal with bills relating to particular fields of governmental activity, as are the committees of the United States Congress and of many continental parliaments. But it would be a mistake to conclude from this that the standing committees contain no members with special knowledge of or interest in the subject of the bill which is referred to them for consideration, or that if any members should have such special knowledge or interest, their presence on the committee is purely a matter of chance . . .

The committees by adjusting their membership to members' interests give much more scope to special knowledge and interest than might seem possible at first sight. In fact, one might say that the essential contrast between the British system of committees and the American and French systems in the matter of bringing special knowledge and interest to bear on bills is that whereas in the French and American systems the bills go to the members with special knowledge and interest, in the British system the members with special knowledge and interest go to the bills, pursuing them to the committees to which Mr Speaker has referred them . . .

It might be added that the Opposition's labours in standing committees are conducted without much hope of reward or success, for they can never expect, if the government has a workable majority, to carry an amendment against the government.[6] But it would be wrong to judge proceedings in standing committees by the number of times the Opposition fails to carry a division. It should be remembered that many of the amendments put down by the Opposition are put down in order to obtain information or assurances or explanations from the Minister, and are withdrawn when his statement has been made. On some occasions an Opposition amendment is accepted. On other occasions, a minister will refuse to accept an amendment but will undertake to reconsider the matter and propose an amendment on the report stage. On many occasions, the Opposition's amendment is clearly unacceptable to the Minister and is moved and resisted in order to bring into the open the difference of political opinion which is involved. It must be

[6] It happens occasionally. In the session 1953–4 the government was defeated twice in Standing Committee A on the Mines and Quarries Bill.

emphasized always that the standing committees like the House itself are party organizations; they are based on the principle of party government. If the government cannot command a majority in the House or in the Committee something is wrong. If it continues in this state for long, it should resign and make way for others. On British parliamentary principles, it is not merely the usual thing but also the normal thing for the government to win.

But it is sometimes asked whether party discipline could not be relaxed a little in standing committee. Should not the government be prepared to accept amendments there more freely than, as a rule, it is? It may be admitted that there is a tendency for governments to be too rigid in refusing to reconsider their proposals, though this differs a good deal from one minister to another. On the other hand, if controversial bills are to be taken in standing committee, it cannot often happen that a government will be able to give way on a point of importance, at any rate to the Opposition's criticism. It may find itself obliged to modify a bill in response to the complaints of members on its own side. But this rigidity and unwillingness to accept amendments applies throughout the stages of legislation in modern Britain, and it is possible that if amendments were accepted in standing committee, they might be rejected later in the whole House at report stage. The strength of Whitehall has no doubt some effect upon this also. The combination of strong party discipline with strong official support for a minister makes it relatively easy for him to refuse to give way. He can be supplied with an armoury of arguments with which to resist every criticism that is made. Yet considered as a whole it seems fair to say that the proceedings in standing committee, little as they may change a bill in important details, ensure a reasoned defence of it and reasoned criticism of it. They are seldom if ever, reduced to mere voting machines, nor is the government's majority used with cynical disregard of the Opposition's case. Both government and opposition behave responsibly—and indeed it may be suggested that for the efficacy of standing committee proceedings a responsible Opposition is even more important than a responsible government. Standing committees provide a valuable element in the British system of government by discussion.

83. MORE COMMITTEES FOR LEGISLATION?

[*Select Committee on Procedure*, H.C. 161 of 1931. Extracts from evidence of Rt. Hon. David Lloyd George. Questioned by Mr Hore-Belisha 937–938]

You think every Bill ought to be sent upstairs to a small Committee?—Yes, I have absolutely no doubt about that.

Except the major Bills?—Yes . . . my suggestion is that you should have many more Committees. You would have Committees, first of all, to deal with administration. You would have Committees to deal with legislation, and then one Member would say: 'I am a Member of the Budget Committee or the Finance Committee'; another Member would say: 'I am a Member of the Committee which deals with the defence of this country'; and so on. There is no doubt at all that it gives an absolutely new status to a Member, and enables you go give him a blue ribbon without making him a Member of the Administration . . .

84. SPECIALIST COMMITTEES ON LEGISLATION?

[*Select Committee on Procedure*, Third Report, H.C. 189, 1946. Extracts from evidence of the Right Hon. Herbert Morrison, M.P., Lord President of the Council. Questioned by Mr. Messer, para. 134]

Now, as to the matter of specialisation of members, I think that the principle which now obtains, whereby there is a Committee A, B, C, and so on, with a number of members on it to which a number of members are added who want to go on, or are supposed to have special knowledge and probably very often have special knowledge about it, is right. But I would not myself favour the principle that you tried to turn the Standing Committees into specialists on a Bill. I think a lot of long-haired planners on a Town Planning Bill, all of them long-haired, would be a dreadful thing. A substantial body of commonsense citizens would be a good thing. I think a body of 100 per cent educationists on an Education Bill would be a dreadful thing, or a body of doctors on a Health Bill. The great quality of

Parliament is the quality of sense, of average intelligence, exammining into these matters, being a sort of Jury, and I do not favour the specialist committee too much; but a specialist element on a Committee is a good thing . . .

85. ANOTHER VIEW ON SPECIALIST COMMITTEES

[from K. C. Wheare, *Government by Committee*, Oxford, 1955, pp. 157 sq.q.]

It is worth while to add, perhaps, that some criticisms of specialized standing committees, based upon experience of them in foreign parliaments, should not be accepted as inevitably applicable to Britain. This is true particularly of the assertion that a system of specialized standing committees is likely to weaken the control by the government over the House of Commons. This assertion appears to be based upon the experience of the French Parliament and the American Congress particularly. It may be conceded that in France and the United States the committees do weaken the government, but they weaken a government which is already inherently weak in its relation to the legislature. The committees provide, indeed, just one more illustration of the weakness of these executives. The weakness of the French Executive is primarily the result of the French party system—a system which itself is not easily explained—and the weakness of the American Executive is the result of the independence of Congress, which enables it to defy the Executive if it chooses. There can be no doubt whatever that if a system of specialized standing committees were set up in Britain and were composed in proportion to the party strengthens in the House, the government would control the committees, just as it controls the House. If its majority in the House were small, the business of controlling the committees would be all the more difficult; but it would not be more difficult than it is under a system of non-specialized standing committees. Governments with small majorities will always be reluctant to use standing committees where a majority of one or two is very difficult to keep in being. But specialization will not make the difficulties any greater. It must be remembered also that French and American committees deal with administrative matters, which gives scope to harry the Executive that is not possible when legislation only is under consideration.

The case against specialized standing committees cannot be founded upon any supposed weakening of the Executive's control over Parliament. Nor should it be based upon some extreme dogma of the infallibility of the layman, which would frown upon those with special knowledge finding their way on to committees dealing with matters which they understood. On the contrary, it would seem that the British system, with its flexible provisions for adding and removing members to and from a committee in respect of a given bill, does in practice give considerable opportunities for members to get on to committees for bills about which they know something. The discussion comes down in the end to a question of which is the better method for ensuring that the greatest use is made of members' knowledge while at the same time making it possible for all members who wish it to acquire some specialized knowledge. Under the British system no member need be relegated for a whole Parliament to an obscure field of public affairs; he has a chance of getting on to a committee dealing with an interesting bill. It is true that the process of steady education which specialized committees can provide is not ensured in the British system, but at the same time there are greater opportunities for using and acquiring specialized knowledge than are often realized. On balance it may be doubted whether a change to the specialized system would be an advantage.

86. SCRUTINY OF DELEGATED LEGISLATION—A WASTE OF TIME?

[*Committee on Ministers' Powers* 1932. Cmd. 4060. Extracts from evidence of Sir Maurice Gwyer, H.M. Procurator General and Treasury Solicitor. Questioned by Professor H. J. Laski, paras 562–564]

Have you thought at all whether the suggestion that has been made from time to time by Members of Parliament and others—consideration of these rules by a Committee or a Joint Committee of the two Houses—would be a valuable way of assuring that Parliamentary attention was drawn to them, in the light of the fact that they are made under powers given by Parliament?—

I have only considered the question to this extent. It seems to me quite impossible for any Committee to get through the work within any reasonable limits of time.

Supposing instead of a single Committee, or a single Joint Committee, you grouped the different Ministries in some way according to their functions, and had Committees to deal with groups of subjects. Do you think it would be possible then on the point of time?—I am rather doubtful about it. But what I feel about any such suggestion is that a large bulk of these rules are very small stuff indeed, and I really think that Parliament has many more important things to occupy the attention of its Members. I think the real remedy is that if Parliament does not like something that a Minister does, it should tell him so, and take care that he does not do it again. I think it would really be a great waste of time for Members of Parliament to go through a great deal of the stuff which appears in a year's volume of the Statutory Rules and Orders.

As an entire outsider, both to Parliament and Ministries, may I put the kind of problem that a layman like myself feels when you say that Parliament when it objects to what the Minister has done, should tell him so? Can, in fact, Parliament seriously tell a Minister that it does object, in such a way that a Minister will always take care, without turning the Government out?—You put a point that I have thought a great deal about lately. I say it with a good deal of hesitation, but I think that there is more difficulty about doing that than, according to the theory of the Constitution, there ought to be. I think it is more difficult now than it was sixty years ago . . .

87. DELEGATED LEGISLATION—SERIOUS APPREHENSION?

[from L. S. Amery, *Thoughts on the Constitution*, Oxford, 1947, pp. 50–52]

Far more controversial is the question of how far the time of Parliament has been or should be saved by taking the details of legislation out of its hands altogether and leaving them to be dealt with under Orders in Council, Provisional Orders or Regulations by Ministers—in other words by civil servants. Much of our social and economic legislation covers so vast and detailed a field that no statute, however, cumbrous—and many of them are already cumbrous and unintelligible enough—could possibly provide for all contingencies. Some power of ministerial variation or interpretation is obviously necessary, subject to the attention of Parliament being drawn to what is being done. In war the need to give Government the widest powers to regulate the activities of its citizens and to provide for continually varying emergencies is such that parliamentary legislation can only provide the framework of principle and leave the detail to be covered by regulations.

But delegated legislation of this type has developed to an extent which has created serious apprehension. A Select Committee of the House of Commons was recently set up to examine these orders, rules, and regulations and, without discussing their merits, to call attention to those which seem to demand particular scrutiny. What is of particular importance in this connexion is to distinguish between the orders which should merely 'lie on the table' and those to which the special attention of the House should be directed by requiring positive confirmation. As the total number of these orders in 1942 reached the figure of 2,937, while 1,744 were issued in the eleven months ending last June, the Committee has found itself almost over-whelmed by the task. One member complained not long ago that the agenda for a single meeting weighed one pound seven ounces.

But it is not merely the spate of these regulations that gives cause for anxiety. It is even more the extent to which they tend to supersede law in the ordinary sense by ministerial edicts which, covered by statute, are not open to question by the Courts, or by ministerially appointed tribunals from which there is no appeal . . . The whole question was examined by the Committee on Ministers' Powers which reported in 1932. It concluded that there was nothing radically wrong in the exercise of judicial or quasi-judicial powers by Ministers and of judicial powers by ministerial tribunals, but that the practice was capable of abuse and that certain safeguards were essential if the rule of Law and the liberty of the subject were to be maintained. The subject is too technical for me to discuss the Committee's suggestions or the extent to which they have, in fact, been always complied with.

88. OPPORTUNITIES TO DISCUSS DELEGATED LEGISLATION

[*Select Committee on Procedure*, Third Report, H.C. 189 of 1946. Extracts from Report, paras 25–30]

While the time spent on discussing administrative detail in the House has decreased, the field of administration itself has steadily increased. Much modern legislation is of an administrative character. Moreover, an increasing number of statutes confer upon a Minister or some other authority power to legislate upon matters of administrative detail. How great this field of administrative activity has grown is indicated by the fact that Statutory Rules and Orders . . . exceed in volume the annual output of statutes. Leaving out of account the war years as exceptional, the number of Statutory Rules and Orders registered in 1937 was 1,231, in 1938 1,661 and in 1945, 1,706.

The form of parliamentary control applicable to a Statutory Instrument is laid down by the Act under which it is made. For the great majority of Instruments, the governing Act provides no parliamentary control at all. In the year 1944, 291 Instruments, out of a total of 1,483 registered, were subject or liable to parliamentary proceedings.

Parliamentary control, where it is provided, broadly stated, may take one of two forms. Either the Instrument has to be confirmed by a resolution of both Houses (sometimes by the House of Commons alone); or the Instrument remains in force unless a motion to annul it is carried by either House within a period prescribed by the Act. In either case the proceedings are exempted business and are usually taken at the end of the day.

Thus, apart from the relatively few Instruments which require an affirmative resolution, only those in which a Member may discover cause for objection are discussed in the House. Until 1944, there was no provision for systematically scrutinising Instruments. In that year the Select Committee on Statutory Rules and Orders, etc. was set up . . .

. . . —the opportunities for discussing delegated legislation in the House are extremely limited and not altogether satisfactory. On an average the actual time so spent has amounted to the equivalent of 1·6 days per session. In view of this fact and in view of the impossibility of finding much more time for the discussion of Statutory Instruments in the House, Sir Gilbert Campion suggests that part of the task of supervising this form of administrative activity might suitably be entrusted to a select committee. He suggests that the existing Select Committee on Statutory Rules and Orders, etc., might be empowered to consider and report on any Statutory Instrument in force from the point of view of its efficiency as a means of carrying out the purposes named by the governing Act. Such a Committee would be precluded by its terms of reference from criticising the policy of the Act under which the Instrument was made. Its task would be to inform itself of the various practical considerations which the responsible Departmental officers had in mind in framing the Instrument and on the basis of this information to consider whether the Instrument was well designed for its purpose and whether the method chosen was the least injurious to the rights of the citizen ...

Sir Gilbert Campion's proposal would go some way to supplement the inadequate and unsatisfactory opportunities which the House at present possesses for exercising, its control over one aspect of administration. Your Committee consider, however, that the delegation of legislative power raises issues beyond the scope of the present investigation ...

89. DELEGATED LEGISLATION INESCAPABLE

[from H. J. Laski, *Reflections on the Constitution*, Manchester U.P., 1951, pp. 42–44]

The growth of delegated legislation, with its consequential expansion of the sphere of administrative law, has evoked, I am well aware, loud indignation from the Bench and the Bar, and piteous cries from a number of members, most of them also in fact lawyers, that the rule of law no longer has any real meaning in Great Britain, and that the House of Commons has been compelled to transfer a large part of its authority to the Departments whose use of what is, in fact, the power to legislate is so exercised to prevent the proper Parliamentary scrutiny of the use made of delegation. An irresponsible Lord Chief Justice, like Lord Hewart, and an academic lawyer whose hatred of change is even greater than his persuasive rhetoric, like Dr C. K. Allen, are only the best-known names in a dramatic rearguard action that has been fought for many years now against a phantom army of bureaucrats lusting for power which has never had any existence outside the imagination of those who warn us of impending doom and disaster. I can remember vividly that, when I was a member of the Committee on Ministers' Powers, I watched my colleague on that body, the eminent legal historian, Sir William Holdsworth, watching every witness from the Civil Service with anxious care to see if he could detect in the official mind a desire to amplify its jurisdiction beyond what was fit and proper. I do not think I am guilty of exaggeration if I say that the climate of Sir William Holdsworth's thinking did not lead him to regard radical innovation, whether against the historic supremacy of Parliament, or against the sacred right of the judges to interpret statutes, with anything that could fairly be called enthusiastic affection; I doubt, indeed, if I should go beyond the mark if I said, that, for him, the Common Law had passed the zenith of its perfection if not with Mansfield, then certainly with Eldon. Yet at no point did it ever occur to Holdsworth to dissent from our *Report* which, whatever its weaknesses, did forthrightly conclude that delegated legislation is quite inescapable, and that there is no effective evidence to suggest that the Departments are seeking to abuse the rule-making powers which have thus been put into their hands.

Anyone who is sceptical of these conclusions might, before he rushes to hasty denunciation, peruse, and seek to answer, the two books, as learned as they are delightful, into which Sir Cecil Carr has distilled the quintessence of his incomparable experience. There is no need for me to traverse the ground which not only he has covered so admirably but which has been mapped, after the closest scrutiny, both of geological detail, and of natural and established fauna and flora, by my friends Professor W. S. Robson and Sir Ivor Jennings. On the side of this problem that concerns the delegation of rule-making powers, there are four simple facts that I wish merely to note. First, I would emphasise that the habit of delegation is not new; the House of Commons has not hesitated to use it any time in this last century and a quarter when it seemed clear that it was a convenient way of operating a statute efficiently. Second, the so-called 'Henry VIII Clause' about which the critics have written as though it were the fount and origin of original sin, has not been employed a score of times altogether, and then quite unexceptionably either to bring a complex statute into efficient life, or to alter some minor detail which, on Departmental consideration might have made it more difficult to give full effect at the proper time to the announced will of Parliament. Third, it is remarkable to note that, except in emergency cases like an outbreak of foot-and-mouth disease, care is taken by the Departments to see that no Order or Rule is made until they have consulted every possible interest—and a good many impossible ones—affected by its promulgation. Fourthly, the House has not only the safeguard of the Select Committee which examines all proposed Orders and regulations; it has also the protection that the Act may require a confirmatory resolution to give effect to the use of the delegated power, or, save for emergency cases, it may require the proposed regulation to lie on the table of the House for periods that vary from twenty-eight to 120 days. I know that many members of Parliament say, often with great warmth, that they cannot hope to prevail by means of a 'prayer' against a regulation they dislike in a thin House, with the Whips on, and all of those present except the praying member himself anxious for nothing so much as the chance to go home as quickly as possible; but, I think the sufficient answer is that, after the brief debate on the prayer, it is the rarest possible occurrence for the very member who moves it to refer to the matter again. He has done what he was asked to do by those who brought the matter to his notice; and having satisfied them of his energy and zeal in their service, he turns to other matters which he almost certainly regards of outstandingly greater importance.

90. ALL STATUTORY INSTRUMENTS ARE CHALLENGEABLE

[from Morrison, *Government and Parliament*, O.U.P., 1954 pp. 152–153]

Statutory Instruments do not have to go through the same lengthy process as an Act of Parliament before they become law. They are, however, subject to a measure of parliamentary control. With particularly important Regulations, it is customary for Parliament to stipulate that the Government cannot act under such authority until the proposed Regulations have been submitted in draft to both Houses, and have been approved by affirmative resolutions. In most cases, however, the Minister can make the Regulations and bring them into force, but either House of Parliament can within forty sitting days challenge them by a Motion praying Her Majesty to annul them, and if either House passes a Motion to this effect the Regulation is null and void and cannot be further acted upon. These Motions are known as Prayers, and are quite frequently moved, sometimes to get information without the intention of pressing them to a division, and sometimes to give a straight challenge ending in a division. Regulations in a third group, quite minor ones, need only be laid on the Table and that is the last that is heard of them in the House (if indeed that is heard), unless an M.P. raises the matter by Question and possibly on the Adjournment or otherwise thereafter.

All Statutory Instruments, therefore, are challengeable in some form or other, so that Parliament is in a position to assert itself both at the time the authorizing legislation is under consideration and at the time the Regulations are proposed or after they are made. The missing element over which argument frequently takes place is that Parliament has no means to amend a proposed Statutory Instrument, only to pass or reject it.

If the two Houses of Parliament were to have the power to amend a Statutory Instrument, it would be difficult not to go through all or most of the stages of legislation again, and then all the details might just as well have been put in the Statute itself. There is more to be said for the proposal to give a Select Committee power to revise and amend, though it is difficult to see how these powers could be completely delegated to a committee without giving Parliament the right to consider and revise the revisions or to restore the Statutory Instrument to its original form on the Floor of the House (or Houses) at what would constitute something in the nature of a Report Stage. So that the idea is not easy either.

91. THE SCRUTINY COMMITTEE

[Ernest H. Beet, Parliament and Delegated Legislation, 1945–53, *Public Administration*, XXXIII, 1955, Extract, pp. 331–332]

This survey would not be complete without some evaluation of the work of the Scrutiny Committee. A study of its reports and special reports provides the clearest evidence of the meticulous care with which every S.I. is examined by the Committee, ably advised and assisted by Sir Cecil Carr. Most S.I.s reported for serious faults were debated, though one would wish this to be the almost invariable rule. It seems a little surprising that the one order in all this time which imposed a charge on the public revenues was not debated. The influence of the Committee has led to a number of useful procedural reforms, e.g. the signing of S.I.s at proof stage, not in typescript, and the issue with S.I.s of more adequate explanatory notes. In other matters—such as over the use of the 'all other powers' clause—it has been less successful.

One important suggestion made for improving the Committee's work is to give it power to examine S.I.s on the ground of merit. Members of the Committee itself have always resisted this proposal, both because of the weight of work involved, and through fear of the Committee being drawn from its non-partisan quasi-judicial approach into the vortex of party politics. The record shows consistent care in remaining within the terms of reference, though on occasion the boundary of merits has been trodden. The Committee's own objections seem (to this writer at least) conclusive; the Committee is not concerned with a field of administration as is the Estimates Committee, but with a constant stream of fresh material from many spheres, and to try to estimate merits would be an impossible task. The Committee has a salutary affect on Departments and it would seem a great risk to alter, in the way suggested, its terms of reference. (This is not to deny the strength of the argument for an overhaul of Parliamentary procedure; it is only to assert that there is everything to be said for a Scrutiny Committee as it stands.)

The conclusion which emerges from this inquiry, is that Parliamentary knowledge of, and action on, delegated legislation, is probably somewhat greater than many critics suggest. In the period reviewed, almost one in ten of all S.I.s examined by the Scrutiny Committee was subjected to some form of discussion in Parliament. Nevertheless, the system of control is far from adequate. Much might be done by an extension of the affirmative procedure. Other reforms of machinery are possible. But lack of time remains as the main enemy and the finding of extra time as the greatest problem.

PART IX
Finance

92. PARLIAMENT AND FINANCE

[from J. S. Mill, *Representative Government*, Everyman's Edition, 1910, p. 230]

The duty which is considered as belonging more peculiarly than any other to an assembly representative of the people, is that of voting the taxes. Nevertheless, in no country does the representative body undertake, by itself or its delegated officers, to prepare the estimates. Though the supplies can only be voted by the House of Commons, and though the sanction of the House, is also required for the appropriation of the revenues to the different items of the public expenditure, it is the maxim and the uniform practice of the Constitution that money can be granted only on the proposition of the Crown. It has, no doubt, been felt that moderation as to the amount, and care and judgment in the detail of its application, can only be expected when the executive government, through whose hands it is to pass, is made responsible for the plans and calculations on which the disbursements are grounded. Parliament, accordingly, is not expected, nor even permitted to originate directly either taxation or expenditure. All it is asked for is its consent, and the sole power it possesses is that of refusal.

93. THE HOUSE HAS NO SPECIAL FINANCIAL FUNCTIONS

[from Walter Bagehot, *The English Constitution*, Fontana Library, ed. 1963, pp. 154–155]

Some persons will perhaps think that I ought to enumerate a sixth function of the House of Commons—a financial function.

But I do not consider that, upon broad principle, and omitting legal technicalities, the House of Commons has any special function with regard to financial different from its functions with respect to other legislation. It is to rule in both, and to rule in both through the Cabinet. Financial legislation is of necessity a yearly recurring legislation; but frequency of occurrence does not indicate a diversity of nature or compel an antagonism of treatment.

In truth, the principal peculiarity of the House of Commons in financial affairs is nowadays not a special privilege, but an exceptional disability. On common subjects any member can propose anything, but not on money—the Minister only can propose to tax the people. This principle is commonly involved in mediaeval metaphysics as to the prerogative of the Crown, but it is as useful in the nineteenth century as in the fourteenth, and rests on as sure a principle. The House of Commons—now that it is the true sovereign, and appoints the real executive—has long ceased to be the checking, sparing economical body it once was. It now is more apt to spend money than the Minister of the day. I have heard a very experienced financier say, 'If you want to raise a certain cheer in the House of Commons make a general panegyric on economy; if you want to invite a sure defeat, propose a particular saving'. The process is simple. Every expenditure of public money has some apparent public object; those who wish to spend the money expatiate on that object; they say, 'What is £50,000 to this great country? Is this a time for cheeseparing objection? Our industry was never so productive; our resources never so immense. What is £50,000 in comparison with this great national interest?' The members who are for the expenditure always come down; perhaps a constituent or a friend who will profit by the outlay, or is keen on the object, has asked them to attend; and any rate, there is a popular vote to be given, on which the newspapers—always philanthropic and sometimes talked over—will be sure to make encomiums. The members against the expenditure rarely come down of themselves; why should they become unpopular without reason? The object seems decent; many of its advocates are certainly sincere: a hostile vote will make enemies, and be censured by the journals. If there were not some check, the 'people's house' would soon outrun the people's money.

That check is the responsibility of the Cabinet for the national finance. If any one could propose a tax, they might let the House spend it as it would, and wash their hands of the matter; but now, for whatever expenditure is sanctioned—even when it is sanctioned against the Ministry's wish—the Ministry must find the money. Accordingly, they have the strongest motive to oppose extra outlay. They will have to pay the bill for it; they will have to impose taxation, which is always disagreeable, or suggest loans, which, under ordinary circumstances, are shameful. The Ministry is (so to speak) the bread-winner of the political family, and has to meet the cost of philanthropy and glory, just as the head of a family has to pay for the charities of his wife and the toilette of his daughters.

In truth, when a Cabinet is made the sole executive, it follows it must have the sole financial charge, for all action costs money, all policy depends on money, and it is in adjusting the relative goodness of action and policies that the executive is employed.

94. REFUSAL OF SUPPLIES A 'CONSTITUTIONAL FIGMENT'

[from Sir Sidney Low, *The Governance of England*, Allen and Unwin, 1904, pp. 89–91]

Mr. Bryce[1] tells us that 'the House of Commons is strong because it can call the Ministry to account for every act, or by refusing supplies, compel their resignation.' But the refusal of supplies is a constitutional figment. 'The ultimate legal sanction,' says Sir William Anson,[2] 'which the House of Commons could bring to bear on a Ministry of which it disapproves, the refusal to pass the Mutiny Act or grant supplies, has never in fact been applied.' And even if the House were willing to take this course, it could not do so, unless it were ready to turn out a Ministry; that is, unless the majority would consent to defeat itself and allow a triumph to its rivals. Nothing can be better in form than the separation between the functions of the Committee of Supply, and the manner in which the Estimates are brought in, presented, and discussed. But in practice the control

[1] *The American Commonwealth*, i. 266.

[2] *Law and Custom of the Constitution*, i. 130.

of the House is largely inoperative; first because of the feverish scuffle against time, which forbids deliberate and prolonged examination of detail; and secondly, because a serious attempt to refuse a Vote, or alter an item in an account, can usually be foiled by setting the party machinery to work. A strong Unionist and Anglican would be reluctant to instal in power a government of Home Rulers and patrons of the Nonconformist conscience, because he wished to prevent an isolated piece of extravagance in the War Office or the Admiralty.

The province of private members in regard to finance is limited to criticism, and there are special reasons why such criticism should be ineffective. The details are often highly technical, and most members are ignorant of the complicated questions which arise in connection with the financial and departmental measures presented to them. Debate on these subjects is almost abandoned to the handful of experts, who are too few in numbers and too little influential with the outside public, to be able to force their views on unwilling ministers.

Who is not familiar with the farce of a debate on the Army or the Navy in Committee? Millions are voted away, vital questions of Imperial importance are discussed and disposed of, in the presence of a minister and an under-secretary or two, an ex-First Lord, a couple of thoughtful hobbyists, and a dozen or so of growling colonels and grumbling captains. The bulk of the House—busy, fatigued, bored and idle—is out at dinner, or on the terrace, or in the smoking-room; its members will come and vote if required, but otherwise will know no more of the debate than the newspaper readers, who will glance languidly the next morning over the array of unintelligible figures and unimpressive names. Here, again, the function of the House of Commons is no longer active. Other organs could, and in point of fact do, supply its place. Which would command the more attention—a speech on some military or naval topic, in Committee of the House of Commons: or a letter in large type in the newspapers, by a public man who is a recognised authority on the subject? Several times, in recent years, it has been shown that it is far easier to compel a Government to change its naval or military policy, as the result of a 'scare,' or an agitation got up in the press, than by means of votes and speeches in Parliament.

95. SUPPLY—A MEANS OF CRITICISM

[from Laurence Lowell, *The Government of England*, Macmillan, 1908, Vol. I, pp. 343–345]

In proposing his new procedure for supply in 1896, Mr Balfour spoke of the belief that the object of debating the appropriations is to secure economical administration, as an ancient superstition no longer at all true. Members, he said, now move reductions in order to get from ministers a promise of future increase; and the danger is that the House will urge too much extravagance. He insisted that the real object of the Committee of Supply is the chance it affords to private members of criticising the executive and administrative action of the government; that it is an open platform for members, where the ministers, for the sake of getting their appropriations passed, are bound to keep a quorum. This is, indeed, manifest to any one familiar with the debates upon the estimates. They are not to any great extent discussions of financial questions, of what the nation can, or cannot, afford to do. They are a long series of criticisms upon the policy of the ministers, and the conduct of the departments under their control. From this point of view Mr Balfour suggested a method of making the debates more valuable. He described the futility of the old system of taking up the estimates in their numerical order, pointing out how much time was wasted every year in discussing the earlier votes in Class I.,—repairs of royal palaces, etc.,—while some of the largest appropriations were always hurried through with little comment at the fag end of the session. He promised in future to bring forward the important votes in the earlier part of the year, and in fact to give precedence to estimates that any group of members might wish to discuss.

Adding together the days regularly allotted to supply under the standing order, the additional sittings used for the purpose, and those devoted to supplementary estimates, the better part of more than thirty days are spent every year in Committee of Supply. This would appear to give time enough for a thorough overhauling of many branches of the administration; and under Mr Balfour's practice, which will, no doubt, be followed by future cabinets, the question what departments shall be examined is determined by the critics themselves.

96. MINISTERIAL CONTROL OF FINANCE

[from F. A. Ogg, *English Government and Politics*, Macmillan, 2nd ed., 1936, p. 450]

In the broad field of finance, control by the ministers is more absolute still, because, as we have seen the House of Commons will give no consideration at all to any request for money that does not come from, or at all events with the express approval of the crown—which means, the cabinet. Indeed, its consideration of even these proposals is often a mere matter of form. Granting of supply has so far lost its earlier importance as a check of the legislature upon the executive that, as we have seen, millions of pounds, are voted every year with no debate whatever, even in committee of the whole. It is true that most of the restrictions mentioned arise from rules which the House of Commons has itself made, and that they could be thrown off by simple amendment of the standing orders. But the point is that even these regulations—including the whole body of rules relating to closure—have, in effect, been dictated by the cabinet, which could be depended upon to offer successful resistance to any effort to relax them.

97. WATCHING OVER THE EXPENDITURE—THE LEAST EFFICIENTLY PERFORMED FUNCTION

[from L. S. Amery, *Thoughts on the Constitution*, O.U.P., 1947, pp. 52–53]

One longstanding criticism of the work of the House is that its original and unique task of watching over expenditure is the least efficiently performed, if, indeed, it can be said to be performed at all. A committee which reported in 1918 on control over estimates pointed out that there had not been a single case in twenty-five years in which an estimate had been reduced on financial grounds, and that 'so far as the direct effective control of proposals for expenditure is concerned there would be no noticeable difference if estimates were never presented'. The twenty supply days of the session are, in fact, selected by the Opposition to raise issues of policy; rightly in my opinion, for policy comes first and governs expenditure. Nor is the House, as a body, capable of judging whether the actual execution of the policy which it approves is being economically conducted. Personally I doubt whether much can be achieved in this direction beyond the useful work already done by the Select Committee on Estimates. The real remedy seems to me to lie in the nature of the Estimates themselves and of our budget system as a whole and to come within the sphere of government itself.

98. FINANCIAL CONTROL NOT A SEPARATE AND SPECIAL FUNCTION

[from H. J. Laski, *Parliamentary Government in England*, Allen and Unwin, 1938. pp. 145–146]

It will be noted that I have assumed here that the examination and control of *finance* is not a separate and special function of the House of Commons; properly regarded, I believe that to be the case. Finance is not something apart from policy, but an expression of it. By deciding what to do in other spheres, the House largely decides by inference what it is to do in the financial sphere. Of course, the Chancellor of the Exchequer must cut a big figure in the House—after the Prime Minister, perhaps the biggest figure. But most of what he does is, in fact, less subject to, or, indeed, capable of scrutiny than what is done by most of his colleagues. A big body like the House of Commons cannot discuss estimates; it can only concern itself with the general policy which lies behind estimates. Members can say 'we wish more were being spent on secondary education'; they cannot usefully say in debate, save by way of general illustration, that more money ought to have been provided for nursery schools in Essex. That will interest, whether by attraction or repulsion, the members for Essex constituencies; but the members for Lancashire or Glamorgan will soon begin to protest that the House does not exist to spend its precious hours upon the particular grievances of one part of the country. If the House of Commons is ever to look at estimates seriously, from the sheer aspect of financial adequacy, it will have to develop organs for their examination quite different from any it now possesses.

The same applies to the problem of ways and means. A discussion of the Budget can never, in the whole House, be much more than a close application of the general principles of taxation to the Chancellor's proposals. He can be urged to recognize that he has set the income tax too high, or that he is not taxing millionaires enough. He can be warned, with graphic illustration, that he is placing too large a burden on the food of the people. It can be insisted that his duties on motor-cars discourage the production of the kind of vehicle likely to penetrate the foreign market. He can be urged to remember that he has a fruitful source of neglected revenue in the taxation of urban land values. Members can be eloquent upon his characteristic tenderness to the farming interest. He can be warned that he is depending too much on raising money by way of loan, and not enough, in proportion, by way of taxes. But however skilful and knowledgeable the criticism he receives, its real impact, in a miscellaneous assembly, is bound to be general, and not specific in character. He has to retain the control of major outlines in his own hands. The alternative is legislation by the chamber itself, and the experience of both France and the United States suggests comprehensively that this will mean bad legislation. The responsibility of a committee for the construction of a Budget is too diffuse to give it either the unity or the coherence that are requisite. Again, it is possible that, with different organs of control from any it now possesses, the House of Commons might be able to assert its primacy over the Chancellor. We may doubt whether, if it did, that would mean a better financial system. But it does not possess them; and their absence means that either the Budget must be his Budget, in whatever form he is ultimately willing to accept responsibility for it, or it must obtain another Chancellor and, in all probability another Government. It is normally unwilling to take this step; and this, in effect, means both that its dislike of his general financial methods must be part of any case it makes, through the Opposition, against the Government; and that the real verdict will subsequently be delivered by the electorate at the polls.

99. A PRE-NATAL CONTROL OVER ESTIMATES?

[from H. J. Laski, *Reflections on the Constitution*, Manchester U.P., 1951, pp. 38–42]

I cannot . . . agree that the House of Commons should exercise a pre-natal control over Estimates and I find it easy to understand why the Committee on Estimates from which, a generation ago, some members hoped so much, has, in fact, been an obvious failure.[3] In the first place, Estimates are the reflection of policy, and the making of policy is the function of the Cabinet which seeks approval for what it proposes from the House. Once you give a committee or committees of the House any serious right to investigate Estimates, you take away from the Cabinet and from the Department the responsibility that is properly theirs. That can be seen by examining the parallel process in the United States Congress. There, in both Houses, a series of Committees examine, with what is often minute particularity, the proposals of each Department, not least in their financial aspects. They may make a cut here by the removal of some item they do not like . . . Or they may insert an item by a process of give and take between members of a particular Committee which the Department itself feels to be quite unnecessary; it would be interesting to know how many federal buildings are due not to governmental needs but to the insistence of some powerful member of the Committee that in the process of general endowment his particular bailiwick should not be overlooked. Finance and policy cannot really be separated from each other; and the Estimates Committee, even with its sub-committees, can neither cover the range of the Departments, nor hope to change seriously the mind of a Minister who knows that he has the backing of a Cabinet which, in its turn, knows that, in the last instance, it can rely upon the support of a majority in the House of Commons. To make the Estimates Committee a really successful instrument of control, it would need, first of all, an official with a status like that of the Comptroller and Auditor-General, with a staff at his disposal with the experience of the Treasury, which could count on receiving Departmental Estimates sufficiently early to be able to have examined them

[3] Since 1947 the S.C.E., in fact, has done much useful work.

fully, and to have discussed them at length with the Minister and his officials in time for these to reshape them in the light of such discussion before they were finally presented to the House of Commons. Not only, as I believe, is this administratively imposible, but it would eat both into the Minister's time and responsibility in a way that would, in the long run, alter the relations of legislature and executive quite fundamentally. I know nothing to suggest that this alteration is possible; and, if it were, I know nothing to suggest that it is desirable. And were it to be adopted in any thorough-going way, it would involve very grave and questionable changes in the whole ethos of Parliamentary government.

A wise House of Commons, therefore, will, in my view, be satisfied with the post-natal control it exercises through the Public Accounts Committee, and that vital officer of the House, the Comptroller and Auditor-General. The fact that the latter is independent of the Departments, that his scrutiny cuts deep and commands wide respect, that he has, so to say, the visible authority of the House behind him, gives him a mandate the power of which makes his rulings, decisions, and suggestions, matters which the Treasury will see are fully honoured by the different Departments. The reports of the Committee command great weight also; and there is massive evidence to show that none of its conclusions go unattended, and that many of its proposals will be put into operation after the Treasury has convinced itself that they are workable. There is no external check upon Departmental habits which renders officials more scrupulous in the economies that make wise spending. For, first of all, they know that the Committee's investigation will have been built upon a careful scrutiny of the evidence. They know, in the second place, that full publicity will be given to its findings, so that if they are denounced as guilty of grievous error, they will get into trouble not only with the House, but, in all likelihood, with their own Minister, and the Treasury, as well; that they will have to find an answer to the Committee's charges; and that they may well have to change traditional routines in order to satisfy their critics. It is, no doubt true that the Committee is only able to cover a small area of the national expenditure in each year; but there is obviously a healthy respect for its operations even among the most eminent civil servants whose long careers tempt them to regard the outwardly majestic procession of their Ministers as in fact hardly more than a march of transient and embarrassed marionettes, whom the eminent civil servants themselves move in the proper direction. Anyone who doubts all this, and is tempted to regard the House of Commons, as an eminent Professor [Ramsay Muir] of this University regarded it, as a minor dependency of the Cabinet, a frustrated chorus of voices unable to choose its own songs, even when it was permitted to sing at all, ought to read, first of all, the remarkable Ninth Report of the Select Committee on National Expenditure in the first World War, and, secondly, the examination of Professor Muir by the House of Commons Select Committee on Procedure in 1931. If I may say so with all possible respect, those who regard the House of Commons, in this connection, as a defeated regiment which has surrendered its arms to its natural enemy, the Cabinet, have either never been in the House of Commons at all, and are constructing a literary stereotype like Bagehot's famous 'retired widow' at Windsor, or are politicians, sometimes politicians of great eminence who are, for some reason or other, out of office when they think the country urgently needs their services, and insist upon the powerlessness of the House as a way of sublimating their own deep sense of frustration. It is always urgent to remember, in reading any account of the House of Commons by an eminent Minister who is out of office when he wants to be back there, that he is pretty certain to be glad to announce his conviction that, while he is in opposition the country is bound to go to the dogs.

100. THE HOUSE IS NOT ECONOMY-MINDED

[Sir Frank Tribe, 'Parliamentary Control of Public Expenditure', *Public Administration* XXXI, 1954, Extracts pp. 363–364, 370–371, 380–381]

I

There has certainly been a change even in the last quarter century in the general attitude of back-bench Members of Parliament to questions of expenditure. The number of Members who now consistently press economy on the Government is much smaller than it was. Even those who press for economies in some directions, such as reduction of staff in Government Departments, may well press for much greater expenditure in other directions, such as building new roads. There appears to be a growing feeling that the back-bencher is free to press for additional expenditure in any particular way that appeals to him and it is the Government's duty to obstruct or at least to point to the financial consequences. The financial conscience of the nation, which, so far as one can gather, was in Gladstone's day shared broadly by the whole House of Commons, is now largely the prerogative of the Crown and the Executive though some back-bench Members and certain organs of the Press do spasmodically urge the cause of economy. How completely has the position changed from that recorded in our history books, whose pages show that for some six centuries up to the end of the nineteenth the constant fight was between the King and his Government who wanted to spend more money and Parliament who wanted to limit their grants so as to prevent more taxation!

A full examination of the reasons for this change would merit a paper in itself. They appear to be bound up primarily with the growth of democracy and the enlargement of the franchise. Is it possible that, with the vast growth and complexity of public expenditure in recent years and the inevitable interest of the Treasury in nearly every political issue, individual Members of Parliament have unconsciously lost some of their old sense of financial responsibility, feeling that financial issues are safely left to the Treasury?

II

There is, however, a much more fundamental reason why the Estimates Committee can secure no reduction in the Estimates of the current year. It is a reason which goes to the heart of our constitution, under which the Government can only remain in office so long as it commands the support of the majority of Members in the House. A snap division on some minor matter may not lead to the resignation of the Government, but by tradition finance is not a minor matter. If any House of Commons voted on a Supply Day to reduce an Estimate the

Government would almost certainly resign forthwith. Having this in mind it is of course very unlikely that any Estimates Committee, on which the Government party are in a majority, would ever make such a proposal. Even if they recommended a cut in some Vote they would not expect immediate effect to be given to it, and if it became an issue of confidence in the House and a three line Whip were issued (as it would be in the circumstances) Members' loyalty to their party would outweigh their support for the views of their Committee.

Under our constitution there is always a healthy check between the Legislature and the Executive. If the Government cannot persuade Parliament to vote what it wants, the Prime Minister can recommend the Queen to order a dissolution—which is generally very distasteful and expensive to most Members.

On the other hand, if Parliament does not approve the actions of the Government, it can reject major Bills or in the last resort refuse to grant supply and so force the Government to resign. The result is a reasonable give and take or typically British compromise between the conflicting views which may be expressed.

All this must seem strange and not very logical to people brought up under an entirely different constitution like that in the United States of America, but I imagine that there are very few British subjects, to whatever political party they may belong, who would wish to change our practice.

Nevertheless, if we accept this view, we must, I submit, accept also the view that Parliamentary control over current expenditure is from a machinery point of view virtually nil. Any Government is obviously influenced by the trend of opinion in the House and, if it became obvious that the opinion of the majority were against some particular form of expenditure, the chances are that the Government would not proceed with it. At the same time they would most strenuously resist any overt act designed to cut the Estimates they had presented.

If, then, Parliament is so incapable of controlling current expenditure, wherein does its control really lie?

The answer, I submit, can be found in the two associated practices of Audit and Accountability. No one, of course, would claim that by these means a Government intent on increasing our level of expenditure by large scale developments in welfare services or defence plans and commanding the necessary support in Parliament could be deterred from doing so. Parliamentary government is government by the majority, and, if the Government and the majority in Parliament both want more money to be spent, then any democrat must recognise that it is the people's will and, unless there is a swing of the popular pendulum in the direction of economy, it is right and proper, whatever economists and financiers may say, that the money should be spent. Parliamentary control is not therefore concerned with the total volume of expenditure but with narrower issues on which Members of all parties can reasonably be expected to see eye to eye. For instance, there can be few, if any, Members of Parliament who do not agree that the Executive ought to explain fully to Parliament the reasons why they need grants for this, that and the other object; that the Executive should never spend taxpayers' money without getting the prior sanction of the House of Commons; that the grants given should be prudently and economically administered and that the House should in due course be given a detailed account of how the grants have been spent and the reasons for any excess of expenditure over grant. These are the kind of things which in a modern state constitute Parliamentary control over expenditure—and they do not differ in essence from the objects which Parliament sought to achieve in the centuries of conflict with the Crown, to which I referred earlier.

III

Our Parliament therefore does not set out to control public expenditure to any great extent by examining and pruning the Estimates it is asked to approve. It exercises its control by the more subtle methods which I have attempted to describe. Although, apart from the functions of the Comptroller and Auditor General in approving, on behalf of Parliament, all issues from the Exchequer before they are made, these are largely of an *ex post facto* nature, they are none the less effective. All Government Departments are very conscious of the fact that a continuous watch is being kept on behalf of Parliament on the way in which they use the grants voted to them. The audit of accounts of all the large Departments is a continuous process and queries are being raised long before the accounts are closed. Departments know that, if they use money in a way which was not intended by Parliament or if they use it wastefully or extravagantly, their sins will be brought to light in reports which are widely read and studied. There is a very healthy respect in the Civil Service for the Public Accounts Committee, and Accounting Officers, apart from their own financial responsibilities are most anxious to avoid any slurs or reproaches on the reputation of their Departments. This fear of adverse criticism is perhaps the most potent influence operating to secure proper control. Intangible as it is, it is rooted in age-long traditions and could hardly be nearly so effective in a new-born State. Like so many other aspects of our public life, this system of Parliamentary control of expenditure has grown gradually over the centuries and is not contained in any written constitution. It is indeed continually being adopted and adjusted to meet changing conditions. But one may doubt whether any other system would be nearly so effective for our own country, and also whether the Parliaments of other countries, using other systems, have really as effective a control over expenditure as the Mother of Parliaments.

101. POSSIBLE ECONOMIES—A 'MERE BAGATELLE'

[*Select Committee on Procedure*, H.C. 161 of 1931. Extracts from evidence of Rt. Hon. Stanley Baldwin. Questioned by Mr Chuter Ede, paras 243–244]

We are trying to carry on in the twentieth century a system that is based on a theory when the composition of the House in relation to the Executive was entirely different? Yes.

Is there any remedy for that, that will enable the House to recover control of finance and to examine for necessary economies itself, without the dreadful alternative of having to throw the Government out to do it, and getting a Government that quite possibly it does not want in return?—I quite see what you mean, but all the economies that you are talking about, and all the economies that can be obtained, or that you could hope to obtain by what you call control of Parliament, are a mere bagatelle compared with the power that the House of Commons has itself of spending money. There, I think, your observation comes in perfectly truly, Mr Hore-Belisha. It is broad policy that means, I will not use the word 'extravagence,' but that means expenditure. Over that the House of Commons has complete control, but, of course, that control is whether or not it accepts certain Bills. As you were saying, it means the dismissal of a Government if they do not like to spend money. The amount of subjects to which the control of Parliament, in the way of examining the details of expenditure extends, is really very limited.

102. THE HOUSE DOES NOT REDUCE ESTIMATES

[*Select Committee on Procedure*, H.C. 161 of 1931. Extract from evidence of Rt. Hon. Herbert Samuel. Questioned by Captain Bourne, para 2536]

We found that for twenty-five years on no occasion had the House of Commons ever of its own motion reduced any Estimate presented to it on financial grounds, and I believe that during the years that have elapsed since 1918 the same condition has applied. The law of the Constitution does not allow the House of Commons to increase any of the Estimates that are submitted, and the practice of the Constitution has not in fact allowed the House of Commons on any occasion to reduce an Estimate. The currents of opinion within the House of Commons may influence the amount of expenditure, but there is no formal direct control over expenditure by the House itself. The Treasury control was in our view not adequate. The Treasury is part of the Executive. If the Minister who wishes to increase expenditure under any head secures the personal assent of the Chancellor of the Exchequer, the Treasury is necessarily silent...

103. FINANCE: WHAT PARLIAMENT CAN AND OUGHT TO DO

[*Select Committee on Procedure*. H.C. 161 of 1931. Extracts from evidence of Sir Malcolm Ramsay, Comptroller and Auditor-General, para 3686]

'... The present system has, I believe, been generally criticised on the ground of its ineffectiveness in controlling the Executive, especially as regards expenditure. Such criticism is, in my opinion, to a large extent misdirected as proceeding from an imperfect appreciation of the functions of Parliament: of what it can and ought to do...

'... If on the other hand "Ineffectiveness in controlling the Executive" is used merely in a general sense, then I should say that during the past thirty years, and specially since the outbreak of the European War, Parliament has allowed the Executive a freer hand in financial matters.

'This result is due not so much to defects in the financial procedure, which still allows the House opportunity in plenty of financial criticism, but to other causes. On the one hand, there is the enormous growth both in volume and complexity of expenditure and the financial and economic difficulties arising out of the War: on the other there has been a change in the attitude of Members at large...'

PART X
Questions

104. THE SEARCHLIGHT OF CRITICISM

[from F. A. Ogg, *English Government and Politics*, Macmillan, 2nd ed. 1936, 453–455]

First—starting with the mildest—is the device of the 'question'. Subject to conditions, any member of the House may address a query to a minister, actually or ostensibly to obtain information . . . Until three-quarters of a century ago, the right of questioning ministers was not much used, but nowadays the number of questions put to them at every session runs into the thousands; and . . . 'question time' is a regular, and usually an interesting, portion of every daily sitting. Sometimes the questions have no object whatever except to elicit information; and the questioner may be entirely satisfied by what he hears. They may come from the minister's political friends no less than his foes. More often, however, they are intended to imply criticism, and to place the minister and his colleagues on the defensive. It is the minister's privilege to decline to answer if he likes; all he needs to say is that to reply would be contrary to the public interest. But arbitrary or too frequent refusal will, of course, tend to create an unfavourable impression. The process of answering questions, as Lowell remarks, gives to the Treasury Bench an air of omniscience not wholly deserved, because, the queries having been put on the 'question paper' in advance, opportunity has been given for the minister's subordinates to look into the matter and supply him with the necessary data. In most cases, all that the minister has to do with the replies is to read them to the House; although after he has finished members may aim 'supplementary questions' at him from the floor, and it behoves him to have as much personal familiarity with the matter as he can muster . . .

The question privilege is undoubtedly liable to abuse; the questioner is sometimes actuated by no very lofty motive, and a good deal of time is consumed on trivial matters. As an English authority testifies, however, 'there is no more valuable safeguard against maladministration, no more effective method of bringing the searchlight of criticism to bear on the action or inaction of the executive government and its subordinates. A minister has to be constantly asking himself, not merely whether his proceedings and the proceedings of those for whom he is responsible are legally or technically defensible, but what kind of answer he can give if questioned about them in the House, and how that answer will be received.'

105. MAKING ADMINISTRATION INTELLIGIBLE

[from H. J. Laski, *Parliamentary Government in England*, Allen and Unwin, 1938, pp. 151–153]

The process of questioning has important results. It brings the work of the Departments of State into the public view. It makes them realize that they are functioning under a close public scrutiny which will continuously test their efficiency and honesty. It mitigates, even if it cannot wholly prevent, the danger that bureaucratic habits will develop in the civil service; men who have to answer day by day for their decisions will try so to act that they can give a good account of themselves. No one can read the question-period over any length of time without the clear impression that whatever the light of day can do to make intelligible the business of administration this process is in a high degree likely to do. But its merit, great as this is, does not end there. Some questions will reveal a defective state of affairs. The minister is made aware that his answers have proved unsatisfactory. He feels that he must go further than the answer his Department is able to render. He is anxious to placate a special or general public opinion which continues to insist that more should be known. He appoints a select committee, a departmental committee, or a Royal Commission to report upon the problem. Or he thinks that some question ought to come into the public view upon which there is inadequate knowledge, or confused or irritated public sentiment. A Committee will discover the facts and trace the outlines of a policy upon which, at a later stage, action may become possible.

106. THE ADMINISTRATIVE SYSTEM—OPEN OR CLOSED

[Nevil Johnson, 'Parliament Questions and the conduct of Administration,' *Public Administration*, XXXIX, 1961, Extracts, pp. 139–140, 143–144]

I

One of the most important ways in which systems of administration differ is the degree to which they are open or closed. If administration is open it should mean, amongst other things, that those responsible for carrying on the activities of government are liable to be asked what they do and why. Some account must be given in public to persons not within the administration of why this or that was done or was not done; there must be some opportunity for public consideration of proposed measures and policies. There are various ways in which these ends can be achieved, and Parliamentary Questions in Britain is only one of many methods, and indeed only one of the methods used in this country. The peculiar characteristic of Questions is that they provide a means of submitting the Government to a continuous stream of Questions about practically anything for which a minister is responsible, and that in practice an answer must be given. Sometimes replies can be and are refused on grounds of security and public interest, or because preparing a reply would involve 'a disproportionate amount of work.' Indeed in theory the Prime Minister could announce that henceforward his ministers were not going to answer any more Questions, although such an announcement is unlikely. What it comes to is that all ministers and civil servants work in the knowledge that most, if not all, of their activities might be the subject of Questions, and that it will be necessary to provide some sort of reply. Even if it is possible to get away with a very tenuous reply, it still remains important that Questions cannot merely be brushed aside. Furthermore open and public argument by way of supplementaries must be faced as the almost inevitable consequence of a Question.

In Britain the habit of questioning the executive has, as its obverse, willingness to allow some discretion to the government. In fact, Questions underline the situation of the British legislature, which has, except on one occasion, not aspired to share in the task of executive government. On the whole it is true to say that in most Western countries and those closely influenced by them, where there is a democratic form of constitution, legislatures rarely accept such a passive role. They have been more anxious to share authority with the executive, both in defining the lines of policy and the content of legislation. In contrast, the House of Commons has tended to leave decisions entirely to the executive, reserving to itself the right to criticize and to question and ultimately to withhold confidence. In most foreign legislatures questioning in anything like the form in which we know it is absent. But these legislatures may have other means of influencing or controlling the executive, the chief of which is some form of specialized committee system. Where there is formal separation of powers the legislature will call upon the members of the executive authority to appear in person before the appropriate committee to justify proposals; or, without formal separation of powers as in the American constitution, legislatures may have highly developed committees to examine legislation and to specialize in particular areas of government work, and they will generally require detailed information from ministers and officials before legislation or financial proposals are passed. This procedure subjects governments to checks and to a balance of power which have never been part of British constitutional practice.

II

Probably many Members of the House would agree that there are strict limitations on the Question as an instrument for influencing government decisions, or for finding out in any detail the background to many acts of the executive. They would accept that the Question can be used successfully to obtain information on precise and limited points, and that as a result a minister may justify or even modify his decision or correct a mistake. But immediately the Question strays on to wider issues involving more general policy matters and issues of political concern, then little, if anything, of practical significance can be achieved. The most that can be hoped for is that the Government of the day will suffer a loss of prestige due to its performance in the face of a stream of Questions, and that public confidence in it will be diminished. Today it is hardly possible to agree with Lowell, writing in 1908, that Question time turns 'a searchlight upon every corner of the public service.' The public service has become too extensive for the searchlight to cast anything more than a diffused light which becomes intense only if it happens to fall upon a more flagrant mistake or abuse. And even then it must be some matter which is fairly precisely defined and does not involve the political standing of the Government too seriously. The famous Question in May, 1928 about the behaviour of the police towards a Miss Savidge, and the Questions in 1959 about the Waters case, illustrate this point. Both were concerned with alleged injustices to individuals, both raised matters of principle which could be argued without much reference to purely political considerations, and both were at least initially limited to a particular action affecting one person. They are classic examples of the effectiveness of a certain type of Question, and it is worth noting that in one of these cases (Waters) the degree of ministerial responsibility was open to some argument.

To regard Questions primarily as a means of 'controlling' the executive, which is the role enthusiasts have cast them for, is misleading. The whole concept of the legislature controlling the executive has found little favour here, and we have preferred to trust the executive, subject to the right to criticize and question. It is within this context that Questions are really significant. What Questions help to do is to keep Governments and their officials responsive to the opinions and feelings of the House of Commons. Responsiveness does not mean that much is conceded to the House, but it does mean that no Government which is prudent will neglect its standing in the House and particularly amongst its own supporters there. Owing to the existence of Questions it is constantly faced with the necessity of justifying politically what it is doing. A Government has to be able to defend itself against attack, and in so doing maintain the confidence of its own supporters. Question time is one of the most important occasions for achieving all this. Both for ministers and officials another significant result of Questions is that answers have to be given in terms comprehensible to the layman. This is often an essential characteristic of an answer which is politically defensible, and it is a healthy check on the activities of government that this effort has constantly to be made to explain in relatively simple words why this or that is so.

107. A BACK-BENCHER ACTIVITY

[from D. N. Chester and N. Bowring, *Questions in Parliament*, O.U.P., 1961, pp. 270–272, 281–282, 284–285, 286–288]

I

If an institution or device is praised and generally regarded as 'a good thing' one would expect it to flourish and its use to expand. In this particular case two other factors would add to that expectation. On the one hand there has been the great growth in the powers and activities of Government Departments, a big increase in the number of voters and a changed public attitude towards state intervention. Inevitably these have led to an increase in the number of 'individual grievances', and have provided Members with many more matters about which they need to take action, or, at least, to ask for information. On the other hand the opportunities for the back-bencher to play an active, public and independent role in the proceedings of the House of Commons are not as great as they were in the early years of the century. In so far as Question time remains primarily a back-bencher activitiy and in so far as 'individual grievances' are largely constituency matters which in turn are the bread and butter of the back-bencher's life it might be expected that an increasing use of this procedure would have led to more time being made available for it. Instead, the number of minutes available are the same now as they were in April 1906 and though the number of supplementaries has increased in the last fifty years this has been at the expense of a more than corresponding decline in the number of Questions receiving oral answer. This in turn has inhibited growth of the number of Questions on the Paper . . .

II

So far we have been assuming that the inability of Question time to provide for oral answers to all, or at least the great bulk of, starred Questions is a serious defect which needs remedying. It will indeed come as a surprise and a shock to many whose knowledge of the working of Question time dates from an earlier period to learn that the opportunity to question the Foreign Secretary in the House occurred on only nineteen occasions during the Session of 1959-60 and that the possibility of questioning most other Ministers was even less. It is, however, worth considering whether there may not be quite another way of looking at the change for may not the present working of Question time reflect more faithfully the current needs of Members than would a return to an earlier usage?

It is, of course, true that the House has got itself into its present position by chance and not by a clearly expressed wish. It was inevitable that the Members asking starred Questions would more and more take advantage of the 'right' to ask a supplementary. As the number of supplementaries increased, the number of starred Questions reached decreased, leading to the development of the rota system. In order to make sure that their Questions were reached Members were bound to use the rota system intelligently, thus leading to a bunching of Questions for Departments at or next to the top of the list. As it became more difficult to get a Question answered orally and more difficult to reach a particular Minister, Members inevitably wanted to make the most of the occasions when he was reached. The more they did this the more difficult it became to get a Question answered orally or to reach a Minister. Thus step by inevitable step there may come a time when only one Minister will be reached at the most sittings. Question time will have become 'the Foreign Secretary's day' or 'the Minister of Transport's day' and so on, rather like Supply days.

There is little or no reason to believe that the recent trend will, or could be, reversed. Question time has on many occasions been referred to as a safety valve in the procedures of the House.

The present use of the supplementary is a kind of safety valve, for Question time is one of the rare occasions when back-benchers can create an opportunity both to address the House and to deal with a specific matter that interests them. The supplementary developed and was allowed to develop in the late nineteenth century because other forms of expression were being curtailed. The way it is now used and the inability of Mr Speaker to restrain this use reflect in part an unsatisfied need on the part of back-benchers. The device of Question and Answer, strictly interpreted is sometimes unsatisfactory, for both parties would like a little more elbow room—the questioner to explain the back-ground of his questions or complaint, the answerer to give more information and fuller explanation. Two post-war developments illustrate this desire for something fuller and yet still reasonably specific. First, there is the greatly increased use of the daily Motion for the Adjournment for the purpose of a very short debate on a specific issue, during which usually only the opener and a Minister take part. Second, there is the use of Ministerial statements followed by questions. Procedurally this is bad and Mr Speaker quite often has to stop such occasions degenerating into 'irregular debate'. But the general idea of there being an occasion for a short airing of a particular issue appears to be attractive to Members . . .

III

A procedure has been perfected and accepted for dealing with the great mass of personal and local matters. In a sense it is an extra-Parliamentary device and possibly becaues of this has received too little attention from writers on the Constitution. In most Departments Members' correspondence is of much greater consequence than Questions as a means of calling attention to matters needing reconsideration and as an indicator of the reactions of public opinion to the activities of the Department.

In the long run, the greater use of correspondence should have the effect of emphasizing the significance of starred Questions or, at least, of changing their character. Such Questions are likely increasingly to become a device of last resort, other 'behind the scenes' methods having failed; or be concerned with major issues which must be ventilated in public and cannot be dealt with adequately except on the floor of the House; or be from Members who wish to embarrass or score over the Minister. There will, of course, remain the attraction of the publicity which Questions receive, though so far as the local press is concerned a Member's correspondence with a Minister is available to receive just as much publicity if the Member passes a copy to the local editor.

Question time devoted to supplementaries is seen not as a deterioration but as an adaptation to the changing needs of the House. Correspondence and unstarred Questions provide ample opportunity for the gathering of information and the raising of individual cases and constituency matters for the consideration of Ministers. The House has had to choose between oral answers and supplementaries and has compromised, trying to get a good many starred Questions reached but still allowing more and longer supplementaries. A rota system has been evolved which makes certain that each Minister will be available for answering on days stated well in advance. Matters about which Members feel particularly strongly are accumulated until the particular Minister becomes available and then he has to undergo thirty to fifty minutes of questioning. Having regard to the many other claims on the time of the House it can be argued that this is a reasonable use of Question time. But it could equally be argued that the House is getting the worst of both worlds, for present procedure ensures neither that Ministers are frequently and regularly available for questioning, say once a week, nor that, once available, there is time to cross-examine them thoroughly. It can hardly be denied that the trend of events has favoured Ministers and that once again the procedures of the House have failed to keep pace with the increasing powers of the Executive.

Nevertheless it is still significant that Question time has remained important in the lives of most Members during a period when more and more of the proceedings of the House have become dominated by the two Front Benches. It still remains one of the few elements in the Parliamentary timetable in which the newest or the humblest or the most disliked Member has the same rights as any other. In this respect, comparatively speaking, Question time is more important and more unique a feature of procedure than it was at the beginning of the century. Moreover, its ultimate value as a sanction and control depends not so much on the precise number of starred Questions reached and supplementaries asked, but on the ever present possibility that they may be asked. This also applies to Questions for written answer . . .

IV

It is also possible that the significance of Question time was over dramatized in the past. It is, of course, a colourful period with the House fairly full, a wide variety of matters dealt with in a short time and always the possibility of an angry scene or roars of laughter. It is seldom, however, an occasion that attracts the most thoughtful and most ambitious among the back-benchers. As for Ministers it is seldom the ordeal that most writers on the subject appear to think it is. It can be a great nuisance when a Minister is engaged on an urgent and important problem to have to give time to framing thoughtful answers about something else, but much of this drafting can be done by the Civil Service. A Minister who is not by training a politician may find it difficult on occasions to deal with the House but the majority of supplementaries present little if any terror for the experienced politician. There are some who would have lasted longer as Ministers or risen higher in Government circles had they been able to answer Questions better. But it is likely that their inability to handle Questions was but a reflection of their general inadequacy as Parliamentarians.

Most writers on Questions quote some spectacular example in which a major change of Government policy was brought about or a great wrong redressed because of Questions asked in the House. As there have been some half a million starred Questions answered on the floor of the House since 1902 it would indeed be remarkable if a few examples of spectacular results could not be found. Moreover Questions are by no means a unique method of achieving such results; probably as many are achieved by Members privately without resort to any Parliamentary action.

The significance of Questions and Question time is to be found in three other directions. First and foremost it is pre-eminently a device for emphasizing the individual responsibility of Ministers. In the House of Lords Questions are addressed to the Government, there being so few Ministers available. When it was proposed to introduce Question time into the American Congress it was made clear that Questions would have to be addressed to the President. In the House of Commons Questions are addressed to and answerable by the Minister responsible. No other Minister can regularly answer for him. His personal responsibility for his actions and for those of all the civil servants in his Department is pinpointed. In the ever increasing scale of governmental activity and the great strength of the leaders of monolithic Parties this stress on personal responsibility stands out as being of the utmost significance.

Second, Questions enable a large number of miscellaneous issues to be dealt with quickly within the framework of Parliamentary procedure. Opinions may differ as to the extent that Question time is 'abused' but few would deny that if this occasion were abolished some other opportunity would have to be found for handling such matters and that this would probably be more consuming of Members' time. It may be a matter of regret that fewer starred Questions are now dealt with at each sitting but nevertheless forty to fifty items dealt with in less than an hour on each of four days a week is a pretty high rate of productivity. The rest of the time of the House is at best no more productive.

Third, there can be little doubt that some Questions are not worth the upset to the work in a Department and the general trouble involved in preparing the answer. Some Questions are still put down for oral answer when a written answer would give the Member most of what he requires. Many supplementaries are clumsily worded, irrelevant and merely time-consuming. Some Members waste the valuable minutes of Question time on points of order of no immediate significance. These things cause annoyance and do not add to the efficiency of the Departments. But these criticisms are not peculiar to Questions. A good deal of debating time goes in speeches that might with advantage have been shorter and more to the point. It would be demanding a standard of excellence and thoughtfulness not found in any large group of men and women that everything each did should be well considered.

There are some 550 Members who are not part of the Administration or leaders of the Opposition or involved in running the business of the House. Nowadays some 12,000 to 15,000 starred and unstarred Questions are put on the Paper each Session, an average of twenty to twenty-five per Member. This can hardly be said to be a large number. After all, each of these Members represents a constituency of some 50,000 voters and each has to concern himself with the mass of decisions and activities of over twenty Government Departments and the great power for good or ill which now resides in them. Moreover the House has large responsibilities for the welfare of Colonial territories. Any annoyance and reduced effectiveness caused by inconsiderate Members seem but a small price to pay for a method of bringing to public notice, with the minimum use of Parliamentary time, the grievances of individual citizens and of groups and the matters about which Members feel strongly. Notwithstanding the changes brought about in recent years Question time and Questions still continue to perform this function effectively. Whether they secure results must always depend on the willingness of Ministers and civil servants to reconsider their decisions and policies and to take account of criticism. There is no reason to believe that they are less willing to do this now than they were thirty, forty or more years ago. There is even less reason to believe that they would be more willing to do so if Questions did not exist.

PART XI

The Use of Committees

108. PARLIAMENTARY CONTROL BY COMMITTEE

[*Report on the Machinery of Government*, Cd. 9230, 1918. Extract from Report, paras 48–53]

. . . Our terms of reference direct us to frame our recommendations with the primary object of promoting the efficient and economical working of the public service. But we have throughout our deliberations borne in mind the fact that any action directed to this end would fail to achieve its purpose if it were to have the effect of disturbing the balance of authority between the Legislature and the Executive.

It would, we think, be generally felt that any improvement in the organisation of the Departments of State which was so marked as substantially to increase their efficiency should have as its correlative an increase in the power of the Legislature as the check upon the acts and proposals of the Executive . . .

We should hesitate to enter . . . upon questions of procedure which Parliament alone can examine or determine with authority, were it not that it has been definitely suggested to us that the efficiency of the public service would be improved if steps were taken to secure the continuous and well-informed interest of a Parliamentary body in the execution by each Department of the policy which Parliament has laid down.

It has been suggested that the appointment of a series of Standing Committees, each charged with the consideration of the activities of the Departments which cover the main divisions of the business of Government, would be conducive to this end. Any such Committees would require to be furnished with full information as to the course of administration pursued by the Departments with which they were concerned; and for this purpose it would be requisite that Ministers, as well as the officers of Departments, should appear before them to explain and defend the acts for which they were responsible . . .

109. COMMITTEES ESSENTIAL FOR EFFECTIVE CONTROL

[*Select Committee on Procedure*, H.C. 161 of 1931. Extracts from evidence of Rt. Hon. David Lloyd George, paras 350, 353, 356]

The Committee would like to know whether you consider there is any justification for the public criticism of the present system of procedure . . . ?—. . . I have no doubt at all there is a good deal of criticism of Parliamentary institutions altogether, and I think there is a very great and growing disappointment with Parliament . . . The only real endeavour made in recent years to secure economy has been in consequence of pressure from outside on the Executive. I am referring to the Geddes Committee. There has been no examination by the House of Commons itself of the Estimates . . . That will be my first criticism on the procedure of the House of Commons, and one of the reasons why I think on the whole it is losing a good deal of prestige amongst the masses of the people . . . My [second] criticism would be that the control of the Executive by the House of Commons is confined to rather perfunctory discussions which do not excite any real interest, apart from an element of censure which is conducive to excitement, but does not achieve the real purpose of establishing control over the Executive . . . The fact of the matter is that the House of Commons has no real effective and continuous control over the Executive . . . I noticed that questions were put—I forget whether to Mr Baldwin or to the Prime Minister—with regard to the setting up of Committees and the analogy of the municipalities was referred to. I think there is a good deal to be said about that. Every municipality in the land has committees which consider every important detail of administration, and report upon it to the council. The general discussions take place there. The examination in detail takes place in the committees which are set up for that purpose. You have a finance committee, a surveyors' committee, a police committee and a health committee, and there are all kinds of committees. On questions of principle you have a debate in the council chamber, but the close examination takes place by committees where the officials are present and questions can be put to them, and if the committees would like to have any outside opinion, if they think any other opinion would enlighten them upon the topics they are studying. But you have no machinery of that kind in the House of Commons, and until you have it the House of Commons will have no effective control over the Executive . . .

That committee would control the Departmental affairs in regard to administration?—No. I would not like to say that. The control must rest with the Minister because he is responsible, to Parliament, and through Parliament to the Crown. The Minister must have the ultimate say, subject to what Parliament says, but it would enable the House of Commons effectively to supervise, and not only that, but to keep itself informed.

Do you envisage the Minister being Chairman of such a committee?—No. The Minister is in the House.

He is summoned before the committee?—Yes; he comes before the committee.

And a Civil Servant might also be summoned?—Certainly. I would suggest that you have power to send for anybody.

And no information could be withheld?—Oh, no . . .

110. CAN COMMITTEES CONTROL POLICY?

[*Select Committee on Procedure*, Third Report, H.C. 189 of 1946. Evidence of Rt. Hon. the Speaker. Questions 3024–3029]

Members have the right to interfere with administrative processes in the normal way in the House of Commons, have they not, and very often where policy is involved?—Yes. I would not dispute that.

Would it not be a logical extension of that principle that a committee of this type would go into matters rather more closely with the Departments?—I should have thought that, once they had got beyond a certain line, the Minister would pull them up and say: 'This is not your business; it is mine. It is policy.' He would put his foot down—and I think rightly, too. He cannot share responsibility with anybody else.

But in these days of heavy pressure of legislation, when so

many extra powers are being given to the Government, do you not think it right that Private Members of the House should have some machinery for going closely into questions in the Departments which result from that legislation, whether or not policy is involved in the interpretation by the Departments of that legislation?—I think they have their remedies in the way of Questions; they have Supply Days, and various other Parliamentary forms.

What is undesirable, Mr Speaker, is that civil servants should be questioned on matters of policy, is it not? Yes, that is most undesirable. It is the Minister's responsibility only and they are his servants.

Precisely. It is not so much the existence of the Committee, which might get involved in matters of policy, to which you object so much as to the fact that this Committee would be examining civil servants on policy? Is that right?—Yes. That would be entirely wrong, in my view. You want to cross-examine a Minister and nobody else.

Would there be any objection, supposing it were practicable, to the Minister being cross-examined by a committee of this kind?—No. I should have thought not. Of course, a Minister often calls a meeting of Members upstairs (it is unofficial) and there he is cross-examined.

III. PARLIAMENT IS NOT ORGANISED FOR CURRENT ADMINISTRATION

[*Select Committee on Procedure*, Third Report, H.C. 189 of 1946. Evidence of Rt. Hon. Herbert Morrison. Questions 3258–3268]

You would never suggest that in the final resort the House of Commons was responsible to the Government of the day?—To the Government of the day?

Yes?—That would be against the whole doctrine. The Government is responsible to the House. On the other hand, the Government has to try to lead the House.

Then why is it, that when you get into the field of departmental inquiry, you take the attitude that the civil servant is a superior person, and that the power of the representative of the House, the power of the trained clerks, I think you said, would be too great, and would be resented in the Departments.

Why do you reverse the constitutional doctrine when you get into the realm of the Departments?—Because then we get into the argument as to who is responsible for executive current administration, the Government or Parliament. I say it is the Government that is responsible. It is responsible to Parliament, but if Parliament is going to set up another duplicating set of administrative experts to take an interest in current administration, there is going to be a clash between Parliament and Government, which I think would be bad. That was the fear. I speak without prejudice about it, because, as I say. I got on very well with them. I only know that this term 'trained clerk' in Sir Gilbert Campion's memorandum did cause certain reverberations in Whitehall, in the light of the experience of the Select Committee on National Expenditure, I take it. I do not know quite why, but I suspect because there was beginning to be another rival administrative set-up in the Palace of Westminster, side by side with Whitehall. I think that would be bad. Parliament's business is to check the Government, throw it out if it wants to, go for it, attack it, criticise it, by all means, but Parliament is not a body which is organised for current administration—not in this country. They have had a go at it in France and the United States, and I do not think too much of it.

112. AN EXPERIMENTAL COMMITTEE?

[*Select Committee on Procedure*. H.C. 92 of 1958. Evidence of Sir Edward Fellowes, Clerk of the House. Questions 274–280]

And if one had a Committee of that sort, what is your view, from the point of view of the House, as to the position of the Secretary of State? He would normally be invited to attend, or to send representatives?—No, I should not think that a Minister would normally be invited to attend, unless it is meant that he is to be a member of the Committee; that is one possibility, that he would be an ordinary member of the Committee. I should rather doubt that. One of the advantages of that sort of Committee is that it does get behind politicians and gets to the administrators. It has the right to call them and to examine them, but not their political heads, because the Committee would not be dealing with political issues.

Not, perhaps, always to fetch a Governor from a remote Colony, but to deal with the officials in the Colonial Office?—Yes, the head of the African Department, or whatever it is, in the Colonial Office.

In fact, the idea you had in mind was something not unlike the Estimates Committee, I suppose?—Yes—perhaps more like the Public Accounts Committee.

Yes, following the sort of lines that those two financial bodies take; and no doubt with a power, which I do not think they have and which they certainly do not exercise, to ask Ministers to attend occasionally?—Oh, yes. I remember the Public Accounts Committee asking the Secretary of State for War to attend on one occasion; so that it is not unknown; but it would be a request, and could only be translated into a command if the Committee reported the fact to the House and the House ordered the Minister to attend.

Of course, they would differ from the financial Committees, because they would only be dealing with one Minister and one Government Department?—Yes, but a very widespread one.

Then with reference to the India Committee to which you have referred us, is this a fair summary of your view; that they did do useful work although their hands were rather tied by the Resolution you quote?—That is my view, though I was never a Clerk to that Committee, so I cannot speak from experience of it. It is true that they considered a Bill in the course of their first session as well as the only occasion on which they produced a Report during their latter years, but they did make other Reports on other matters.

It would perhaps be wise if one were to try the experiment of making the terms of reference rather wide?—That would be my view; that it would be worth trying as an experiment with wide terms of reference, and if the Committee and the Government got at loggerheads with each other, then clearly the experiment would not be repeated.

113. COMMITTEES MUST NOT CHALLENGE POLICY

[*Select Committee on Procedure*, H.C. 92 of 1958. Evidence of Rt. Hon. Herbert S. Morrison. Question 461]

The Clerk of the House has made the suggestion for one or two specialist committees: one, for example, a Colonial Committee. What do you think of the suggestion?—There is now the Estimates Committee, and the Public Accounts Committee. If the Colonies are of such importance—and the other suggestion is Defence—that there ought to be committees set up, I would be prepared personally to accept it, if it is a breaking off—a departmentalisation—of the functions of the Estimates Committee or the Public Accounts Committee, as the case may be. Therefore there would be *vis-à-vis* the Colonial Office a committee discharging the same functions as the Estimates Committee in relation to the Colonial Office, and the same thing in relation to the Ministry of Defence and the Defence Departments. That would not much worry me. But I think the terms of reference of those committees in that case should be in principle the same as those of the Estimates Committee; that is to say, they could not challenge or interfere with the policy of the Government of the day. Otherwise you will be importing into our Parliamentary system something like that which the United States and the French have, whereby government departments can be put on the spot in a committee over policy and everything else, and the Minister will inevitably have to be called in; and in the case of the Secretary of State for the Colonies, he is a very hard-worked man, not noticeably far behind the Foreign Minister himself. Therefore I do not think I like policy in this sort of matter going to committees. But if it is a matter of doing the work of the Estimates Committee in these two cases and they are so important that we must ensure an annual look at them, then there is something to be said for it. But I would not myself recommend that they should go wider than the Estimates Committee can go. The other point is that not only will it tend to make ministers tired and, indeed, increase the labours of Members, which one must try to avoid, but it would tend to take away the dignity of the floor of the House on these matters of public policy, which I think it is important should be retained by the floor.

114. A SPECIALIST COMMITTEE ON THE COLONIES?

[*Select Committee on Procedure*, H.C. 92 of 1958. Report, para 47]

The main argument against the proposal, and one which convinces us, lies in the nature of the committee, which in our view would constitute a radical constitutional innovation. The parallel with the Scottish Grand Committee is not exact, since that committee is composed of members who represent constituencies whose affairs they are debating. Notwithstanding that the order of reference might be drawn in general terms without conferring any express powers of direct interference, there is little doubt that the activities of such a committee would ultimately be aimed at controlling rather than criticising the policy and actions of the department concerned. In so doing, it would be usurping a function which the House itself has never attempted to exercise. Although the House has always maintained the right to criticise the executive and in the last resort to withdraw its confidence it has always been careful not to arrogate to itself any of the executive power. The establishment of a colonial committee would not only invade this principle, but would also lead to the establishment of other similar committees.

115. A DEROGATION OF PARLIAMENTARY AUTHORITY?

[from Morrison, *Government and Parliament*, O.U.P., 1954, pp. 155–156]

It is noticeable that broadly speaking (though there can be exceptions) the function of examining and challenging important Government policy is reserved to Parliament as a whole. This doctrine has, I imagine, been preserved for two reasons: the wish of Parliament not to weaken its own powers and authority, and the desire of Governments not to become (to put it crudely) the victims or creatures of committees.

In the United States and in France things are very different. American Secretaries of Departments may be summoned to give evidence and to be examined by Committees of the Senate or of the House of Representatives in Washington, and in France the Parliamentary Committees have considerable powers over

French Ministers. The result may indeed be fatal for the Minister, or what the United States calls the Official, concerned. In the United States the President's nominees for his Secretaries of Departments, Ambassadors, and even delegates to the United Nations Assembly, are subject to approval by a two-thirds majority of the Senate and can be summoned before Senate Committees and severely examined in Committees of the U.S. Congress. And in the French Parliament [committees] would often appear to have even more decisive powers and influence than the parliamentary institution as a whole.

I once had the experience, exceptional for a foreigner, of giving evidence before a Committee of the United States Senate, on the late Senator Wagner's Housing Bill. It was an interesting and fascinating experience: a crowded room, some seated, some standing, including local government officers who had come long distances. The Chairman of the day was evidently hostile to the Bill and he handled me with some degree of American frankness and hostility. By the time we had reached nearly the last question I was beginning to feel at home and equally frank, so that when he asked me, 'Well, Mr Morrison, what *is* this London County Council, anyway?', I thought I had better be a little boastfully British and I replied, 'Sir, it is the greatest municipality in the world—that's what the London County Council is'. I forget whether the Chairman snorted or said, 'Uh, huh'. However, it was a most interesting and for me happy experience. But if you ask me whether it was anything like the procedure or atmosphere of a Select Committee of the House of Commons or the House of Lords, the answer is in the negative.

Our own Parliament has not gone in for these procedures. I feel sure that it would regard the practice as a derogation of parliamentary authority.

116. IS LORD MORRISON RIGHT?

[from David Widdicombe, Review of 'Government and Parliament', *Fabian Journal* No. 13, 1954, pp. 20–23]

The methods which could be adopted to deal with this situation have received a good deal of discussion in the past. Mr Morrison examines one or two of them. He is probably right in dismissing the ideas of Fred Jowett of the I.L.P., who wanted to replace Cabinet Government altogether by a form of government by committees of Parliament rather on the lines of the method used in our County Councils. This would mean the abandonment of Ministerial responsibility altogether, and the proposal has not been considered seriously since Laski advised the Labour Party against it in 1924. Some authorities, including Sir Winston Churchill, at various times have advocated subsidiary Houses of Parliament to deal with certain matters, such as economic affairs. Lloyd George advocated Committees of the House of Commons on a modified Jowett pattern, and did so, not only as a powerless back-bencher, as Mr Morrison believes, but in his heyday as a Minister in 1916. But it is probable that Mr Morrison is right to dismiss those proposals too, because Lloyd George envisaged the attendance of Ministers before his committees, and this is not very reasonable in view of the enormous burdens Ministers must shoulder today.

But something short of that could be considered. It has been suggested that it would be possible to have committees of Parliament studying aspects of Government action without the necessity for Ministers to attend, for this is the way the present Committees of the House in fact work. This suggestion is not considered by Mr Morrison, but is, in my view, the most obvious way for Parliament to develop. During the two World Wars the House of Commons had a Select Committee on National Expenditure, and although such a powerful committee is not necessary in peacetime, it is hard to see why some modified form of it, such as was recommended by the Select Committee on the Procedure of the House of Commons in 1946, cannot be adopted. Mr Morrison discusses the recommendations of this Committee on Procedure but omits to mention this particular recommendation; the omission is perhaps significant.

There is a problem here, and it is a pity that we have not been given Mr Morrison's views, except so far as they are implied by his evasion of it. All he says is, 'Maybe light will descend on us'. (P.160). This is a polite way of saying that the Government has an entrenched interest in preventing the extension of Parliament's function. What we want to know is whether the Government is right, and if not, what should be done about it?

117. MINISTERS WOULD GAIN FROM COMMITTEES

[from L. S. Amery, *Thoughts on the Constitution*, O.U.P., 1947, pp. 53–55]

More useful, to my mind, as a method of supplying the House with better information in many subjects than can be supplied by occasional debates and by questions, and of keeping Ministers more closely in touch with members on their special subjects, would be the institution of committees, either of the House of Commons or of both Houses, presided over by the Ministers concerned, of members interested in the work of individual departments. The objection has usually been made to this suggestion that similar committees in France or the United States have tended to be a great burden on the time of Ministers and, indeed, to have seriously impaired their responsibility. The objection, I think, overlooks the fact that the relation of Ministers to committees only reproduces in miniature their relation to the House as a whole, and that Ministers with us, unlike French or American Ministers, are unquestioned masters of the House and are supported in their position of authority by a solid majority there which is naturally reflected in the composition of its committees.

My own experience in the offices which I have held is that I should have gained by such regular opportunities of giving information and explaining my policies and of gathering the views of those interested, and that the effect upon the quality of debates would have been equally beneficial. To some extent, indeed, the need for this type of contact has been increasingly met in recent years and particularly in the present Parliament, by party groups or committees on departmental subjects. Liason committees keep the work of these bodies in touch with the leadership of the parties. There are also the increasing weekly meetings of the parties as a whole. The drawback to this system is that Ministers may be too liable to one-sided pressure by their own supporters, while the Opposition Committees may miss some of the sense of responsibility which goes with official information.

118. THE USE OF SELECT COMMITTEES

[from K. C. Wheare, *Government by Committee*, O.U.P., 1955, pp. 205–206; 209]

I

There have been proposals from time to time that the House of Commons should be given an opportunity through the use of committees to exercise some sort of control over what Whitehall does. It is admitted that while the House has important and valuable opportunities to criticize administration through debate, it lacks any chance of close and continuous examination of what is being done. Its standing committees set up to consider bills, as we have seen, are confined purely to that function, and though in the course of debates on a bill some discussion of administration may be in order, there is not much scope for it. There is no allocation of particular subjects to committees, as in the Parliament of France or in the Congress of the United States or in the town and county councils of this country. It has seemed to some students of the working of standing committees in Britain that their functions should be extended from the consideration of bills to the study of administration, and that they should be organized according to a division of subject-matter and authorized to deal with both legislation and administration in their allotted field. Though proposals of this kind have been put forward and supported by people of authority and experience, they have always been rejected, and usually emphatically. The Cabinet will tolerate no rivals to its authority in the House of Commons. Whether it is justified in its attitude or not, the outcome has been that standing committees have been confined to the consideration of Bills. The only opportunities which members of the House of Commons have for inquiring into administration have arisen through the establishment of the [Public Accounts Committee, the Estimates Committee, the Statutory Instruments Committee and the Select Committee on the Nationalised Industries]...

II

What these four committees are authorized to do and what they do in practice are not always the same thing. The line between scrutinizing the application or legalization of policy and discussing the formulation of policy is not easily drawn and indeed it is sometimes quite genuinely impossible to discuss the one without encroaching upon the other. More particularly is this true in the case of the financial select committees, where wise spending, economy, waste, and misappropriation of funds can hardly be discussed without some discussion of policy. It will be seen in fact that they have not always in practice kept clear of the discussion of policy. In estimating the use of these committees, it will be necessary to consider how far their exclusion from discussing policy or 'the merits' reduces their usefulness, and whether an authorization to consider them would increase their usefulness.

119. ADVISORY COMMITTEES

[from A. H. Hanson, *Parliament and Public Ownership*, pp. 130–131]

The general tendency is to make increasing use of Select Committees. A Select Committee on Statutory Instruments was first appointed in 1944, and the Estimates Committee, re-established in 1946 after a war-time interregnum during which a National Expenditure Committee conducted vigorous and often unwelcome investigations, proved far more effective than its somewhat effete predecessor of the period between the wars. In general, Select Committees to investigate the behaviour of government departments were not exactly popular with Ministers of the Crown or with civil servants, but they did seem to offer a useful method of supplementing Parliament's more normal and traditional methods of bringing 'the bureaucracy' to account. New Select Committees tended to acquire something of the prestige already won by the formidable Public Accounts Committee, and also to reproduce the 'non-political' atmosphere which surrounded that body. The process of hearing, sifting and weighing evidence, by a small number of Members in a committee room where parliamentary reporters had no right of entry, made for 'responsibility'; and the necessity of producing a Report which had to be unanimous or near-unanimous if it were to carry much weight discouraged the pushing of mere party arguments to the point of a division. These factors tended to prevent a Select Committee from getting too deeply involved in matters of policy and thereby, as the opponents of constitutional innovation feared, undermining ministerial responsibility. They were also responsible for the growing habit, on the part of Members, the Press and the public, of treating Select Committee Reports as weighty, if not completely authoritative documents whose criticisms and proposals deserved serious consideration. Many, therefore, regarded Select Committees as offering a way out of the *impasse* in which Parliament appeared to be involved as a result of the growing size and complexity of the administrative apparatus. Some believed, and continue to believe that the House of Commons ought to equip itself with a positive network of specialized committees, each attached, in an advisory and critical capacity, to a department or group of departments.[1]

GREATER COMMITTEE SCOPE FOR M.P.S

[by Michael Ryle, *The Times*, 17 April 1963]

A hundred years ago Bagehot could properly write of 'parliamentary government'. Today the phrase is less appropriate. Increasingly, through their control of party machines and thus of the House itself, Governments have secured the power both to initiate policy and to carry it out. But, as Mr Leo Amery once put it, 'the main task of Parliament is still what it was when first summoned, not to legislate or govern, but to secure full discussion and ventilation of all matters'. Therefore, if Parliament is to perform this role effectively, the increasing power of the Executive in initiating policy and controlling its execution must be matched by an increasing ability on the part of Parliament, and particularly the House of Commons, to scrutinize and criticize both the policies themselves and their implementation.

[1]See A. H. Hanson and H. V. Wiseman: 'The Use of Committees by the House of Commons', in *Public Law*, Autumn, 1959.

And if, as has been suggested, the power behind the scenes of both the Prime Minister and Civil Service is increasing, there is an even greater need for those immediately responsible to be subjected to parliamentary scrutiny, so that the very real dangers of government behind closed doors may be averted.

So long as there is an effective Opposition the major policy decisions, for which Ministers are directly responsible, can be effectively challenged within the present procedures of the House. But these procedures are less well adapted for scrutiny of how policies are administered. Question hour is a vital and vigorous part of House of Commons proceedings and an invaluable occasion for the public examination and testing of Ministers. But it is an inefficient method of discovering and setting out in a concise and readily digestible form the essential facts upon which scrutiny of administration must be based. Nor, in the course of general debates, is there opportunity for detailed explanation by Ministers.

Fact Finding

The need for more information is central to the problem of ensuring effective parliamentary scrutiny. Fortunately the House already possesses an efficient instrument for fact finding by which such scrutiny could be conducted, but at present its use is unduly restricted. Select committees consider the Estimates, the Public Accounts and the affairs of the nationalized industries. These committees have shown themselves well suited for examining the large range of government that lies below major policy decisions but above the day to day decisions of individual civil servants. Typical inquiries have dealt with trooping, the price of drugs and the fixing of coal prices, and their reports have proved valuable. But the work of these committees has been primarily concerned with finance; committees of this type could also be used where finance is not so directly involved.

Previous proposals for greater use of committees have tended to urge either committees claiming a right to exercise effective control over the work of departments or committees where Ministers could answer points raised in debate. Criticism of such proposals has centred on the dangers that such committees would interfere with the running of departments, concern themselves with major policy issues—for which small committees dividing on party lines are not well suited—and put undue demands on the time and energy of Ministers. In general, it is argued, they would alter the role of Parliament in relation to the Executive; hence such proposals have found little favour with Ministers of any party. Committees of this type it has been said, would be like those of the French Assembly or the American Congress, and alien to the British constitution.

Purely Advisory

Although these objections may be valid in relation to committees concerned with the *formulation of policy*, they lose their force if applied to committees examining the *implementation of policy*. Such committees would be mainly concerned with hearing evidence, not debating. This follows from their primary concern with fact finding. They would also be purely advisory, so in no way exercising control over the Executive, and therefore totally different from the French and American committees.

What should the committees examine and how should they set about it?

(i) Their *subjects* could eventually cover almost the whole field of government, but it would be advisable to start with a few committees—to be reappointed each session—concerned with those topics which already concern many members, such as agriculture, education, health, home affairs, science and Service matters. Typical inquiries might be agricultural research, training of teachers, hospital amenities and buildings, prison reform, atomic energy and soldiers' quarters; these are all matters in which members have frequently shown their interest in questions or debate. A special case can also be made for colonial affairs so that practical problems of small territories which do not normally come before the House might be examined, and the citizens of those territories made directly aware, as they are not at present, of Parliament's concern for their welfare.

Work In Private

(ii) They should be *empowered to call for oral and written evidence*, and to visit government establishments, schools, hospitals, &c. They should examine civil servants and other expert witnesses, including representatives of bodies affected by the subject of the inquiry. They should not normally examine Ministers.

(iii) Their *membership* should consist of between eight and 16 back-bench Members drawn from both sides of the House, in accordance with party strengths, especially members known to have a special interest in the subject concerned. There should be little difficulty in finding members willing to serve.

(iv) They should *meet in private*. This is important if the informal, non-party nature of their deliberations is to be maintained, and if witnesses are to give evidence freely.

(v) At the end of the inquiry they should *make a full report to the House* with as much of the evidence as possible, which should be published, as should the replies of the Government departments.

(vi) *The committees' staff*. As they would be essentially concerned with lay criticism, the committees' non-expert status would be a positive advantage. Their members' own standing would be significantly weakened if they came to rely on their own expert advisers on the American model. And it would probably destroy the necessary good relations with the departments if responsible civil service experts were, in effect, to be examined by non-responsible, unofficial experts. The committees should therefore obtain their expert advice from those giving evidence. They could, however, each be served, as the present select committees are, by a House of Commons Clerk who is able, on the basis of experience gained serving his committee over a period of years to advise the best lines of inquiry, analyse the evidence and undertake the drafting of reports. Technical expertise, for example from a statistician, could also be called on where necessary.

New Thinking

Other advantages would flow from the appointment of such committees. The information and arguments set out in their reports would lead to more informed consideration of policy matters by the House itself. And the very conduct of the inquiries, apart from the specific recommendations made, would often serve to stimulate new thinking within the departments concerned (experience of the present select committees supports this—the Estimates Committee inquiry into Treasury Control led to the Government review of control of public expenditure by the Plowden committee).

The establishment of such committees would also enable members with special interests to find a constructive outlet for their experience and talents in a way that the rare debate on their particular topic and the occasional chance to ask a couple of questions cannot possibly provide.

Reform of the House of Commons on these lines—designed to increase its efficiency, not its powers—might command greater general support than more wide-sweeping changes. It could at least be tried.

Subject Index

Index of Persons